KV-419-044

HH.

STOKE-ON-TRENT PUBLIC LIBRARIES

PUBLIC LIBRARY

HOURS OF OPENING—The Adult Lending Libraries at Tunstall, Burslem, Hanley, Stoke, Fenton and Longton are open as follows:—

Monday, Tuesday, Wednesday, Friday	**9 a.m. - 6.45 p.m.**
Thursday	**9 a.m. - 1.00 p.m.**
Saturday	**9 a.m. - 6.00 p.m.**

Hours of opening for the Junior, Part-time, and Meir Libraries will be supplied on request.

BORROWERS' TICKETS—All borrowers are entitled to tickets as follows:—

(a) Two General Tickets (on which any book may be borrowed).

(b) Additional Students' Tickets (with a maximum of four) available for all books except English Fiction.

(c) One Parent's Ticket (where applicable).

Borrowers' Tickets are available for use at any of the City Libraries, irrespective of the Library from which issued.

Any change in the residence of a Borrower MUST be notified to the Librarian immediately.

TIME ALLOWED FOR READING is 21 DAYS, excluding the day of issue and the day of return.

RENEWAL—If it is not required by another reader a book may be renewed three times for a period of 21 days each, giving a maximum period of three months continuous loan.

FINES—Unless books are returned within the time allowed, borrowers will be fined **TWO PENCE** per week or portion of a week for the period beyond that time.

DAMAGE TO BOOKS—Any damage done to books will be charged for Borrowers are requested to examine books on receiving them, and call attention to any fault in order that they may not be charged for it.

In case of any infectious disease occurring in the home of the borrower, Library Books must be handed to the Sanitary Inspector, and NOT returned to the Library.

By Order of the Committee,

K. D. MILLER, City Librarian.

Phone: Stoke-on-Trent 25108.

TE: The above Rules are correct at me of issue but may subsequently dified. Copies of the Rules in t any given time may be seen Library.

4/59

A Corner of High Green *c.* 1800

A

HISTORY

OF

WOLVERHAMPTON

to

THE EARLY NINETEENTH CENTURY

By

GERALD P. MANDER, M.A., F.S.A.

EDITED AND COMPLETED

by

NORMAN W. TILDESLEY

Published by
WOLVERHAMPTON C.B. CORPORATION
1960

and Printed by
W. GIBBONS AND SONS, LIMITED
WOLVERHAMPTON

Contents

List of Illustrations

Foreword

In June 1956 the Council adopted unanimously a recommendation that the invaluable work by the late Mr. Gerald Mander on the History of Wolverhampton should be published by the Corporation for the benefit of the town.

It is now my privilege, as Mayor of the Borough, to welcome most warmly the appearance of this volume. I hope and believe that Mrs. Mander and the other members of her family, to whom the Corporation are deeply indebted for their willing consent to publication, will regard the finished book as worthy of the author.

In that belief, I congratulate the Honorary Editor, Mr. Norman W. Tildesley, and those who have helped in this enterprise. I offer to them the thanks of the Borough for a job thoroughly well done.

I commend this book, not only to those with a special interest in the subject, but to the people of Wolverhampton as a whole. I have, as I am sure they have, a great affection for our town. I believe that this History will add to our pride in its past, our confidence in its future, and our determination that its present shall be worthy of both.

NORMAN F. BAGLEY, Mayor.

Introduction

❦

No history of Wolverhampton has been published since 1836, when the Rev. George Oliver, D.D. published "An Historical and Descriptive Account of the Collegiate Church of Wolverhampton". The author of this present work, the late Gerald Poynton Mander, M.A., F.S.A. spent a great part of his life collecting historical data to make a history of the town possible, but the manuscript was not complete at the time of his death in 1951.

When the Corporation decided, with the willing consent of Mrs. Mander, to proceed with the printing of Mr. Mander's "History of Wolverhampton" the hon. editor volunteered to finish the incomplete chapters. These comprised the mediaeval period, the 18th century, St. Peter's Church, and the Saxon Pillar. In completing these chapters he has drawn extensively on Mr. Mander's rough notes and has had the able and ready help of Mr. J. S. Roper, M.A. and his staff who were responsible for the typing of the MS. The Editor is also indebted to Mr. M. M. Rix, M.A. for the use of his MS. on the Saxon Pillar.

The decision of the Corporation was that the History should end in the present volume with the accession of Queen Victoria, 1837, as it was generally agreed that the modern history of Wolverhampton should be contained in a separate volume.

The younger son of the late Sir Charles Tertius Mander, 1st Baronet, Mr. Mander was educated at Eton and Trinity College, Cambridge, where he read history and law, and graduated M.A. in 1907. He then joined the family business, becoming a Director in 1910, but ill health restricted many of his activities and he turned to history and other similar pursuits as an outlet for his energies. His knowledge of mediaeval Latin was considerable and in the field of palaeography he had few rivals.

His first important work, a model of its kind, was the "History of Wolverhampton School", which he published in 1913. The "Wolverhampton Antiquary", which appeared in parts and contains much miscellaneous material concerning the town, first appeared in

1915. From 1923 to 1945 he was the Hon. Editor of the "Collections for a History of Staffordshire" published by the Staffordshire Record Society and during that time he saw through the press many important volumes relating to the history of his native county, on many occasions contributing articles himself.

For his work in the field of historical research he was made a Fellow of the Society of Antiquaries. As time went by he assiduously gathered data for his projected "History of Wolverhampton" but he did not live to see its completion.

The editor wishes to express his indebtedness for the help he has received from Mrs. Gerald Mander, Sir Geoffrey Mander, the Rector of Wolverhampton, Mr E. L. Cotterell, and many others who have placed material at his disposal for the completion of this work. The friendly encouragement of the Town Clerk, Mr. R. J. Meddings, has been most helpful, and thanks are due to the Borough Librarian, Mr. F. Mason for assistance in seeing the volume through the press.

N.W.T.

CHAPTER I

WOLVERHAMPTON ORIGINS

It is only necessary in order to explain the position of Wolverhampton for the purposes of History to say that it is in South Staffordshire in the hundred of Seisdon and its own parish—now much sub-divided. It took little place in pre-history. In 1928 the half of a sand-stone axe was found in the playing field of the Grammar School near the brook at Merridale, of date B.C. 1200. A bronze "palstave" or edged instrument of no more recent date then 600 B.C. was found in a garden at Finchfield (inside the present Municipal boundaries) within a mile of the last. There have been reported palstaves found at Bushbury and the Laches to the North of the town and recently from Cannock; one from Wrottesley to the N. West of Tettenhall is in the British Museum: while a polished flint axe-head was found at Ashmore in Wednesfield in the eighteen eighties.[1]

Thus there is evidence of some prehistoric rambling in the virgin forest of this neighbourhood. The high ground stretching from the Clent Hills by way of Dudley, Sedgley, Bushbury to Cannock "Castle Hill' must have provided a track-way in primitive times taking the site of Wolverhampton in its way.

Of Barrows of this period there were many in the neighbourhood and they were conspicuous enough to receive and even give names (Lowe de la Lowe of Bushbury), but their position is only approximately known and no reports of excavation have been made to explain their date. Yet we may assume that these were of the pagan Anglo Saxon period until other evidence is brought to bear, for the district owes something to pagans of the pre-Christian kind. Such barrows are indicated by North Low, South Low, Great Low, Horselow, Tremelowe, Ablow and Stowman's Hill or Low.

They named Wednesfield (and indeed Wednesbury some five miles distant) after Woden, who heads the pedigrees of all self respecting Anglo Saxons[2] and the names must obviously be taken as a survival from pagan times. If then, as seems certain, Wednesfield existed as a name before the battle between the Saxons and the Danes in 910 it cannot well have been so named as a result of the battle.

The artificial formation of the county is probably rather later (C.1000) than this;[3] the conditions which controlled or modified and distinguished this district from other, notably Eastern parts of England, were normal in localities where the British were numerous. South Staffordshire is a county of hamlets as opposed to the nucleated village. The former inhabitants cultivated when the nature of the land was more inviting: the Saxons took over their homes and grouped them as part of their organization. Of this many hamlet district Wolverhampton forms a conspicuous example. It is sufficient here to point out that Wolverhampton is in its original structure British.

There are several survivals of British names in the district in hill and stream, but Wolverhampton had no British name that has come down to us, and there is no reason for suggesting that it existed before the Saxons called it (in the dative) aet Heantune. Yet

1 There was also one found in Stafford Street, Willenhall about 1920.
2 Searle.
3 Staffordshire Historical Collections—various articles.

Penn may be British, as Penkridge and Trysull (Tresel), the latter taking its name from its stream, as does Trescote (aet Treselcotum). Cannock (Cnoc)[1] also has a distant origin. We learn on good authority that the boundary from which the Mercians took their name "boundary people" was probably that belt of high land joining Cannock Chase with the forest of Arden. This leaves Wednesbury and Wednesfield—Woden's fortress and Woden's plain to the East,[2] and also the lands of the bishop which (as being the subject of early grants) stretch significantly southward East of this line and so influenced the shape of the latter 9th century Offlow hundred.

The early history of Wolverhampton is so obscure that we cast about for some signposts of suggestion. One of the earliest documents which we have to guide us is of course the foundation charter of 994. A study of this is instructive. Although the physical features of the place have been much disturbed, it is still possible to follow fairly closely the boundaries set out so many years ago. The aged thorns and boundary stones have disappeared but some names remain.

For example in the description of the "land boundaries of Bilston and Wednesfield" we know where Wolverhampton, Bilston and Ettingshall meet, also where Wolverhampton Bushbury and Wednesfield meet (which happens to be at an old land mark called Spa Well): the dykes and thorns between these two points marked the original eastern boundary of Wolverhampton proper. (The way lay over the East Park, the Dean's or Old Heath Collieries and thence along the Smestow Brook). The northern boundary of what is now Heath Town is more certain along "Penwie" to Bury Brook, and further on on the S.E. we have the Port Street which becomes the boundary at Kirnesford (by Moseley Hole Farm, in 1240 called Kircles-ford). Here we have the names of two Saxon roadways. What information can we gain from them?

Firstly the Portstrete or Portway, coming from Warwick via Wednesbury seems to have every intention of missing Wolverhampton completely. It points with considerable certainty at Bushbury and Stafford, joining the two, not perhaps very ancient but certainly Saxon burgs. In this Wolverhampton plays no part. It is still too early to suggest that it could have been the "port" in question.[3]

Let us now examine "Penwie" which means, doubtless Pen-way; the way to Penn. At this point it is what was the old Cannock Road, running from the N.E. to S.W. and joining at Bushbury the old[4] Stafford Road. We need not follow it over the ground on which Wolverhampton now stands, but will pick it up again at Goldthorn Hill (anciently Goldhoard) where the parish boundary follows the road southwards. Certainly this is the ancient way but not the modern one; it has almost disappeared. But persevering along a track, then a footway, we come out where? At Penn Church itself. Thus was ancient Bushbury joined to ancient Penn.

It is not the only link. These were strong manorial ties. Before the Conquest Moseley and an unnamed estate (probably Seawall) in Bushbury and the part of Penn designated Lower Penn were owned by Godeva Comitessa, the Lady Godiva (as was Upper Penn by her husband Adfgar[5]) and along this road she would with all propriety, if she visited the place at all, have ridden.

After the conquest the manors were all part of the fief of the Dudley lord, and the under tenants of Bushbury and Upper Penn long remained the same. The de Bushburies probably built Penn Church. One more point, and here we see the road as an approach to Stafford:

1 This has been mistaken for Clent, and caused that Worcestershire manor to have been placed in Staffordshire.
2 F. M. Stenton: Anglo-Saxon England, 1943: p. 40.
3 "Port" meaning simply "town".
4 More direct and more modern roads having superseded them in places.
5 With part of Sedgley, and later their son Edwin's.

the owner of Penn, alone of South Staffordshire landowners, had burgages (mansions) in Stafford Town itself.[1]

Wolverhampton, as Heantun, is first mentioned in 985; it is true that neither Penn nor Bushbury (Bishop's Burg it has been suggested after some Mercian bishop) nor yet Wednesbury (for its identity with Wansborough has been disproved) appear in the written form so early, not indeed until Domesday Book. But it is evident that these roads ignore Heantun, which came later to be crowned at last (perhaps even because of its central position) with a church.

(There is another small straw floating in the same direction. The Anglo Saxon Chronicle mentions the battle in which Edward the Elder defeated the Danes in 910 alternately as being fought at Tettenhall or at Wednesfield. Perhaps the truth is that it was fought midway between on the higher ground at Wolverhampton; but as this place was then nameless, so the suggestion is that the Chronicle mentioned those lying near).

The history of Wolverhampton may really be said to begin with the grant by the lady Wulfrun in 994 of lands to the monastery or minster there. There is no surviving reference to Wolverhampton (in form of Heantun) earlier than the year 985 when King Aethelred granted to the lady Wulfrun lands there and at Trescott (aet Treselcotum).[2] This subsequently formed part[3] of her endowment to the Church at Wolverhampton; how and when she obtained the remainder we are not told.

There is more than one Wulfrun known to Saxon records, and it is important to give credit to the right lady if it is possible to identify her. It seems as if this can be done even though it upsets the previously conceived view and that expressed so steadfastly at the celebration of the 900th anniversary in 1894.

The only appearance of a lady called Wulfrun in the Anglo Saxon Chronicles was when Anlaf the Dane stormed Tamworth with much slaughter in 943: "There was Wulfrun captured in this harrying." The very mention in this much truncated record is proof of her importance and she was doubtless the Wulfrun mother both of Wulfric Spot, who founded Burton Abbey in 1004, and also of Aelfhelm, ealderman of Northumbria, and associated with Northampton[4] (not Staffordshire) who married the other Wulfrun known to history.

Who the other Wulfrun was in origin is not so easy to say, but tradition has by no means deserted her.

When Dr. Wilkes had a copy of Erdeswick, incorporating additions by later antiquaries, Hurdman, Loxdale and Huntbach in 1720 (or thereabouts) made for him[5] this note was written on p. 242:—

"Some of our Historians tell us that King Canute had a Concubine that was born in this town on whom he begat Harold Harefoot.

Speed calls her Algive, Ulfranc's Daughter; Weever says her name was Alice and that she was a Shoemaker's Daughter. p. 444."

The gloomy Weever can be found to confirm this on the page mentioned[6] for Harold King of England had helped to name St. Clement's church "Danes" from his burial there in 1040.

1 Domesday Book: Willielmus fitz Ansculfi habet in comitatu quatuor mansiones que pertinent ad Pennam manerium comitis (Edwini). Ex his una tantumodo est hospitata.
2 S.H.C. 1916, p. 101–4. It also gives the first known form of Bilston "Bilsatena", and is interesting as having been witnessed by Archbishop Dunstan.
3 It is described as "the ten hide book" in the rubric, and was evidently one of the three X jugera cassatorum (ten estates of householders) referred to in her later grant.
4 Known at this date as "Hampton"—an additional complexity (S.H.C. 1916, pp. 62–3; 65). The "Hampton" attacked by the Danes before Tamworth is identified with Northampton. (See: Victoria County History of Staffordshire, Vol. I).
See also: Camb. Mediaeval Hist. Vol. III.
5 It is now William Salt copy No. XXI.
6 Funeral Monuments: Edn. 1631.

"This Harold was the base son of King Canut, by his concubine Alice of Wolverhampton in Staffordshire, a Shoemaker's daughter . . . ." And this he obtained from Stow's Annals.

There is a suggestion of a changeling; thus Higden, edn. 1495. Book VI ch. 20. "This Suanus (Sweyn) was holden ye sone of Canutus and of Elgina of Hampton. Some men sayd that this Elgyna myghte conceyve noo chylde by ye Kynge. And therefore she toke this Suanus when he was new born of a preestis wyfe, and layd herself downe, as it were in chylde bedd and the chylde by her: and begyled King Canutus: and brought hym in witte that it was sooth."

"Whenne Canutus was deed thenne was made grete stryfe at Oxenford who sholde be King and his successour. For Leofrycus Consul of Chester and other lordes of the northside of Temse and the Londoners also toke Harolde Haseforte that was holden the sone of Canutus and Elgyna of Hampton and made him Kyng though Goodwyn made him besy for Canutus & Marianus. Some men sayen that this Harolde was a Souters sone. And falsl . . anone as he was borne brought to ye bedde of this Elgina and leyd by her as though she hadde borne hym: And brought hym forth. Right as Suanus was layed by her somtyme. But Harolde was made Kynge." (and that was of course the important fact).

It seems likely that Wulfrun was advanced in age when she made her famous grant. Where she is buried is not known. If this had occurred at Wolverhampton some tradition of the fact would have remained. An alternative burial place is Tamworth, where there was formerly the convent mentioned in Wulfric's will, which she may have founded.[1]

But the legend of her beneficence lived on, for besides giving the prefix to Hampton by which it is now distinguished, her name lingered among the fields and meadow lands lying to the north of the town near Dunstall (or Tunstall) where she might have lived, and is attached to a well—Wulfrun's well—now overwhelmed by a railway embankment, but once a living spring.[2]

The rediscovery of her charter in 1560 restored her tradition to modern times. Holinshed would seem to be the first historian to use this evidence, and it is probably through him that Michael Drayton half remembered her as St. Wilfrun. In his map of Staffordshire river sources in his Polyolbion (1613) he depicts Wolverhampton and St. Wilfrun's Well with a lady with a water jar sitting by it, the source of the River Smestall, described by these lines at the end of his 12th song (p. 208).

"Thus though th' industrious muse hath been imploy'd so long.
yet is shee loth to doe poore little Smestall wrong.
That from her Wilfrune's Spring neere Hampton plyes to pour
The wealth shee there receives into her friendly Stour
Nor shall the little Bourne[3] have cause the Muse to blame.
From these Staffordshire Heathes that strive to catch the Tame."

The County of Stafford did not exist when Wulfrun made her gift; but the collection of townships into Hundreds had already taken place. This formation of the Hundreds was artificial, and followed ownership rather than natural boundaries (which however were important in forming the constituent parts). Wulfrun's gift was too late for this process, so its main portion lay in two hundreds. The site of Wolverhampton itself fell wholly within the hundred of Seisdon, and the hundred boundary which cuts it off from Wednesfield and Willenhall (but not Bilston) ran along its east side, having a bulge westward at this point. Wednesfield and Willenhall were assessed at 10 hides, and this solid block was

1 S.H.C. 1916, pp. 10, 15, 40. Wulfrun's relationship is briefly considered in the Wolverhampton Antiquary, ii, 93.
2 A stone fountain head erected in 1895 by A. Staveley Hill stands near the site.
3 The Bilston Brook, rising in Coseley. See: W.A. ii, 93.

carried in its entirety to the hundred of Offlow. Actually this dispersal of jurisdiction did not matter, as Wolverhampton with its 'parts' formed, as it were, its own hundred and was independent of the hundred courts.[1] It has been shown[2] that the normal hundred in Staffordshire was the 'long hundred' comprising 120 hides, made up of six subdivisions of 20 hides, representing the landed possessions of so many families.

In the present case it will be noticed that the charter itself uses a form of the word 'casata' (a house with land sufficient to maintain a family) to describe the particular lands given, there being nine at Hampton and one at Trescote. A 'hide' of land can be understood in the same sense, and the same term is used for assessments in 'Domesday'—the fiscal hide—where the same place or area is reckoned as equivalent to 120 acres (the land appropriate to a plough team of eight oxen). It is not easy to say how the original assessment of Wolverhampton, the town on the hill, was calculated. The one hide representing the value of the priest's holding here, with $\frac{1}{4}$ hide (one virgate) at 'Cote', *i.e.* Trescote is a meagre total. Nor is it easy to account for the hides of the phrase 'ten hide book' of the document now under consideration. The writer of the rubric (following probably an endorsement on the original charter) may have understood the position, but it is not clear to posterity.

It is probable that the lay estate existing alongside that of the church in this neighbourhood in the eleventh century, consisting of Tunstall, Woundon[3] and the village of 'Mora' (mentioned in a 13th century Survey) which may be Monmore, was omitted from the calculations of the Commissioners, being either freed from taxation or of low taxable value, the state in which nearly the whole of Staffordshire found itself at 'Domesday'. Walsall also is not valued. On the other hand the Wolverhampton church endowment represented by numerous estates widely dispersed within this region, reckoned at the 'Domesday' value, $27\frac{1}{4}$ hides, comes very close to the original 30 hides of Wulfrun's gift. If however the other nine parts of the 'ten hide book' are valued like Trescote (at $\frac{1}{4}$ each) they are seen to equal $2\frac{1}{4}$ fiscal hides in all. There was certainly a lay estate here in the 12th Century, and this may well represent its value at an earlier date; but it is likely that the land 'aet Heantune' on its hilly waste required only a low assessment.

Modern research has revealed that the town is fairly well furnished with the evidence of later charters, which though mostly still unpublished, have become available for study in the last 25 years. Foremost of these are the Huntbach M.S.S. (H), the collections of John Huntbach (1639—1704) the "nephew and pupil" of Sir William Dugdale. His headquarters was from Brinsford in Featherstone; but the ground he covered, besides extensive materials for the history of Seisdon Hundred, included Moseley, Coven, Seawall (and its valley). Second only come Sir Richard Paget's "Gough" M.S.S. (R.P.) belonging to the Oldfallings Hall Estate (now preserved at St. Chad's College there), a rich mine of information for the N.E. boundary of the old parish from Bushbury to Ashmore, with some important evidence of the land west of Chapel Ash, where Paget Road commemorates the connection. Mr. Vernon's Hilton and Essington deeds (Hilton Ess.) help with the N.E. of the parish; Major Davenport's Bushbury manor papers, partly used by S. Shaw, throw much light upon the Coven, Elston and Wybaston district; Mrs. R. Fowler-Butler's Pendeford deeds, mostly of the late thirteenth century (when the estate was given to the priory of St. Thomas, Stafford) join with and complete that area. The recent discovery at Trentham of the Duke of Sutherland's Penn Manor Charters (Penn) dating

1 But not of the sheriff and his 'tourn'. A 14th century Wrottesley deed was dated at Wolverhampton but he was there perhaps only for convenience.
2 S.H.C. 1919, p. 154; The Staffordshire Hidation.
3 S.H.C. 1911, pp. 143–4; in. 1919, p. 167.

from the twelfth century, (they are now deposited at the William Salt Library, Stafford [W.S.L.]) bring much new information about the southern boundary of the town from Bradmore to Muchall and Coton.

Numerous place names are found in the wills of those of the townsmen who invested their savings in land in the 16th and 17th century, and some complicated exchanges of land are shown in deeds of the late Elizabethan period when considerable enclosure of open fields took place.

WOLVERHAMPTON—THE MEANING

HEA-TUN, dative Haen-tune, means High Town, and to state as much as hitherto been regarded as a satisfactory and sufficient explanation: "Wolverhampton stands on a high table-land" says W. H. Duignan (Staffordshire Place Names, p. 175). But it is not so simple. If a comparison be made between the heights along the chain of hills in this area, it will be seen that the site of the church and town centre is by no means the highest point on the skyline. The facts are interesting. From north to south we find from the Ordnance data:—

	Hilton Park (and Windmill)	600 ft.
	Bushbury Hill	590 ft.
	The valley between	373 ft. at the brook.
	Dunstall (about)	370 ft.
	Dunstall Hill (Woundon)	472 ft.
Wolverhampton	Church Porch	529 ft.
	Princes Square	510 ft.
	Snow Hill (which has been lowered) ..	513 ft.
	Goldthorn Hill	610.4 ft.
	Colton Hills, Penn	608.1 ft.
	Sedgley Park Hill	600 ft.
	Sedgley Beacon	700 ft.
	Sedgley (High Street)	756.7 ft.
To the West lie:—		
	Wrottesley Old Park	506 ft.
	Tettenhall (Upper Green)	457 ft.
	Tettenhall Wood	500 ft.
	Compton	342 ft.
The valley at the brook at Newbridge	.. .. ..	345 ft.

From this survey it will be seen that the town centre, as recognised by St. Peter's church, is by no means as high as some of the surrounding terrain, but it would be true to say that Wolverhampton stands astride part of a long undulating range of hills running from Rowley and Dudley in the south to Bushbury in the north.

Staffordshire in the eleventh century was very thinly populated. Its wooded condition accounts for this. Its map shows it was composed of British hamlets, not villages, (a Saxon feature) which was a condition expected where forest abounded. These hamlets at Wolverhampton can be pointed out, although some of their names were of later application. Our map shows them: Tunstal, Broadmeadow, Oxneford, Merridale, the Lea, Graseley, Blakenhall, 'Mora', Seawall, atte Low, Gosebrok, Woundon—satellitic hamlets round 'the town on the hill'.

This list is confirmed by the names of those assessed for the Subsidy, granted in 1327 to meet the expenses of the Scotch War.[1] These, after a rather doubtful start, are evidently presented in an order which runs clockwise round the town. I select the following:—[2]

1 Printed S.H.C. VIII, p. 249. Richard de Hampton, who might reasonably have appeared, was one of the collectors.
2 Hervey Page and Adam Swetelove probably represent the origin of Pages Croft and Page Tenement, and Swetelove Tenement, both burgage houses. Thomas the miller was probably of Gosbrook mill, according to the order of the names. It is too early for a windmill.

Hervey Page
Thomas the miller
John atte Wynde
John atte Lowe
Adam atte chirche gate
Thomas in la Lone
Richard in la Lone
John de la Hethe
John de Monnemere
Stephen ad novum pontem (i.e. Newbridge)
Hugh de Tunstal
Eva de Woundon
Alice atte Lone
Nicholas atte Wynde
Adam Swetelove
Clement de Coton (also John and Robert)
Geoffrey de Graselye
John atte Lee
Richard atte Knolle
John de Barndeleye
William de Oxneford
William de Saltford
Richard Levesone
Richard de Coven

Total assessed here 38.

One noticeable feature we find on all sides. The Anglo Saxon braec, developing into breche, bruche, birch, means 'newly cultivated land'; but how new? That we are not told, but it was certainly a very general term for all parts of 13th century Wolverhampton, and the process was continuous. Most local place names, some derived from the ancient holder, have 'bruche' (or the equivalent) attached to them; thus we get:—

Knolle bruches
Sydersbruch (1404)
Cross byrches
Wagebyrch
Oxnefordbruche
Newboldesbruches
le Blakebruche
le Morebruche
loneendebruche
Wollemerebruche
le Muridale bruche (1516)
Harpers bruche
Guddebruche
Jonkysbruche
Gamulesbruche
Sexteynesbruche
Gemmebruche
Stywardesbruche
Patersbyrch (1629)
Slade byrch
Can burche

and the district can produce many others.

There is confusion in the meaning, and the word is not fully noticed in N.E.D. where the examples are late.[1] The various spellings over the centuries result in words of opposite meaning, and place names are derived from both, one used in the sense of a thicket, brushwood, and the other as a cleared space, an oasis in the forest. 'Fernie bruch' means 'breaks of fern, undergrowth, bracken'. 'Breeches' means a cleared or open space *e.g.* in 1592 "a meadow called Clare breeches". Also there is 'Birchen Byrch' (1656). Professor Eckwall shows that two words braec and braec are probably involved.[2]

OLD ROADS AND BOUNDARIES

At the time when Hampton emerged from the twilight of Antiquity it had no need for a way to Stafford, for the County was not yet formed. The tie was with the Hundred, the hundred of Seisdon, and the road to the hundred moot, once held on the highest hill there, is well marked. Yet some close touch must have been maintained with Penkridge, a very ancient centre, on the way to Stafford, and head of its own hundred (Cuttlestone).

The old Stafford Road is not the present one, which is the product of the 18th century turnpikes. They way from Wolverhampton lay towards Bushbury from the ford at Gosebrook; thence to Northicote and so on N.N.W., the way here being the western

1 See under Break (12), breeches, bruche, breach.
2 Dict. English Place Names, p. 56.

boundary of Moseley (Mollesley) manor, the northern side of which is formed by the brook, crossed at "Warwicksford" a name preserved in the adjacent meadow. It is the Stafford-Birmingham road and so on to Warwick; but it misses Wolverhampton. This road runs one side of Bushbury Hill,[1] the Cannock Road lies on the other, the eastern side. The way to Cannock is likely to have been the more ancient; a parish boundary, often a sign of antiquity, runs along it at "Park Lane", indeed has kept it on the map, as part had become only a footpath in modern times.

The old Stafford Road is called "the highway from Stafford to Warwick" in a Coven deed of c. 1280[2] and "the way leading from Stafford to Birmingham" (a less distant mark) in another of about the same date *i.e.* 1290.[3] This is the road through Northicote and Wednesfield, which further north forms the western boundary of Moseley manor. The new Stafford Road was not made in 1747 (Bowen's Map), though there were the makings of it (Fordhouses).

I do not feel happy about the antiquity of the road running from 'le Goldhord' to Merryhill (the hill here is inconsiderable, a gentle slope, but a deed of 1340 preserves the name Murihull); the road called Coalway road served as an outlet to the west for the people of Bilston in early Victorian times. The more ancient way is the one which forms the boundary here, and is known by a local deed of about the year 1300 (a grant by Henry de Bissebury lord of Overpenne to Robert Payn of Mughale, Penn deed W.S.L. bundle 2 No. 9) as the "King's way which leads from Goldhord towards Bridgnorth (Bruges) as far as another royal road which divides the manor (feodum) of Penne and the manor of Hampton" (that is by Coton). This is supported by another deed of the same date (a grant of Richard le Fox of Mugehale (Muchall), Benigna his wife and Elena their daughter) mentioning "the way between Coten and Wolvernehampton" and "the King's way which leads from Cumpton to the Goldhord". Another deed (no. 12) is a grant by Walter de Coten to Robert son of John de Muchehale in free marriage with Alice his daughter of all his purpresture "at the lane of Muchehale", etc.

Two other deeds also concern this area. One, an agreement about the "wood of Penn" dated 1291 (but confirming another of the 12th century) mentions "that wood which extends from the hedge of Walter de Cotes towards the Goldhord by a 'sichet' which is called 'Woluedon' " (Bundle III no. 1) and the other concerns a purpesture of Richard le Fox lying between the outer road (exteriorem viam) of Burnildelow (Brunhild's tumulus) and the hedge of the field of Penne, and extending from the purpresture of Richard fitz Osbert of the Knolle as far as "the brook of the boundary ditch" (runilum de la Horesiche—bundle II No. 10). Let us add that a purpresture is an illegal encroachment on the land of the manor, an enterprise which the manorial courts watched and regulated by fine or restitution. The modern widening of roads reverses this process.

In the course of centuries the firmest boundaries tend to alter. The straightest road may be caused to wobble on account of various physical features that may arise, a soft patch, a tree growing up, a rock disturbed. In the same way a watercourse may alter or be diverted or drained, and become no longer a definite boundary obvious to the eye.

The time came when the manor's unmeasured wastes became valuable and this would tend to make tenants stake them in, or claim them by hedge or ditch—purprestures and assarts they were called—increases often disallowed by the manorial court or denied by a neighbour; or perhaps the subject of settlement by agreement or force. The need of more

1 The bounds of Bushbury manor in 30 Eliz. mention "the portway" here.
2 S.H.C. Vol. 1928, p. 50, deed 100.
3 ibid, p. 108, deed 200.

rapid transit first for coaches then for motor cars leading to much alteration and the construction of completely new roads has resulted inevitably in the obliteration of many of these old landmarks. Nevertheless the mapped boundaries of the town of, say, 100 years ago as shown in, for instance, the Tithe Map of 1844, must bear a not very distant resemblance to its shape 900 years earlier. One cannot insist on exactitude, and it is evident that there exist some examples of probable divergence.

1. The river (or brook) on the north and west of the town is likely to have been interfered with, on account of the canal which runs beside it. At Dunstall (now built over) the boundary is shown some distance to the north of the brook marked by stones and trees across the meadows. This may be accounted for as the site of the original stream.

2. The boundary on the east of the town has been overwhelmed by railway lines, and coalmines, and building has blotted out five of the extensive manorial open fields, Quabbfield near the Culwell (which suggests marsh, as does Causey or Causeway Lake[1] a pool where the Wednesfield road begins). In the 16th century Quabb (or Quebbe) field became "alias Windmill field", the windmill standing once in Lower Stafford Street a short distance after the turn into Cannock Road. From this the ground slopes down gently towards the east.

Rather more to the south is found Horselow field, named it may be supposed after some long forgotten tumulus in that area. Whether Horseley Fields (now a street) is the same name in origin is uncertain. Finally there is Windefield near Blakenhall, also on the eastern slope. Such ancients as Clement atte Wynde (fl. circa. 1327) took their name from it. The name is not yet extinct in the north country *i.e.* a wynd (see N.E.D.).

What then is to be our vision of the origin of the town? We see in retrospect a bare and windswept slope stretching from north to south subject to icier blasts from the higher ground of Essington and Hilton on the north east. To the west is meadow ground and moor, much moor, with some swamp near the brook. Its western side is sunny and rain from the Atlantic favours it upon occasion. To the east it is swampy too and the river Tame is fed from these fields and hills.

The Romans did not concern themselves actively with these parts; so far as it was settled it was British. The Pagan Saxons, worshippers of Woden, stayed their march[2] for a time at this range of hills. It was not until the early ninth century that the tribes, now Christian, with their talent for organization, surged westward to the Severn, and took note of and organised the scattered steads. Hampton later to become Wolverhampton was one of these.

Charter of King Ethelred A.D. 985

The aforesaid land is seen to be surrounded by these boundaries.

First from the goose brook[3] shooting (i.e. extending) to Saeffan moor,[4] thence against the stream from seven springs brook,[5] from the brook to one spring,[6] from the spring to the other spring, from the spring into the dike, along the dike to one boundary-mark,

1 Now gone, though the name lives in that of an infant school.

2 Bilston, in its ancient form, contains the name of one of these ancient tribes.

3 Goose-brook, Gosebrok (1300), eventually (and wrongly) Gorsebrook: the stream bordering the Dunstall estate on the North. It gave its name to a hamlet and mill on the Wolverhampton-Stafford road.

4 Saeffan moor. The name occurs as part of the boundaries of King's Tettenhall in 1300, in the form "Saffemor". The present "Saltmoor", in Oxley, on the northern side of the above-mentioned stream, retains the name in a corrupt form.

5 "Seofan Wyllan" is the origin of the curious and very ancient name of Sewell, Seawall, Showell. Vide Ekwall's Concise Oxford Dict. of English Place-names, p. 391. "The seven wells": A tradition of seven springs is common. There used to be a strong spring running through Seawall moat (filled in in 1935). The name Showell is also found at Springhill on the road from Penn to Lower Penn.

6 The spring was doubtless the source of the Smestow and the Culwell, situated in "Springfields". The course is now southward to Bilston.

from the boundary-mark to Bilston boundaries, thence to the boundary of Sedgley, along the boundary so to Scurf's moor,[1] from the moor to the hill-side brook,[2] along the brook so to wet lea,[3] from wet lea up to the snows,[4] from the snows straight over the plain[5] till it comes to where the path[6] shoots on to the street that lies from Byrngyth's stone, along the path so to the gallows tree,[7] from the tree to the broad street[8] till it comes to the meadow, thence along the meadow sitch till it comes to Tresel[9] (water), up along Tresel (water) so again[10] to the goose brook shooting on to Saeffan moor.

1 The name is preserved in "Moorfields" to the south of the town. In the tithe map of 1840, this district was called the Moors stretching to Goldthorn Hill.

2 This may be the Graiseley brook, running west, but it is not now the boundary at this point.

3 The wet lea. The name may have been preserved in the ancient homestead lying west of the hill called "The Lea". The name is still found in Lea Road.

4 The snows. Though perhaps rather out of our route, the name may be found in the high land in Wolverhampton known as Snow Hill.

5 The plain: now called Bradmore, where the Penn Manor open fields were.

6 The path: probably the parish boundary known as Stubbs Lane.

7 Perhaps later the site called "Gospel Tree" where the above lane joins the Finchfield Road. (Tithe map).

8 The Wolverhampton-Bridgnorth Road. We are now turning north.

9 Tresel is the ancient name for the Smestall (and later) Smestow brook.

10 This stream in its higher reaches is the Goose brook. We thus complete the circuit.

CHAPTER II

BEGINNINGS: WULFRUN AND AFTER

OF Wulfrun we have already spoken: it is the history of her foundation which concerns us here. There will probably be always able writers not fully informed who date this occurrence in 996;[1] Mr. Duignan[2] writing in 1888, followed by the rector, Mr. Jeffcock in 1894, and confirmed by Mr. Bridgeman in 1916,[3] emphasize the fact that King Aethelred's confirmation belongs to the year 994. The month was probably October. The benefaction itself cannot have been later than this date, but may have been earlier by several months or even years. The archbishop while fortifying the gift with the chain of apostolic authority, spoke of "the venerable monastery of Hamtune, which has now in modern times been built" and "with longing" desires "the religious purpose . . . . should with God's help be fulfilled without any delay". The intention is set forth in the next paragraph: "that as regards all the urban places, towns and rural fields, just as her aforesaid monastery had kept them from ancient times" so she ought to possess them now the more peaceably, she and her successors, abbots, clerks or female nuns.

This is the sense of the document. The building then may have been but recently erected, the monastic scheme is only now settled and confirmed, but the foundation had been an accomplished fact of unspecified duration.

There has survived one clue to limitations within which this gift was made, namely the grant in 985 of King Aethelred to the lady Wulfrun of lands at Heantune (Wolverhampton) and Treselcotum (Trescott) for her to enjoy during life with free power of granting them in her turn.[4] The description of the land then granted tallies with some of the land specified in the grant 994. In fact it comprises one third of her donation—ten estates of householders, or as the Anglo Saxons concisely term it a "ten hide book".

Without wishing to cast any slur on the value of the gift or of the piety which inspired it, we may suggest that it was made towards the end of her life; indeed she states that it was partly made for the good of her soul.

The purpose of Wulfrun's benefaction was the propagation of the Gospel from her college of priests. It has been shown elsewhere[5] that Staffordshire was a backward waste and the least important part of the Mercian Earldom. There were no parishes in Staffordshire at this date and religious houses were only just being formed. There was of course Lichfield which had been a centre of some ecclesiastical importance for 200 years. There was probably some reason for the inconvenient arrangement of the lands of the endowment which comprised some fifteen estates, half of them quite small, dotted about South West Staffordshire—the most remote (Earnleia: Arley) being 15 miles away from the college. Presumably by this system of missionary priests who must go far afield to collect their dues, if for no more laudable purpose, the teaching of Christianity was spread in those

1 V.C.H. Worcs. iii, sub Arley; and Camb. County Geogr. Staffs. 1915, p. 151.
2 Charter of Wulfrun, p. 7. Record of the 900th Anniversary of the Collegiate Church, p. 15.
3 S.H.C. 1916, pp. 43, 114.
4 S.H.C. 1916, pp. 101–4.
5 S.H.C. 1916, 147, 165, etc.

days. This arrangement had however, its disadvantages, for it took the full resources of the Church to hold possessions so widely dispersed in turbulent times.

Whatever may have happened to the original charters of this church, and in 1640 they, or copies of them, would appear still to have been in the Dean's possession, they were entered on the Charter Rolls of the realm at the time of their "inspection" in 1328[1] and so have been preserved.

The first charter is one of King Edward the Confessor, and if the bishop and earl addressed were Leofwine (1053—1067) and Leofric (d. 1087) as is probably the case, it belongs to some date between 1053—7. He pledges his troth to his priests at Hampton and wills that they and their monastery be free as well as their possessions, even as he first had it; and he grants them whatever was rightly granted to them. It is a deed of a jealous and scanty character but much could be read into it.

The next is a charter of William the Conqueror, addressing L(anfranc) the archbishop, G(osfrid) bishop of Coutances, P(eter) bishop (of Lichfield), R the sheriff and others faithful to him in Staffordshire. He grants to Sampson his chaplain the church of St. Mary of "Wlurenehamton" with its land and all other things and customs as in the time of King Edward "And see that he holds all these things with honour as I wish well".

King William did not interfere with Staffordshire until the break up of the Mercian earldom in 1071, and the grant is not likely to have been made before this time and probably not before 1078.

The document gives the first recorded notice of the full name Wolverhampton. The words are few but the intention is clear: The King rewards a trusted courtier. Domesday Book (1086) naturally shows Sampson (or Sansome as the name is spelt) in possession as tenant in chief. The priests or canons hold the church lands from him and not, as formerly, direct from the crown. But there have been some changes. Arley the remote has suffered from the unruly attentions of Osbern fitz Richard the powerful Herefordshire baron, for part of it "he took by force from the canons" and still held.

Bilston was now the King's, possibly by exchange for an equivalent Worcestershire manor, Lutley near Halesowen. But Lutley[2] was the church's in King Edward's time, so its acquisition was not quite recent. Haswie which has recently been identified with Ashwood in Kingswinford was then unoccupied—"Waste on account of the King's forest". It was afterwards incorporated into Kinver forest as Ashwood Haye.

A less obvious omission is the apparant loss of a large part of the land granted to Wulfrun in 985. Bilston has been mentioned but apart from this nearly one tenth[3] of the land granted does not appear. The missing portion had no doubt been taken into the King's hands at the same time as Bilston and lay near it, and it may be conjectured that this was the land which formed the King's manor of Wolverhampton, which, though not mentioned in Domesday, was of similar value.[4]

History is silent on these changes which presumably took place before King Edward's day, perhaps under the Danish King Cnut. But would the priests have remained silent had they received no compensation? And assuming they were compensated, what was the bribe? Domesday Book suggests an answer. It is singularly ambiguous about the church lands of Tettenhall. It lists under the chaplain Samson's fief land at Tettenhall and Bilbrook, "the canons of Hampton, or rather the priests of Tettenhall" holding it from him. It is

1 Oliver, Collegiate Church, p. 178; and Shaw, Staffs., following some edition of Dugdale, misdate this event 2 Ed. I instead of 2 Ed. III, an error of 57 years.
2 V.C.H. Worcs. i. 308.
3 Including Lutley there were 27¼ hides in 1086 whereas there should have been 30.
4 S.H.C. 1919, pp. 167–8, 171. The King's possessions would thus stretch from Tettenhall to Wednesbury.

possible that this property passed to Samson under the grant already mentioned and the assumption[1] that the land was King Edward's before the conquest may therefore be wrong. But the Survey attempts an explanation: "This land", it notes, "does not belong to Hampton but is the gift of the King to the church of that vill" (Tettenhall). What had indeed just been accomplished whether or not from the King's or the Church's lands, was the formation of the Collegiate Church of Tettenhall. Eyton[2] moreover suspects in the arrangement of four estates (Hatherton, Kinvaston, Hilton and Featherstone) under the names of two priests, (Edwin and Alric) a design, never fulfilled, of providing for yet another Collegiate Church. But eventually these estates became four distinct prebends of the Church of St. Mary of Wolverhampton.

The Charter of Wulfrun to the "Minster" at Hamtun has hitherto been taken as the basis of the early history of Wolverhampton. That it deals with only part of the endowment of the church, that of the outskirts, the *foreign* as it was called, omitting the town itself (within which a large area of church lands lay), does not seem to have impressed students. Yet no document of this date can be otherwise than impressive and from its very complexity it needs some description. The original has had a history of its own, for after having been lost for some hundreds of years, it was rediscovered in 1560. It remained for a time in the hands of the dean's 'official', William Green, but was at length taken to Windsor where Sir William Dugdale made his copy in 1640.[3] It appears that Sir Henry Spelman made another and independent copy of all except the last two paragraphs and the names of the witnesses, before the original was finally and irretrievably lost.[4] So although there are gaps and mis-spellings, the bulk has reached us much as it was written by the King's notary and secretary on a certain Sunday in October 994 and attested "with joyful visages", diligent pen and signs of the holy cross by King Ethelred, both archbishops, twelve bishops, eleven abbots, five dukes, two deacons, one count, and five thegns, all in the Witanagemot assembled.

The charter is in Latin with the boundaries of the land granted described in Saxon; the meaning of both is obscure, the former from verbosity the latter from terseness;[5] yet the boundaries of the estates so set out must at the time and for centuries after have been quite clear, and even now, with the help of a map (preferably not a recent one), they can be followed to a certain extent. Thorns, alders, oaks, hedges and even boundary stones (hoar or "war" stones) disappear; but roads and watercourses remain, and until recently have been, with the parish and township boundaries, sacrosanct and unchangeable.

Briefly, Sigeric, Archbishop of Canterbury[6] grants a privilege "to the noble matron and religious woman Wulfrun (in order that she may attain a seat in heaven, and that she may found a church[7] in honour of the Lord and Saviour of the world . . . . and of the holy mother of God, the ever Virgin Mary, ... and of all the Saints) that *through it*[8] in the same ancient minster of Hamtun, which has now in modern time been built, firmly with common stability, mass may be chanted unceasingly for ever.[9]" The archbishop greatly desired "that the religious intention, shown to belong continually to the holy

1 Ib. p. 46.
2 By Eyton and his followers. See his Domesday Studies, table III and p. 67. Domesday does not mention the Saxon owner of Tettenhall.
3 W. A. i, 194.
4 Jeffcock, "Record", p. 17 (note) and App. p. 13, where some variations from Dugdale are set out, tending to prove that Spelman made his own copy.
5 Mr. C. G. O. Bridgman's translation, S.H.C. 1916, pp. 105–110, is the most recent, and has been closely followed. Here the author endeavours to shorten the document while retaining the sense (J.S.R.).
6 Died 28 Oct. 994, an important witness as to the date of the Charter, and ruling out the old reading of its date as 996—a change of vi into iv.
7 Basilica.
8 Per eum. Duignan translates: "by her (Wulfrun)"; Bridgman: "by her means".
9 . . in eodem venerabili monasterio de Hamtune, quod in moderno nunc tempore constructum est. n perpetuum missa communi stabilitate firmiter . . . . . in ibi decantetur.

place, should be completed, God willing, without any delay", and that he should ever assist in its defence. It was therefore fitting that all things belonging to the aforesaid minster of Hamtun "of the holy mother of God, Mary, our lady", should be confirmed everlastingly and inviolably. Therefore, influenced by your prayers, we decree . . . . "that all urban places, towns, or rural country, just as your minster held all things from ancient times,[1] so you ought now also to possess them the more peacefully in great security". . . . (and) in no wise shall any man great or small exercise authority over the things or estates of the said minster whether cultivated or not, nor shall he despoil them, but rather let them remain in everlasting right in the same venerable[2] minster, under your power or at the disposal of all your successors, whether abbots or female religious.

The archbishop then warns those who would thwart this his apostolic authority, and blesses the guardian and observer of it. Then Wulfrun gives the particulars of her grant.

It concerns the following estates only: Arley, "Ashwick", Bilston, Wednesfield, Pelsall, Ogley, Hilton (by Ogley), Hatherton, Kinvaston, Hilton and Featherstone.

The charter proceeds to describe in Anglo-Saxon the land boundaries and the vill names of the eleven places which are somewhat widely dispersed over South Staffordshire, and it is perhaps remarkable, considering the violence which was often inflicted upon property owners in the course of centuries, that some half dozen of these manors survived the Reformation as the property of the church. What previous writers do not seem to have noticed is that no land at Hampton itself is included in the grant; the gift of the area which comprised the town must have been the subject of another grant that has not come down to us. Actually then the charter of 994 withholds evidence of the area covered by Hampton in the tenth century; but in setting out the boundaries of Bilston[3] and Wednesfield (which are taken together) the north and south points of the East side of the town can be definitely recognized, although the details of the intermediate boundary are obscure. It is a matter for speculation how far the ownership of the church extended to the north, as we know it did extend, into what became Bushbury parish.

A clue to the area covered by the missing charter is found in King Ethelred's grant to the lady Wulfrun in 985.

First observed by Mr. Duignan[4] under the disguise of "Southampton" in Kemble's Codex Diplomaticus (iii. 213. No. 650), this document has now been assigned to its rightful locality.[5] As the earliest document connected with the town that has survived and is likely to be found, and one which must therefore be regarded with pride and veneration, a full transcript of the Anglo-Saxon description of the boundaries—the earliest boundaries of the town—is set out here, with a commentary, in an Appendix I to this chapter.

Something also should be said about the position of Willenhall which has been misunderstood, or taken for granted. In Wulfrun's grant there is a list of the estates to which the charter refers, including Bilston, Willenhall and Wednesfield in that order. But when reference is made to the section describing the land boundaries "of Bilston and of Wednesfield", there is no Willenhall, and it is seen that this is not included within the boundaries given. We may infer, therefore, that Willenhall was not part of Wulfrun's gift to the

1 . . a priscis temporibus.

2 venerabili.

3 Called "Bilsetnatun", and in 1086 "Billestune". Unfortunately the misspelling, by a printer's error, of a place, as yet unidentified, but near Trysull, called BELSTOW, which appears in Oliver, p. 162, n. (but not in the actual text, p. 174) as Belstona, was seized upon by Mr. G. T. Lawley (History of Bilston, p. 4) as "the undoubtedly correct" Latin for Bilston (when it is certainly no such thing), and such a hold has this error in the public mind, that it would be difficult to dislodge it. An attempt was made to do so in W.A. ii, 85.

4 Jeffcock, p. 6. Kemble marks it as of doubtful authenticity, as well he might if he tried to read into it a Southampton provenance. It is from the Codex Winton (Brit. Mus. 11th cent. Add MS.15350) a Cartulary of the Priory of St. Swithin, Winchester.

5 By C. G. O. Bridgman, S.H.C. 1916, p. 101–4, giving a translation of the whole.

church. It is true that part of it appears as church property in Domesday Book, but that may have been in exchange for Bilston (of equal value) which drops out, though it remained in Wolverhampton parish. So it was then that at some unknown date in the eleventh century the church at Wolverhampton lost the manor of Bilston either by exchange with the King for part of Willenhall or for one of equal value at Lutley in Halesowen. It is impossible to say when this change took place. It may have happened during the upheaval which placed Cnut upon the throne, for Heming the monk of Worcester tells how his monastery suffered then at the hands of the sheriff of Staffordshire, an evil minded man,[1] who had alienated the villages of Swinford, Clent and Tardlbigg, places near Lutley. Lutley duly appears among the clerks of Wolverhampton's possessions in the portion of Domesday Book relating to Worcestershire, and has remained with that church until this day.

That the church was once favoured by a writ of King Edward the Confessor conferring privileges, is evidenced by a copy of that grant made in the year 1328, now preserved among the Harleian manuscripts in the British Museum.[2] The original writ or some document that purported to be it, presumably existed at that date; but as transcribed in the fourteenth century the text is much altered. The Saxon lettering is not attempted; the spelling is not true and some words are ambiguous on that account; there may be omissions, and there is certainly confusion, especially in the last clause, which make the genuinness of the original suspect. It must assuredly have been useful for the clerks of Wolverhampton to have some documentary evidence of their past immunities and privileges to show to the Conqueror and his advisers, or to bolster up claims in the time of Edward I. The fraud was doubtless a pious one. The real or fancied date of this writ falls within the years 1062—1066. King Edward sends friendly greetings to bishop Leofwine and earl (Ead)wine and all his theyns in Staffordshire; he tells them he has given "my priests at Hampton" his pledge, and wills that they and their minster be free and also their property, together with manorial jurisdiction (*sac* and *soc*) in as complete a form as ever he held it in all respects. He ends with a prohibition against anyone doing them wrong.[3]

A convenient vagueness besets the privileges which the church enjoyed throughout its mediaeval history, and discussion of this may be postponed for the present. The next royal recognition which Wolverhampton received is known from the same source; but, being in Latin, the text is preserved in an almost perfect form. The brevity of King William's writ suggests its repetition here:—

W. rex Anglorum L(anfranc) archiepiscopo et G.(osfrid) episcopo Constant'[4] et P.(eter) episcopo et R(obert) vicecomiti ceterisque suis fidelius de Estaffordscire salutem. Sciatis me dedisse Sampsoni capellano meo ecclesiam Sancte Marie de Wlurenehamptona, cum terra et omnibus aliis rebus et consuetudinibus, sicut melius predicta ecclesia habuit tempore regis Edwardi. Et videte ut aic omnia honorifice teneat quoniam bene volo.

Lanfranc was archbishop from 1070; Gosfrid was in England before that date;[5] Peter is styled bishop of Chester as early as 1070, although he was not consecrated until 1072 and the removal of the see there from Lichfield was not formally sanctioned until the council of London in 1075 (Warner & Ellis, Facsimiles of Royal and other Charters in B.M. (1903) vol. i. no. 1).

1 Hemingi Chartularii Ecclesiae Wigorniensis, vol. 2, pp. 276–7.

2 See as to this, W. A. i. 325. It is Harl. Charter 43 E.51.

3 Reading "unriht" for "on rich". Dugdale who knew this grant only in its 1328 form attempts a reproduction of the original Saxon in his edition. (See more fully in App. II).

4 MS. Cisternensi, which Dugdale alters to Cestrensi, suggesting a Bishop of Chester, whereas Gosfrid of Coutances is meant.

5 He signs the grant to the Church of St. Martin the Grand in 1068 (Regesta, No. 22).

The possible dates include the years 1074—85, (Regesta, no. 210) but these extremes may be narrowed.

Samson the chaplain, Samson of Bayeux, as a member of the household of Kings William I and II and in his youth a protege of Bishop Odo, the King's brother, was well established at court and in a position to inspire or suggest the appointment in question, not as a cure of souls, for he was not yet a priest, but as a source of income for a useful official. He is the first on record of a long line of courtiers or civil servants, who found a source of emolument in the "deanery" of Wolverhampton. His brother, Thomas of Bayeux, received the see of York in 1070, and one might expect Samson to have been present at the ceremonies that inaugurated an episcopate of thirty years.[1]

As a guide to the date of the grant the political state of the country may be considered. Events influenced the King's actions, and Staffordshire did not call for notice until the revolt of Edwin, the Mercian earl, first in 1068,[2] and finally, after the easy conquest of Staffordshire,[3] and the building of Stafford Castle[4] in 1070, the final overthrow of Edwin and Morcar in 1071.[5] It was then time for the King to decide upon the division of the county. The Rev. Robert Eyton has dealt fully with this question in his Domesday Studies of Staffordshire (1881). Of Earl Edwin's demesne estates the King retained the lion's share. Large portions went to found and endow the twin Palatinates of Chester and Shrewsbury. Many a Midland Baron got a share of the gain which resulted from the escheat of the Mercian Earldom.[6] After 1070 the monarch's fief or estates in Staffordshire were of three classes, in virtue of his status as King, as earl and as conqueror. Wolverhampton church lands were of the first category: what King Edward had he retained. The bishop's lands do not appear to be upset by the conquest; but at Wolverhampton a definite change was made, the canons were no longer to hold from the crown "in chief",[7] but as tenants of Samson. But in practice probably the change was small, and being in direct touch with the government put the church "on the map".

About the year 1075 therefore, King William greeted Lanfranc the archbishop of Canterbury, Geoffrey bishop of Coutances, Peter bishop of Chester and R. (probably Robert de Stafford) the sheriff, and others his faithful in Staffordshire: "Know that I have given to Samson my chaplain the church of Saint Mary of Wolverhampton,[8] with the land and all other possessions and customs, just as the aforesaid church had them favourably in the time of King Edward. And see ye that he holds all these things with honour since I wish it well".

Domesday Book would appear to show that the adjoining church estate of Tettenhall was also granted him, possibly at the same time; but the instrument to that effect has been lost together with all Tettenhall charters of antiquity.

1 The Norman Conquest, iv. 342.

2 Previously he was in the King's favour and there was talk about a Royal marriage (N.C. iv. 180). William I notified the confirmation of Perton charter to him: "That the land at Perton belongs to the altar of St. Peter of Westminster as fully and freely as King Edward, the King's Kinsman, gave it. Abbot Aegelwy (of Evesham, who owned the adjacent estate of Wrottesley) and Thurkill the Sheriff are to protect the land for the abbey". Regesta, No. 25.

3 N.C. iv. 282,315.

4 N.C. iv. 318.

5 Ibid. 466.

6 Eyton, op. cit. p. 32.

7 As did the 13 prebendaries at Stafford at the time of Domesday. History (says the author) is silent on the pre-Norman Stafford church—but since the death of Mr. Mander, excavations at Stafford have revealed a great deal about the Saxon church of St. Bertelin there. (JSR).

8 This is the first known occurrence of the full name.

CHAPTER III

DOMESDAY BOOK

THE pride shown by Englishmen in the Conquest is repeated in the veneration for those volumes known as Domesday Book. Compiled for fiscal purposes in 1086, they provide a record of a state of affairs just before the Conquest and twenty years later. But besides this they provide material for searching into the more distant past—the "Beyond" of Professor Maitland.[1]

Intended as a "rate book", the Domesday survey shows the assessment of the manors in terms of "hides" (each representing the holding of a family), the grouping of such into "hundreds", and the assembling, quite artificially, of the hundreds into counties.[2] On this basis, the tax, known as danegeld, was levied from 991, though the formation of Staffordshire (one of the last of the counties) and consequently its assessment, date from the 9th century. By arranging here, in table form, a list of the manors associated with Wolverhampton, we can see their relative value in the 9th century.

The Domesday Entries

Only the Latin text is set out here. H. Malcolm Fraser's "Staffordshire Domesday" provides one of the most convenient translations and may with advantage be consulted, especially with reference to the meaning of Domesday terms.

Let us first see what the record says about Wolverhampton (in the original Latin in an extended form). Staffordshire is divided among 17 holders of which the King comes first, followed by the Church. Wolverhampton's section is no. vii, which gives the direct holdings of the canons and of "Sanson, clerk" who is their dean or custos.

VII TERRA CLERICORUM DE HANDONE

CANONICI de HANTONE tenent. I. hidam de Sansone. Terra est. III. carucis. T.R.E. fuerunt ibi. VIII. carucae. Modo sunt. X: et XIIII. serui. et VI. uillani et XXX. bordarii cum. IX. carucis. Ibi. II. acrae prati.

Ipsi canonici tenent in ERNLEGE. II. hidas. Terra est. VI. carucis. In dominio est una caruca. et II. serui. et VII. uillani et III. bordarii cum. IIII. carucis. Ibi. III. liberi homines. Silua.

VI. quarentes longa. et IIII. quarentes lata.

Ad hanc terram perinet dimidia hida in alia Ernlege. quam Osbernus filius Ricardi ui tollit canonicis. Terra est. I. carucae. Ibi est cum. III. uillanis. Valet. X. solidos.

In BISCOPESBERIE habent ipsi canonici. I. virgatam terrae. Terra est dimidiae carucae. Ibi est unus liber homo cum. I. caruca. Valet. XII. denarios.

In COTE habent. I. virgatam terrae. Terra est dimidiae carucae. Hanc habet ibi unus liber homo. et valet. XII. denarios.

1 "Domesday Book and Beyond", 1897.

2 There were in Staffordshire 5 hundreds, and the fact that the Wolverhampton manors (or the main group of them) spread over 3 of them—those of Cuttlestone, Seisdon and Offlow, shows that "hundreding" had preceded Wulfrun's gift (S.H.C. 1916, p. 158). It was otherwise with the church lands (and this is specially to be noted in Worcestershire) where ownership very much shaped the formation of the hundred boundaries. Again, the fact that the adjoining parish of Bushbury lies in 2 hundreds shows that it was of late formation. Evidence that it was originally formed from Wolverhampton will be adduced in another connection.

In TOTENHALE habent. I. hidam. Terra est. II. carucis et dimidae. et ibi sunt. III. carucae cum. I. uillano et. III. bordariis.
Haec terra non pertinet ad Hantone. sed est elemosina regis ad ecclesiam eiusdem uillae. De eadem elemosina habent presbyteri de Totenhale. I. hidam in BILREBROCH. Ibi sunt. II. liberi homines cum. I. uillano et II. bordarii habentes. II. carucas et dimidiam.
Ipsi canonici habent in HASWIC. V. hidas. Terra est. VIII. carucis. Modo est wasta propter forestam regis. Ibi pertinuit medietas siluae. quae est in foresta.
Ipsi canonici habent. V. hidas in WODNESFELDE. Terra est. III. carucis. Ibi sunt. VI. uillani et VI. bordarii habentes. VI. carucas.
Silua pastilis dimidium leuum longitudine et III. quarentes latitudine.
Ipsi canonici tenent. II. hidas in WINENHALE. Terra est. I. carucae. Ibi sunt III. uillani et V. bordarii habentes. III. carucas.
Ipsi tenent dimidiam hidam in PELESHALE. Terra est. I. carucae. Haec uasta est.
Ipsi tenent. III. virgatas terrae in ILTONE. Terra est. I. carucae.
Ibi. II. liberi homines et IIII. bordarii habent. II. carucas.
In HOCINTVNE. I. hida Wasta.

Tota haec canonicorum terra ualet per annum. VI. libras.

IN COLVESTAN HD.

SANSON tenet de rege. et Eduin et Alric presbyteri de eo. III. Lidas terrae in HARGEDONE. Terra est. II. carucis. In dominio est una. et unus seruus. Ibi. I. miles et III. uillani cum. VII. bordariis habent. III. carucas. Silua ibi dimidium leuum longitudine. et quatuor quarentes latitudine.
Valuit. II. solidos. Modo. X. solidos.
Ipsi tenent. I. hidam in CHENWARDESTONE. Terra est. I. carucae. In dominio sunt duo carucae. et III. serui. et III. bordarii. Ibi molina de. III. solidis. et VIII. acrae prati. T.R.E. ualebat. XII. denarios. Modo ualet. X. solidos. Has duas terras tenuit S. MARIA de Hantone. T.R.E.
Ipsi tenent. II. hidas in HALTONE. Terra est. II. carucis. In dominio est una. cum. I. seruo. et unus liber homo cum. II. bordariis habet carucam et dimidiam. et III. uillani habent ibi. I. caruca.

Valuit. XII. denarios. Modo. X. solidos.

Ipsi habent in FERDESTAN. I. hidam wastam.
The King owned Bilston and the other part of Willenhall, and their record is as follows:—
In BILLESTVNE sunt. II. hidae. Terra est. IIII. carucis. Ibi sunt VIII. uillani et. III. borazii cum. III. carucis. Ibi. I. acra prati. Silua dimidium leuum longitudine. et dimidium lat. Valuit. XX. solidos. Modo. XXX. solidos.
Rex tenet WINEHALA. Ibi. III. hidae. Terra est. IIII. carucis. Ibi sunt. V. uillani et. III. bordarii cum. III. carucis. Ibi. I. acra prati. Valuit et valet XX. solidos.
Of manors adjoining Wolverhampton, the following were the King's:— Tettenhall, Compton and Wightwick.
The remainder belonged to the Dudley fief of William fitz Ansculf, being all in Seisdon hundred—with the exception of Essington:—Sedgley, both Penns, Oxley, Ettingshall, Bushbury, Pendeford, Moseley, Essington and Bradley (by Bilston).
Lady Godiva formerly owned Lower Penn, Moseley and an unnamed estate in Bushbury belonging to Essington, and now unoccupied. (uasta est omino, says the record. It was probably Sewall).

The aggregate of 27¼ hides out of the original 30 of Wulfrun's grant, shows how well the assessment of the 9th century, though now out of date and with a decreasing taxable capacity,[1] had been remembered; but monastic bodies (as the records of Burton and Worcester show) made careful notes of these things. Wolverhampton and its dependencies thus paid £3, when charged with a Danegeld of 2s. on the 'hide' in 991; but when William I. taxed his subjects "stiffly" in 1084 at 6s. a 'hide', he would not have been able to collect more than £5 15s. 6d. out of a possible £8 3s. 6d. (formerly £9) working on the Domesday figures, a loss of about one third. Even so the 1084 tax must have been a grievous one, as it represented the whole annual income returned in 1086.

One striking point which one notices in this list is the very small and apparently inadequate assessment given to 'Hampton' (one hide) compared with the neighbouring villages of Wednesfield and Willenhall (5 hides each).[2] The different treatment may be accounted for in two ways; firstly it may be that Wolverhampton was not at the time of the original assessment in the 9th century of any great importance: it was undeveloped economically compared with its neighbours on the east; it is a suggestion that may confirm the theory of the town's late origin. Secondly, there is granted "his priests at Hampton" freedom from burdens to which they had hitherto been subject. Prof. Maitland explains these as "worldly, secular, temporal services" (p. 270) meaning that the land is devoted to services which are "heavenly, sacred, spiritual".

The occupiers of the soil do not benefit. The church merely took what the King had hitherto taken; (ib. 272) and now Samson, it would seem, would take what the church had obtained. But the clergy must be provided for, and the time was soon to come when the canons were to have some definite provision (prebends) made for them.

Domesday Book actually mentions the existence of 13 prebendaries (canonici prebendarii) at Stafford without naming them. At Wolverhampton no number is mentioned and the reference is to "priests" (presbyteri). But in enumerating the church's estates in the hundred of Cuttlestone: those of Kinvaston, Hatherton, Hilton and Featherstone (which latter was then vasta or unoccupied), and the record is interlined, as though an afterthought, or because a little more definite information seems to have been required, are entered the names "Eduin" and "Alric" priests as tenants there, holding from the dean. This represents the legal position in a feudal community, and it seems certain that in these Eadwin and Aelric priests we get the names of two prebendaries of the time (1086), leaving the soldier, miller and freeman (the producing element) as undertenants.

The case of Willenhall is another instance. In Domesday Book this 5 hide manor is divided between the King and the canons, yet it does not form part of the original endowment. Its appearance as church property denotes the foundation of another prebend, Willenhall Prebend.

One note more and we can leave Domesday. In 985 the description of Wulfrun's lands[3] brings them to the boundaries (at least) of Sedgley. The King's manors now isolated this place from the Church's possessions.[4] But under Sedgley the survey hints at its former neighbour; it remarks "Part of the wood of this manor the priests of Hampton claim".

Samson the King's chaplain has been called the first dean of Wolverhampton. "The title is anachronous" writes Eyton,[5] "but probably represents the essence of his position as well as any other".

1 It is believed that the compilation of Domesday Book was intended to provide the materials for a new assessment; but it was found easier to impose a new tax (tallage) than to correct the old.

2 The King also had 3 hides in Willenhall, which with the clerks' 2 make up a "5 hide unit" (the holding of a Saxon thegn).

3 S.H.C. 1916, p. 102.

4 But the lay manor of Wolverhampton was probably part of the Dudley fief (until exchanged with the King in 1204–5), estimated at 3 hides. Cote (trescot) which was the canons' in 1086 was afterwards in the possession of one of the Dudley tenants.

5 Staffs. Domesday, p. 44.

Of noble lineage he was befriended by William I from childhood, took minor orders, married and became the father of two bishops and a lady of fashion at the Court. He did not pretend to any great sanctity and refused a bishopric in 1073, but accepted the position of treasurer and a canonry of Bayeux (1082). There can be very little doubt that he was rarely if ever seen in Wolverhampton: he was a courtier and followed the court. His brother Thomas, Archbishop of York (d. 1100) could speak no English, and this was probably also true of himself and most other Normans. (It was true of his successor at Wolverhampton, dean Peter of Blois in the time of King John). He continued in favour under William II and was on 8 June 1096[1] consecrated bishop of Worcester at St. Paul's London, the archbishop Anselm and Thomas, his brother, officiating. He had been admitted to priest's orders on the preceding day. Without the qualities of a bishop but of a charitable disposition he benefitted Worcester by his gifts and was let down lightly by the chroniclers with some aspersions on his gluttony. It may not have been easy to succeed St. Wulfsten upon whose newly completed church he now entered. That he remained at court may perhaps be shown by his grant of the church of Hartlebury for the support of the monks of Worcester in 1097. (Sir Ivor Atkins, The Church of Worcester from the Eighth to the Twelfth Century. Antiquaries Journal April 1940. p. 212 (citing Hemming, Chart. p. 426)).

Here one of the witnesses is the archdeacon of Bayeux, and it looks as though Samson has accompanied his monarch on his visit to Normandy in that year. Two others of the meagre array of witnesses were Worcester Monks (his chaplains) one being Frederick who witnessed his grant of Wolverhampton to Worcester.

Here began a curious interlude in the history of Wolverhampton College, a crisis which produced other crises, before stability was regained.

Fortunately this period is well documented. At Worcester are preserved in cartulary form an interesting series of charters "hitherto", wrote Eyton in 1881, "sadly mis-stated and sorely misunderstood".

They carry the history of Wolverhampton Church to the reign of Henry II. By the first charter (passed at the beginning of Henry I's reign and before the death of the "terrible" Urse d'Abetot, c. 1106, the witness to King Henry's charter of confirmation) Samson, bishop of Worcester granted "to Thomas the prior and the brothers and our sons the monks of St. Mary of Worcester, the church of Wolverhampton with its lands and possessions as free and quiet as my lord King William gave and granted it to me. Moreover while they keep and maintain this gift let them receive the revenue from every repayment".[2]

Ailric the archdeacon and Frederic and Ailwin the chaplains were witnesses.[3] The King briefly confirmed this in two charters (one omitted by Shaw).

There follows a grant in similar terms of Queen Matilda "on behalf of her lord the King and of herself" witnessed by Roger, bishop of Salisbury (so not before 1107) and Adam de Port.[4] This document when referred to in subsequent deeds seems to have been taken as the act of Matilda queen of Henry I (d. 1118). It is not clear why it was made unless, perhaps, she was acting as regent while her husband was in France.

In 1109 Samson was required to take part against his son Thomas archbishop elect of York who refused obedience to Anselm archbishop of Canterbury. The dispute was a

1 So D.N.B.

2 As leases fell in—if this be the meaning of "ab omnium retributore mercedem".

3 The Latin of these grants is given in Shaw ii, 152, col. 1.

4 This can hardly have been Adam de Port of Arley, whose lands were seized in 1172 for treason. Roger was Bishop from 1107–1139, and sided with Stephen.

High Green looking south-west, 1835

Old House in Exchange Street

long one, but acting on his father's and brother's advice Thomas at length gave way having become "enormously fat and consequently unfitted to bear exile and worry".

On 5 May 1112 Samson Bishop of Worcester died. He was buried in the nave of his Cathedral monastery at Worcester before the crucifix.

The document mentioned above is of interest because it was thought necessary to fortify the gift by the bishop's approval and also for its testimony of the church's privileged position.

Not much later can have been the bishop's confirmation in these terms:—

"Robert[1] by the grace of God bishop of Coventry to all his successors, &c., greeting. By the episcopal authority and by the security of the present charter I grant and confirm that gift of the Church of Wolverhampton which Samson the bishop made to his monks at Worcester, that the brothers themselves may possess it lawfully for ever, and hold it without any disturbance with all their tenures which are contained in the privileges of the aforesaid Church. For this church of Wolverhampton was of old one of the King's own chapels which used to belong to the Crown; but the most pious King Henry (sic) had given it to Samson his chaplain aforesaid. Samson verily when bishop gave it to the Church of Worcester as we have said above and King Henry and Queen Maud all consenting to his gift as their charters bear witness".

It was evidently considered that the grant to Samson was so absolute that it did not end with his life. But doubts on this point were settled by a charter of his son the archbishop, which can be dated 28 December 1113 and 24 February 1114.[2]

"Thomas by the Grace of God archbishop of York to T(heobald) elect of Worcester greeting and God's blessing. I confirm and grant as previously I have granted and confirmed the full alms of my father which he made by giving his fee of Wulrunahantun to church of Worcester and which I, to whom (my) father himself had given the aforesaid fee, have confirmed by my seal and assent".

What followed may be picked up from a letter of the Canons of Wlfruntun (though written apparently from Worcester) to pope Eugenius (1145—53).

It appears that on Samson's death "Roger bishop of Salisbury, who by means of his excessive power did much against right and justice with impunity and greatly oppressed very many churches of the English realm, violently assailed the church (of Wolverhampton) and despoiled the church of Worcester unjustly and without judicial order, the monks themselves continually resisting and showing dissent".

But bishop Roger of Salisbury fell in 1139 and was compelled to disgorge. In a very humble notification which can only have been made between the time of his imprisonment and death in this year (for it, like the rest of the series, is without date except such as can be inferred) he recounts, after allowing his action to be through ambition and secular power: "I acknowledge that on account of this grave sin and my offences the hand of my lord (? the King) has touched and worthily overthrown me. I therefore taking refuge in the pity of the most pious Mary the mother of God, seek forgiveness and pray the brothers of Worcester in order that they may pardon me through God's mercy this grave injury which I have inflicted on them and absolve me in the presence of God before whom I already take my trial".

King Stephen evidently seized this church as part of Roger's property, and not knowing what to do with it, handed it over to the bishop of the diocese. Pope Lucius confirmed

1 Robert (1086—Sept. 1117) and Robert his successor (chosen 1121. Died 1127—Brit. Chronology: Powicke). Oliver, p. 30, assigns this to Bishop Roger, and indeed makes chaos of these charters and the tale they tell.

2 Eyton's Staffs. Domesday, p. 45. He does not seem to have been aware that the Archbishop was Samson's son

this grant to the bishop (R. de Clinton) and Church of Lichfield together with those of the churches of Stafford, Penkridge and Gnosall on 4 May 1144.[1]

King Stephen's charter runs:—

"Know ye that I have restored to God and St. Mary and the prior and monks of the church of Worcester for the soul of my mother's brother King Henry the Church of Wlfrunhamtona, which I had formerly inadvisedly granted to R(oger) bishop of Chester. For I have enquired from many whose it was of old and ought to be and therefore I am unwilling that they should lose or in any way be disturbed on account of any writ which the bishop has there (propter breve alquod quodeps inde habeat) Wherefore I will and order that thus they hold it, well, freely and quietly just as Samson the bishop gave it to them, and Thomas the archbishop granted it, and as the charter of King Henry my uncle bears witness".

It has usually been considered and the probability is that the losses of territory which the Wolverhampton Church is known to have suffered, took place during the Bishop of Salisbury's usurpation.

Arley and Trescote were alienated in or before the next reign, and Haswic which was "unoccupied" in 1086 had probably been incorporated, without protest, into the King's forest of Kinver at a still earlier date. It is curious, as regards the latter, that some hint of its original ownership existed late in the 17th century when the people of the vicinity knew of this deserted area (the "Camp" at Greensforge near Swindon) as "Wolverhampton Churchyard", but at a still later date a legend connecting it with the devil and Kingswinford Church had sprung up,[2] an attempt to explain an archaeological puzzle by an appeal to the supernatural.

It is not at all clear how or by what act the Church of Worcester lost the church of Wolverhampton. This happened in the time of Henry II and may have been accomplished by the charter granted by him as Duke sometime after March 1153 and before he came to the throne in 1154.

This document is a very curious one and its true significance seems to have been overlooked by all commentators on Staffordshire history.[3] This is what probably happened. In January 1153 Duke Henry landed in England to claim the crown. In March[4] he bribes Ranulph Earl of Chester, in return for his support with a grant of a large part of England, including, in the main, all Staffordshire except the Bishop's, Earl Ferrars and Gervas Paganell's baronies.

This was the so called Treaty of Devizes. He evidently regarded Paganell of Dudley as favourable to his party, for the late baron had supported the Empress, his mother in 1138. It was at Dudley therefore that the canons of Wolverhampton met the Duke and his followers and obtained their charter, the Duke being ready to grant anything[5] within reason and the canons (unattached to a bishopric) being left by a turn of fortune woefully out in the cold.

"Henry duke of Normandy and Aquitaine and earl of Anjou to all archbishops, bishops, earls, barons, justices, sheriffs and all his friends and faithful (both) Normans and English, greeting—

1 Dugdale: Monast. Ed. 1846, vi. 1252.

2 Shaw ii, 233.

3 It is listed out of order in the confirmation of the charters in 1328. See Oliver, p. 178.

4 Or thereabouts. See S.H.C. ii, 222, etc.

5 The fragment of Pipe Roll for 1154 (S.H.C. i. 17) shows that Henry had been lavish with his gifts both to clerical and lay. Eyton (ib. 19) notes that Henry visited Dudley during his campaign of 1153, but forgets the evidence of this charter.

Know ye that I have granted to the church of Wluronehampton my chapel all that liberty which it had in the time of King Henry my grandfather and all that quiet in wood and field, in meadows and pastures, in waters and without, in roads and lanes and in all places.

And to the canons of the same church I grant the same freedom and quiet. Wherefore I command and strictly order that the same church be my free chapel exempt (quieta) with all its appurtenances from all customs and taxes, and that the canons possess all their things freely and quietly, nor shall anyone dare to cause them loss or trouble or any hurt.

As witness Roger, earl of Hereford, Walter his brother, Constable, Henry his brother, Gervase Paganell cousin (germans) at Dudley".

There can be very little doubt that when Henry II became King, the canons sought an early confirmation of his grant and that the following writ (whose date lies somewhere within the period dated by the term of Thomas a' Becket's chancellorship, (1154—62) was then made.

"Henry, King of the English, duke of Normandy and of Aquitaine and earl of Anjou to his sheriffs and bailiffs of Staffordshire greeting. I ordain that the lands and the men which belong to the church of Wlurnehamton be in peace and exempt from court attendance (placitis) and fines (querelis) both of Shires and hundreds and from all things except (the fine for) murder and highway robbery, even as they were ever benefitted in the time of King Henry my grandfather.

As witnesseth Thomas the chancellor at Westminster".

With Henry II commences the list of Deans proper. There was probably also some appointment or confirmation of an appointment. In 1172, 31s. 8d. was returned by the sheriff from the King's chapel of Wolverhampton, pointing to a vacancy in the deanery at that date.[1]

Whether Peter of Blois (Blessensis) succeeded then to this preferment is not at all certain; but he is known to have been introduced by the King into England in or before 1173[2] and there is an apparent coincidence of dates. This French nobleman was made archdeacon of Bath (c. 1175) and a canon of Chartres (c. 1176) and the Wolverhampton deanery whenever it came to him can only have represented a little more pocket money for an impecunious diplomat.

Dean Peter has appeared to recent writers[3] as conscientious and righteous. It is possible he was both upon occasion. Known chiefly as a prolific letter writer, a man of undoubted ability and unquestioned learning, fit to be entrusted with missions to the Pope, he was nevertheless greedy of preferment and loud in his complaints. Although certainly dean of Wolverhampton in 1190, when he was having trouble with the sheriff,[4] he was silent on the imperfections of the College until 1198 (for his letter to the Pope Innocent cannot have appeared before) although the scandals were notorious and crying for reform.

The morality of the clergy at this time was medieval, and it may be doubted whether Peter was much of a moral reformer. He had fallen out with his prebendaries and in spite of threats they would not fall in with his views. But he had the advantage of his criminous clerks. They had faults; the townsmen treated them with contempt; while he had the ear of the archbishop whose secretary he was. It is possible his aim was constitutional reform. The primary reason for the college had ceased, the district being then amply provided with parish churches; but an abbey with increased revenues and himself as abbot might still have its uses and fulfil in his opinion a long felt want.

1 Pipe Roll 1172–3 (S.H.C. i. 66–7).
2 This and what follows is taken from D.N.B.
3 Oliver, p. 33. Hall's Coll. Church, p. 14.
4 (Note omitted in MS.–J.S.R.).

The outcome was his resignation. He had taken priest's orders against his will in order to qualify for the archdeaconry of London (c. 1192) when he complained "he must live on wind" moreover "he heard in England a tongue he knew not" and he sighed for his native land. It has been suggested that as no new dean is known to have been appointed until August 1205, Peter's resignation may have been as late as 1204, but in an unimportant lawsuit of 1203 connected with the ownership of Kinvaston a Nicholas "decanus" of Wolverhampton, otherwise Nicholas of Wolverhampton, occurs, and, although this by itself is slight evidence, there is corroboration in a suit concerning the advowson of Penne church in 1292 of which "Nicholas formerly Dean of the Church of St. Peter and Paul of Wolverhampton" was said to have been seised in the time of King John.

The explanation may be that dean Peter resigned at the beginning of John's reign, having received preferment more to his liking in exchange. In the meantime the archbishop's preparation for an abbey continued.

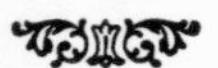

CHAPTER IV

MEDIÆVAL WOLVERHAMPTON

THE history of Wolverhampton during the thirteenth, fourteenth and fifteenth centuries is largely that of the church and its officials and the activities of the important families. Local government as we know it today was almost non-existent for Wolverhampton was one of the market towns which had no charter of incorporation at that time. Local affairs were carried on by the churchwardens, through the Easter Vestry, and by the manor courts, the latter having the more important functions. The Statute of Highways 1555 permitted the vestry to appoint supervisors of the highways but it was not until the end of the reign of Elizabeth I that they could appoint Overseers of the Poor to administer the newly enacted poor laws.

In Wolverhampton there were three manors, two belonging to the church and one to the King. The church's manors were those of the Deanery and the Prebends and the King's manor that of Stowheath. Each of these manors held its annual court, usually in October, when the officers were appointed. These consisted, amongst others, of the lord's bailiff who held office, in his turn, by virtue of his ownership of one of the customary tenements, the constable and his deputy who were responsible for order in the court, the calling of officers and the carrying out of the court's decisions, the pinner or bellman who acted as town crier and looked after the public pound, the ale conners who approved the standard of brewing in the manor and the jury who decided any doubtful cases brought before the court. The court baron and court leet which usually sat together dealt with the appointment of officers, the transfer of land and property and the proving of wills, while the court of the view of frank pledge dealt with misdemeanors of tenants. Such infringements of the laws of the manor as the stopping up of watercourses and drains, refusal to cut the hedges, permitting of livestock to wander about the highway, lack of repairs to the highway and building on the lord's waste or common land were all offences punishable by a fine. It was quite common to build on the common land and many tenants did this, considering the fine (about two pence annually) as a small rent. Many of these squatters cottages can still be seen in the district of Priestfields Road although a much larger number are to be found in the manor of Sedgley where this contravention seems to have flourished.

The officers of the court were chosen from the tenants of the manor and their service was compulsory and without remuneration. Sometimes a man refused to serve as in the case of John son of William Jones who held a house and land in Wednesfield in the Deanery Manor. In 1351 the dean, Phillip de Weston seized his cattle in a field called Middle furlong in Wednesfield for refusing to take the office of Provost[1] and Jones sued at the Hillary Assize for their return, pleading that as he was a tenant of the manor and not a native within it he was exempt from service. The case was adjourned and we do not know the outcome.

1 S.H.C. Vol. XII, p. 110.

As the deans and prebendaries were pluralists and very often non-resident in the town they leased out their interests in the manors for long periods and this practice led in the end to the alienation of a large part of Wulfrun's endowments and the consequent enrichment of the lessees. By this means such families as the Levesons rose to great wealth and the church became the poorer.[1]

A large part of the original parish of Wolverhampton was copyhold of one or other of the three manors, but there were several areas of considerable size which from very early times seem to have been of freehold tenure. Title deeds of properties in the centre of the town reveal small islands of freehold land in Dudley Street, Bilston Street and Victoria Street, and the position is the same in the centre of Willenhall. Larger freehold areas can also be found at Wood End in Wednesfield and Little London in Willenhall and there are no doubt others. Some part of Wulfrun's endowment both in the Deanery and Prebendal Manors lay in districts outside the confines of the mediaeval parish of Wolverhampton and it may well be that at one time the parish extended over a much larger area. There is good reason to believe that the priests of Hampton served Bushbury in the 12th century before it became a separate parish and in that area lay the bulk of the Prebendal Manor of Wobaston, and Featherstone and Hilton were nearby. Kinvaston and Hatherton were near to Penkridge and so lay much farther afield. The same is true of Codsall, Lutley near Halesowen, Ogley Hay near Brownhills and Pelsall, although the latter place was within the parish until the end of the Peculiar. All these latter places were in the Deanery Manor. This large manor covered the northern part of the town of Wolverhampton and also included nearly the whole of Wednesfield, part of Codsall, a small part of Willenhall, Lutley and Pelsall.

The boundaries of the manors were never well defined and we frequently find small islands of one manor scattered about within the confines of another. This is particularly true in the case of portions of the Prebendal Manor in the centre of Wolverhampton and in Willenhall. The Prebendal Manors of Featherstone, Hilton, Wobaston, Willenhall, Hatherton and Monmore were held together, and ultimately farmed together, by the Leveson family and their successors.

At some unknown date the canons of Wolverhampton were each allotted one of the manors which were part of the original foundation, and in addition a house and land in the town itself, towards their support or provision (prebend). One might assume that these estates were distributed no earlier than those of the canons or prebendaries of Lichfield —direct documentary evidence is lacking before the 12th century. There exists, however, a strange tradition, put forward in 1393, about a grant of King Henry I to the six priests serving the church of St. Mary of Wolverhampton and their successors, of a house and 40 acres of land in Wolverhampton worth yearly 10 marks, and 20 pounds of rent receivable from various tenants at Easter and Michaelmas.[2] It is odd that nothing more has been heard of this grant; but the 10 marks, £6 13s. 4d., does represent approximately the full year's value of the crown land in Wolverhampton at the end of the 12th century.[3]

In any case prebendaries were in existence at this date, for the dean, Peter of Blois, in his letter to the Pope, speaks of having the gift and institution of the prebends "by very

1 The Deanery Manor eventually passed into the hands of the Dukes of Cleveland and on the death of the last Duke in 1891 the lease expired and it reverted to the Church Commissioners. The history of the Manor of the Prebends took a different course. This manor was sold for £1,200 by Robert Leveson and Robert his son to Francis, Earl of Bradford. Negotiations for the sale commenced about January, 1702 and the deeds are dated 20 and 21 May, 1702. These are at Raby Castle among the muniments of Lord Barnard who, as heir of the Dukes of Cleveland, succeeded to the property. With the passing of the Law of Property Act in 1925 the manorial system with the many rights of copyhold tenure disappeared.

2 Chancery Inquisitions Misc.: File 254, No. 76. The Rev. George Fisher in his " Sketch " of the church's history gives the date as 1121 [? a guess].

3 S.H.C. II 137. The actual value was £6 - 12 - 0 [ibid. 131].

ancient custom".[1] Robert of Shrewsbury was holding a prebend of Wolverhampton before he became bishop of Bangor in 1197.[2]

The manor of Kinvaston followed a different course from the others and ultimately passed into the hands of the owners of Oxley. As a general rule the property of each prebend lay within the area after which the prebend was named but there were also a small number of island sites in Wolverhampton on which burgage houses were built. These lay scattered about the centre of the town. In Willenhall we find that besides land belonging to the prebend of Willenhall there was also a considerable area belonging to the prebend of Wobaston, one or two small island blocks on the north side of the Market Place in the prebend of Hatherton. The reason for this jigsaw arrangement is now obscure.

The manor of Stowheath was by far the largest of the three Wolverhampton manors, for besides covering a large part of Wolverhampton and stretching as far west as the Halfway House on Tettenhall road it covered the whole of Bilston and a considerable part of Willenhall. It eventually came into the possession of the family of Lovel[3] and was held by them until forfeited on attainder by Francis, Lord Lovel, in 1485. He appears in Shakespeare's play Richard III and was one of the most romantic figures of his time. On 18 December 1489 the King granted the office of Bailiff of the lordship of Wolverhampton to his servitor Thomas Taillour, one of the yeomen of the crown.[4] On the 18 June 1512 Sir John Gifford, a member of the King's household, (being Gentleman Usher of the Chamber)obtained the office of joint bailiff of this manor.[5] Later on the Leveson family purchased the manor, for Joyce daughter of James Leveson brought half of the manor to the Giffards of Chillington, and the Dukes of Sutherland, descended from James Leveson's brother Nicholas, retained the other half and their descendants share the manor in this way until the present day.[6]

Having considered the position of local government in Wolverhampton in the Middle Ages we now return to the doings of the church and the deans. As a result of the efforts of Peter of Blois and Archbishop Hubert Walter, King John agreed to the suppression of the deanery of Wolverhampton and the setting up of a monastery and to this end the King granted a charter on 31 May 1205[7] whereby the manors of Wolverhampton and Tettenhall passed to the new foundation. The change took place and the monks entered into possession, but the death of the Archbishop on 13 July 1207 put an end to the project and the King snatched back his manors and cancelled his grant. "Now for the first time am I King of England" he said.[8] The move had one effect that was important. To obtain the "manor of Wolverhampton" it had been necessary to make an exchange in 1204 with Ralph, Lord Dudley in whose family it had been for generations. This detached Wolverhampton from the Dudley influence.

In 1224 Giles de Erdington was appointed dean of Wolverhampton and he was destined to rule there for the next 44 years. He was a man of considerable ability for besides being an ecclesiastic he was also a lawyer and judge. It may well be that he owed his appointment to the influence of his father Thomas de Erdington who had been a power in the land, not only as Sheriff of Stafford and Shropshire but as a favourite of King John who rewarded him, after a mission to Rome, 3 November 1212, with a grant of the rich manor of

1 Letters cxliii [Edition 1519] otherwise No. 152.
2 Ib. Letters 147.
3 Wolverhampton Antiquary Vol. II, p. 103.
4 Cal. Pat. Rolls. 5 Pat. Rolls. S.H.C. N.S. V., p. 112.
6 The Court rolls of these manors, or copies of them, are at the William Salt Library, Stafford. They are a wonderful source of local history recording as they do the day to day affairs of the local families, very often enrolling the pedigrees of quite humble folk when it was necessary to place on record the rightful title to some property in the manor. The existing court rolls of the Deanery Manor commence in 1603, those of the Manor of the Prebends in 1653 and those of Stowheath in 1645.
7 For charters and translation see History of Tettenhall—J. P. Jones, p.p. 19–23.
8 " John Lackland" by Kate Norgate, 1902, p. 113.

Wellington (Salop). He also held Shawbury in the same county. When Thomas de Erdington died as a monk at Worcester 20 March 1217/18 his eldest son Peter was on the fifth Crusade (1218/21) from which he did not return leaving Giles to succeed to the patrimony while still under age.

As a younger son it is possible that Giles was receiving a training in the law which he subsequently pursued. No patent of his election as dean has survived; but the considerations which weighed with King John seem also to have influenced his son and successor Henry III, and Giles is stated to be holding the church and deanery of Wolverhampton "by gift of the present King". He was certainly dean in 1224 when he was probably of age.

It was not therefore as a humble ecclesiastic that Giles (Egidius) de Erdington appears in history, but as a holder of manors and broad acres in more than one county. His interest in Erdington was shared with a cousin (William Maunsel), but he owned other manors and, more important, the advowsons, it seems, of Aston-by-Birmingham where his brother Henry had been parson, and of Yardley, Worcestershire, and in the latter connection was remembered as a benefactor of the Priory of Newport Pagnel. As a tenant of the Dudley fief, through Erdington, he was of less importance than holder, as knight of the barony of Stafford, of Oakley, near Elford, and in the Barons' Wars (1264—6) this may have influenced him to take the side against the King.

He was a considerable benefactor of St. Thomas's Priory near Stafford, for he and his heirs had the presentation of a canon to celebrate divine service there for the health of his soul; and his name was entered in their martyrology, so that his anniversary could be kept everafter in an ample manner. He was appointed a Justice of Assize from 1250 continuously until 1262 (but not in 1263/4) and in 1265 his judicial services were required both by the barons and the King; he was similarly employed until the middle of 1268. He was "lately deceased" in March 1269. Sir Henry de Erdington, his son, married Maud fourth daughter of Roger de Somery, baron of Dudley. He died in 1280 and a descendant, Giles, stood at Crecy.

It is possible that Giles made Wolverhampton his headquarters, and that the development of his estates there was due to his presence on the spot. For there was not only exploitation but augmentation. The appearance of Codsall manor as part of the endowment of the church begins at this time, and at the far side of Wednesfield he receives (by Royal grant, no doubt) some 32 acres from Bentley Hay "worth 20s. per annum" at a rent of half a mark (6s. 8d.) yearly "for that his successors, the dean and church of Wolverhampton might hold the said land of the King by serjeantry and by one-fifteenth part of a knight's fee".

It has been thought that the church of Wolverhampton possessed no land within the manor of Essington;[1] but a dispute between Giles de Erdington, Dean of Wolverhampton, and Robert de Essington (Esenington) and Robert de Wyston tenants of two acres of wood "with the appurtenances" in Essington, seems to show it had certain undefined rights in that area. The difference concerned "the whole wood within the metes and bounds below written. To wit, from Kirclesford[2] by the entrenched place of Wulfrin (per fossatum Wulfrini) and by the Holeweweye as far as Horestan, and from Horestan in a line as far as Biribrok (usque in Biribrok) and so by the hedge of Esenington and by the high road which is called Stamstre as far as Kirclesford".

1 "Essington never belonged to the Canons of Hampton" says Duignan boldly—Charter of Wulfrun p. 15, note 2.
2 The correct spelling (c and t at this date being indistinguishable) is probably Kirtlesford, agreeing with the two other examples in this respect.
Kirtlesford—see also Essington Deed No. 22, a grant of "a certain meadow which John Wodeman held near Curtlesford"—temp. Edw. I.

It is not easy to identify this area. Biri- or Bury- brook and the hedge of Esenington suggest the neighbourhood of Blackhalves; and Stamstre (? Stonystreet) and Horestone may be the old Lichfield Road and the Horestone (mentioned in 994) in the same area. Alternatively the locality may be somewhere in Short Heath, perhaps crossing Pool Hayes brook near New Invention.

An agreement was reached on 1 December 1240 whereby the wood was divided between claimants, the Dean's portion, "to wit, that moiety which is towards the sun" to be held by him and his successors and the church in frankalmoign.[1]

A further reference to Kirclesford is to be found in a Huntbach deed (Huntbach M.S., Bridgeman copy, W.S.L. p. 50) relating to land at Bentley, whereby John, lord of Bentley grants to Nicholas Underhull of Wodensfeld a place of land called "le olde Borewardes Croft in territorio de Bentley" as was ditched about and bounded thus:—vizt. medietatum que jacet propinquior versus Curtleford". Habendum, etc. Witnesses:— Wm. Hillary de Bertem'cote, Hen. de Prestwode, Ric'o Leveson de Wylenhale, Will'o ad Boscum de Echeles, Will'o Boon del Merch, Will'o ad gardinum de Bentley, Johanne de Lappel' clerico.

The date of this deed is probably late Edward I but it may be earlier. William Hillary seems to have outlived the Edward I period. We know the date of death of Henry de Prestwood.

It was during dean Erdington's time that King Henry III on 4 February 1258 granted his charter for a market and fair. The charter conferred the right of a weekly market to be held every Wednesday and a fair to be held every year commencing on the Vigil of the Feast of St. Peter and St. Paul and lasting for eight days. Although the charter gives no indication of the fact there was undoubtedly a market in Wolverhampton long before this date as the following entry in the Assize Roll for 5 John (1204) bears witness:—

Mercatum de Wulvernhamton remotum est a die Dominica usque ad diem Mercurii, et ideo villata in misericordiam et sit per diem illum.

In 1261 the King confirmed the church of Wolverhampton as an exempt jurisdiction "whereby they were exempt from all ordinary jurisdiction and that no sentence of excommunication or interdiction should be pronounced against them, without especial licence of the Apostolic See".

These changes were not made without clashes with local interests, the Abbot of Croxden at Codsall, and William de Bentley at Bentley. It is of interest therefore to find a suit brought by William de Bentley against the dean's tenants at Wednesfield for depasturing their cattle on his corn. This was on Monday before St. Peter and Paul 1250 and twenty to thirty acres were involved. Giles claimed that the defendants were his villeins and that he held this land as part of a serjeantry he held of the King. Evidently the land in question was in or near Bentley Hay, which was subject to his tenure, and we may have here the germ which became Short Heath. Bentley lay in the parish of Wolverhampton, and at that early date part of it was known as the 'bailiwick of Wolverhampton'.

The considerable number of charters (or their copies) still in existence bear testimony to Erdington's endeavours to strengthen the finances of the church and deanery but it was through some of the long leases which he created that church property ultimately fell into other hands. The annual rent or consideration was generally, by our standards, quite small and as the years went by it ceased to be paid. This is particularly true of the small estate adjoining Watling Street at Ogley near Brownhills which was part of Wulfrun's

1 Feet of Fine 15–26 Henry III, Stafford No. 58.

foundation and was leased by Erdington about 1226 to William Rous lord of Walsall for the rental of 4 pounds of wax given to God and the light of the church of Wolverhampton yearly on the Feast of St. Peter and St. Paul for ever. The text of the charter is preserved in a Walsall Chartulary in the British Museum (Cottonian M.S. Nero, CXII p. 132) and it gives the boundaries as from "Chyancland (? Cannockland) descending as far as the Causeway of Ecleford and thus from the causeway ascending the Wite (sitch?) as far as Watling Street and so from that road to Clianeland (presumably the starting point)".[1]

In the case of Dam Mill[2] we see in operation the process of acquisition, for here Erdington, having purchased 3 acres of land near the Penk from Nicholas of Oaken, dammed the stream and established a mill there. The church of Tettenhall formed a dam higher up the stream and so denied water to the dean's mill. This produced a law suit at Stafford at Ascentiontide 1230 when the dean sued William chaplain of Tettenhall (Cal. Pat. Rolls). All this property afterwards became copyhold of the Deanery Manor.

Towards the end of his long and active life dean Erdington began to prepare himself for the future life. He had built himself a chantry chapel within Wolverhampton Church and in the fulness of time he made provision for its endowment. The deed which recorded this transaction unfortunately perished in the disastrous fire which completely destroyed Wrottesley Hall in December 1897 but fortunately at least two antiquaries saw it and made a note of its contents. Dugdale in his copy of the Aston Chartulary (Dugdale M.S. 15, Bodleian Library) copies it thus:—

f.39.b. "Notum sit (etc.) quod ego Egidius de Erdington Decanus de Wulverhampton ad sustentation em unius capellani imperpetuum in predicta ecclesia divina celebratura (sic) pro anima mea et antecessorum meorum et successorum, unum molendinum cum pertinentiis in Codesale cum vivario etc."

Mr. R. P. Walker, churchwarden of St. Peter's and an antiquary, who saw the deed at the Wolverhampton Exhibition of 1884 records the names of the witnesses as follows:— William de Benetleghe, Clement de Wlvernehampton, Gervase of the same, Nicholas of the same clerk, Robert de Shakelestone, John de Prado(?), Ralph de Hengeham, Jordan de Hengeham, etc. Thus to all intents and purposes we have the substance of the whole deed. Dean Giles de Erdington gives to God and the church of Wolverhampton for the support of a chaplain to celebrate divine service for ever in the said church for his soul and those of his forebears and successors a mill with the appurtenances at Codesale with the fishpool etc.

Sometime in 1268 dean Erdington passed to his rest and was most probably buried in his chantry chapel in St. Peter's. Shortly afterwards the King approved, as his successor, Tedesius or Theodosius de Camilla. This dean ruled at Wolverhampton until 1295 and during his time he continued the practice of leasing the decanal properties as his predecessors had done. We also find him appointing relatives to prebends in the church of Wolverhampton, a practice which continued for many years after his time. Nepotism was not considered irregular in those days. It is on a number of surviving deeds of de Camilla's time that we find early examples of the chapter seal which had then been in use for probably a hundred years previously. It is in the form of a pointed oval. Around the outside is the inscription ✠ Sigillum. ScI. PETRI. DE. WLFRUNEHAMTUNE. In the centre is a figure of St. Peter full length, a crosier in his right hand and two keys in his left. There are signs of decoration on his robes. His headdress is that of a mediaeval pileum, a close fitting cap. The figure stands within a dotted border.[3]

1 Wolverhampton Antiquary, Vol. I, p. 297.
2 **Ibid p. 266 et seq.**
3 For full account of these seals see **Wolverhampton Antiquary, Vol. I**, p. 197 **et seq.**

Several of the Hilton deeds still retain this very interesting seal for it was during de Camilla's time that the property at Hilton and within the manor of the Prebend of Hilton passed to the Swynnertons the ancestors of the Vernons. This latter family have retained the Hilton estate until very recently. Another interesting conveyance at this time was that of the property now known as Chapel Ash Farm. Under the name of Oxford by Hampton[1] this estate was conveyed about 1270 to Henry son of Simon on the payment of 14 pence every half year. The transaction also included the sale of a house in Tunwall Street (now Victoria Street) in Wolverhampton.

During the time of Tedesius de Camilla and his immediate successors there were a number of enquiries concerning the manor and the deanery. The most important was that held 12 March 22 Edw. I (1293/4) when an inquisition revealed considerable alienations and subtractions from the deanery. Large areas of land in Codsall, Pelsall, Wednesfield and Hatherton had passed into other hands and very little rent for these properties (in some cases none) passed into the hands of Master Thomas de Chobham the dean's steward.

Philip de Everdon who became dean in 1295 leaves us a very interesting seal which is appended to one of his deeds. He it was who by charter granted to Henry son of William de Essex a considerable property at Prestwood in Wednesfield. The original deed has long ago become separated from its file, but survives in the form of a certified copy made in 1585 (R. Paget deeds No. 97). The rest of the bundle of deeds concerning Prestwood which were omitted by S. Shaw from his history of Staffordshire "for brevity sake" are still happily preserved at Old Fallings.

The place names mentioned in these deeds are many and remarkable and are welcome as an introduction to the history of this side of the town. Here is a list:—

'Knollebruches' where Henry built a house
'le Nous'
'le Carters Slade'
A watery place in the wood of Prestwood opposite
Henry's gate, where he has made a pool (stagnum)
A place in the same wood called 'Wooderuddinge'
Another called 'chichekyrne heth'
Another called 'prestes bruche' with a certain
increase (incremento) near 'le Port lydiate' for
a way to his pastures of (de) 'Wademore'.
Land on (super) 'le Stowheth' between the road
from 'la Heth' to Willenhall, and the road leading
from Wolverhampton to Willenhall.
Land in seven places – 'Newbold', 'side erlede bruche',
'crossbruches', 'Wagebruche', 'Tromelow', 'Dymmesdale',
and the pastures called 'Wadmore'.

The annual rent was 5s. 5¾d. in silver, with two appearances at the two great courts in the year. The whole shows in brief the many physical characteristics of the town and district in the 13th century, the 'brech', the woods, the moor, the heath, and the watery places *i.e.* fenland.

Philip de Everdon was succeeded in 1303 by John de Everdon who held the deanery for five years. These deans may have been connected with the de Everdons who held property in Bushbury. Dean John de Everdon was an officer of State being a baron of the exchequer and Dean of St. Paul's.[2]

1 Wolverhampton Antiquary, Vol. I, p. 276.
2 S.H.C., Vol. 1928, p. 71.

Let us now consider the chronicles of the sub-tenants, the men on the spot, those who would have been called "landowners" in later times. Of these, as in the case of the principal tenants: dean and baron, there were two. Both took their name from the town: they were 'de Hampton' or 'de Wolverhampton'. But the early tenants are mere names, little more, jurors at inquests,[1] forest officers,[2] witnesses to charters, during the last half of the reign of Henry III, namely Clement and Gervase 'de Wolverhampton'. Though usually mentioned together, there is no proof that they were blood relations,[3] and their origins may have been quite different; each was succeeded by a son and successor—Hervey son of Clement, and Richard son of Gervase, both still 'de Hampton' with separate estates. We will take Clement first.

His son Hervey flourished during the reign of Edw. I and is important only as the father of three daughters among whom the estate was divided:— Agnes who married William de Salford and whose descendants lived at Merridale; Juliana who married John de Lapley probably the same as the 'clerk' or lawyer who wrote and witnessed many local deeds from 1272 up to about 1332[4]; and Margaret who married Richard Leveson of Willenhall and became the ancestress of a very important local family.[5] It can be judged by this that Clement and his descendants were tenants of the church lands of the Dean of Wolverhampton. We will leave this family at this stage and return to Gervase, but not before putting the descent in pedigree form.

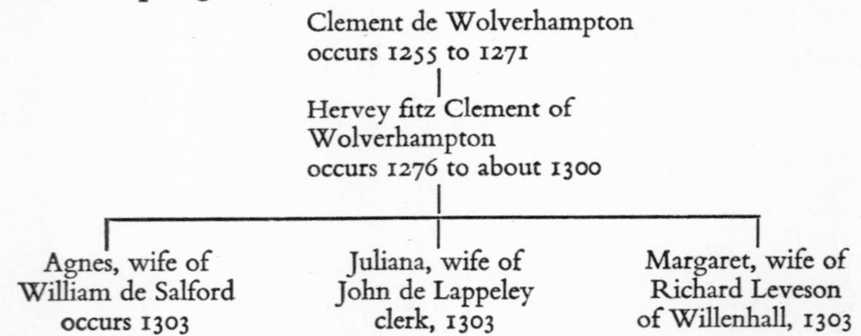

The descendants of Gervase de Hampton were settled at Dunstall, and the origin of the family may be sought in the history of their manor house. In considering the early status of Tunstall, the truer and earlier spelling of Dunstall, a place now overwhelmed by "progress", we are met by one of those dark tunnels through which the road of history sometimes runs. The lay tenants of this manor do not appear by name until the mid-thirteenth century, rather later than their neighbours. Tradition, sounder than usual, associates it with Wulfrun; fieldnames, Wulfrun's meadow, Wulfrun's well, support this; she lived there, in full view of the hill across the meadows a mile distant soon to be crowned by her church.

Until 1204 Tunstall was part of the Dudley fief. It may be that the first member of the family 'de Hampton' who settled at Tunstall in the 12th century was connected by blood with Gervase Paganel, feudal baron of Dudley from c. 1150 to 1194.[6] A tradition voiced in 1242 spoke of the time of Fulk Paganel his father (fl. 1130).[7] The place was regarded with 'Woundon' (Dunstall Hill) above it, as 'ancient demesne' of the Crown. There is

1 S.H.C. 1911, pp. 132.–140. 2 S.H.C., Vol. Vi, p. 116, 138–9.
3 The words 'frater ejus' would have been used in charters had they been brothers.
4 The series of "Paget" deeds allows one to trace a characteristic hand from a clear and firm to an old and shaky one between these dates. The scribe's name appears sometimes. Towards the end of this period William le Newrnon appears as writer.
5 S.H.C. VII, p. 112, a lawsuit of 1303 which settles the relationship.
6 A suggestion by the late Mr. W. F. Carter. A grant by Gervase Paganel about 1175 is the earliest deed connected with this place; see edition in S.H.C.
7 S.H.C. 1911, p. 144.

actually no evidence that it ever belonged to the church. In view of the charter of 985 and the ground that it covered, it is clear that this and much of the town, half in fact (represented by six out of a jury of twelve) was grabbed from the church at an early date. There were ruthless men ruling between 994 and 1066.[1] After the Conquest a dual form, Church and lay estates lying together, was not unusual, as at Tettenhall, Penkridge, Coventry, to look no further; a lay tenure seems to have been found a necessary balance to religious pressure.

It is in accordance with known fact therefore that the first known reference to the owners of Dunstall is a grant from Gervase Paganel, lord of Dudley. This deed does not refer to Wolverhampton property; but it passed with the Dunstall records to the Moseleys of Dunstall and was seen by Huntbach, and Stebbing Shaw prints (not quite correctly) what Huntbach records. It is unfortunate that the original can no longer be seen and admired, for things so remote possess a charm beyond the information they impart. Here indeed we have the names of important members of the baron's household, and they are not all to be found elsewhere.

It was two members of this ancient family who in February 1328—9 founded a chantry in the church of St. Giles, Willenhall. They were Richard and John Gervase who, following an inquisition held at Wolverhampton on 29 October 1327, were permitted to found the chantry and endow it with one messuage, forty acres of land and four acres of meadow and the moiety of one mill with the appurtenances in Willenhall for a chaplain to perform divine service daily in the chapel, for the souls of the said Richard and Felicia his wife, and for the souls of their fathers and mothers, brothers and sisters and children, their ancestors and all the faithful departed. These messuages and lands were held at the will of the lord of the manor of Stowheath, Sir John de Hadloo, kt., and the lord Robert de Dunham and the lord Thomas de Legh, canons of Wolverhampton.

The Church of St. Giles was a chapel of ease to the mother church of Wolverhampton, founded in about 1300 by Richard and John Hampton for the ease of the inhabitants. In 1311 a chapel of ease was also established at Pelsall by William le Kev[2] and probably about the same period one was built at Hatherton. It is of interest to note that the earliest reference to a chapel at Bilston is the founding of a chantry there by Sir Thomas de Erdington in 1458.[3]

Although these chapels of ease were built in the out hamlets of this large and straggling parish for the convenience of the inhabitants care was taken to see that very few powers of the mother church were transferred to them. The Sacraments could be performed but marriages and burials still had to take place at Wolverhampton. The clergy serving the chapels were elected by those inhabitants having property there but it was necessary for them to be presented to the Dean of Wolverhampton for licence before they could exercise their office. The chapelries also appointed their chapelwardens and managed their parochial affairs and at Willenhall they had the right to appoint the trustees (or feoffees as they were called) who managed the Chapel of Ease Estate from whence the income of the incumbent was derived.

During the 14th century there was a long succession of deans many of them holding the deanery for but a brief period. A considerable number were pluralists who held other offices at the same time and they rarely visited Wolverhampton being very often instituted by proxy. Some of them have left traces of their rule, sometimes beneficient at other

1 See, for instance, the seizures of Sheriff Eire under Cnut.
2 S.H.C. Vol. 1915, p. 336.
3 Lawley History of Bilston, p. 24.

times very unsatisfactory. It must have been during the time of Philip de Everdon 1295—1303 or that of his successor John de Everdon that the nave and aisles of the church were largely rebuilt and the present ground plan came into existence. The beautiful Decorated east window of the Lady Chapel and the lower storey of the south porch date from this time. Some deans gained notoriety as when John de Everdon 1303—1308 came into conflict with the King over his appointment to the deanery and the appointment of one of the prebendaries.[1] One of his successors, Hugh Elys 1322—1339,[2] was also accused of wasting the assets of the church and allowing the fabric of the church to fall into decay. On the other hand we find that Richard Postell 1373—1394 was jealous for the rights and privileges of his church and was successful in obtaining a charter from the King in 1376 confirming the grant by one of his predecessors of certain lands in Prestwood in Wednesfield to a John de Telford.[3]

From the 13th century onwards we get an important series of charters granted by the deans of Wolverhampton to various tenants. There is a fine collection relating to Old Fallings and also those relating to Hilton[4] formerly the home of the Vernon family and which they had inherited from the Swynnertons. There must also have been many charters in the priceless collection at Wrottesley Hall which was entirely destroyed in the great fire there in 1897. Amongst the deeds at the Wodehouse, Wombourn are many concerning Wolverhampton[5] referring particularly to the conveyance of land in the north and east parts of the town in the Middle Ages.

Lawrence Allerthorp was dean of Wolverhampton from 1394 to 1406 and was one of the few deans who spent much time in the town. In 1394, the year of his appointment, a hospital was founded in Wolverhampton but few details have survived. The foundation deed was due to the action of Clement Luson, chaplain, and William Waterfall of Wolverhampton who at the cost of £3 6s. 8d. obtained the Kings licence for its establishment in honour of God and the Blessed Virgin Mary and for the support of a chaplain and six poor men.[6] There was also a house and three acres of land in the town which might provide a manse for their dwellingplace. Therein they should daily celebrate divine service and continually pray for the good estate of the founders (and Joan the wife of William Waterfall) while they lived and the souls of all the faithful departed. So King Richard II consented at Nottingham, 4 August 1394.[7] On the 20 May 1402, Lawrence Allerthorp the dean, who was in London, issued a mandate to John Gervys, Canon of Stafford (of whose church Allerthorp was also dean) and Thomas Wrottesley, one of the Wolverhampton chaplains, to induct John Peppard, priest, as perpetual chaplain or custos of the hospital; and this was done accordingly on 27 May.[8] It was at the presentment of William Waterfall. Who then was he? He was probably one of the junior branch of the "de Prestwood" family. His contemporary, perhaps brother, John Waterfall—the two figure among the Wardens of the Light of St. Peter's church in 1385—is described as son of John de Prestwood.[9] Clement Luson (or Leveson) not infrequently appears as a priest at Wolverhampton and was a member of the large and important family of that name.

1 Oliver "History of Wolverhampton Church", p. 45.

2 Wolverhampton Antiquary, Vol. II, p. 7.

3 See copy in the Mander collection from the original in the possession of the late W. H. Duignan.

4 These deeds are now in the William Salt Library.

5 S.H.C. 1928

6 Pauperibus "poor people", not females as Dr. Oliver translates, p. 54, who says it was situated in Lichfield Street. There is no reason to think so.

7 Pat. Rolls 16 Richard II, p.l.m. 14. Dugdale's Monasticon VI. 712.

8 Lawley M.Ss. IV, p. 21, in Bilston Library.

9 In a suit of 1404; S.H.C. XV., p. 117.

John Pippard, chaplain, appears again so late as 1435,[1] and it is probably he who is responsible for the name "Pipers" chapel in Wolverhampton church, also Pipers Croft and Pipers Row (this last still a street name) in the town.

The hospital may have stood by the croft; but it did not survive until the Reformation, and its revenues may have been diverted at a much earlier period.

Wolverhampton at the beginning of the 15th century was a growing and thriving town. Although the Black Death, some fifty years earlier, had no doubt some effect on the population that was all now past and the advent of the wool trade increased the town's prosperity. Many of the leading families were trading in wool and not a few of the more important citizens were members of the Staple of Calais, for it was through that market that the raw and processed wool (prior to the fall of the town to the French in 1558) passed to the markets of the continent of Europe. The raw wool came from the Welsh Marches and was brought to towns like Wolverhampton where it was spun into yarn and woven into cloth. This trade brought great wealth to a number of Wolverhampton families who in former times were yeomen and small traders.

The men who operated the wool trade can be divided roughly into two parts—those who bought and sold the raw wool, the staplers as they were known, and the clothiers or drapers who manufactured the woollen cloth and sold it to the tailors. From various records the following merchants of the staple are found in Wolverhampton:—

Nicholas Ridley "Merchant of the Staple of Calais", 1504
John Nechells "Merchant of the Staple", died 1531
James Leveson "Merchant of the Staple of Calais", died 1547
Richard Creswell of Barnhurst "Merchant of the Staple", died 1559
John Leveson "Merchant of the Staple of Calais" died 1575
Thomas Offley "Merchant of the Staple of Calais", died 1580
Thomas Leveson "Merchant of the Staple" 1567, died 1594
John Cresswell "Merchant of the Staple" 1587, died 1593
Henry Planckney "Merchant of the Staple" 1582–7, died 1608
Richard Creswell of Barnhurst, "Merchant of the Staple", 1592, died 1612
Thomas Huntbach "mercator stapelie", died 1624.[2]

It will be seen from this list that for its last fifty years as an English town Calais served as a depot from which the Wolverhampton staplers distributed their wool in Europe. Afterwards London was used and there was a hall in the city where the sale of wool and cloth took place. The Wolverhampton merchants may have used the Welsh Hall as many of their brethren from Shrewsbury did for much of their wool also came from the Welsh border. It was customary for one of the partners of each firm to live in London so that he could be on the spot to receive the goods and deal with their sale.

The drapers or clothiers dealt with the manufacture and sale of the finished products. These men were also to be found in Wolverhampton. As early as 1459 James Leveson, esquire sued a shearman of Wolverhampton for neglecting to fuller his cloth properly.[3] The following men flourished in the town during the 15th, 16th and 17th centuries:—

William Waring, "Clothier", will dated 1444
John Howlett, "Draper", from 1534
William Creswell, "Clothier", died 1560
John Gough, "Draper", died 1597
Robert Cutt, "Draper", occurs 1560, died 1599
Henry Gough, "Draper", occurs 1602, died 1656[4]
John Hanbury, "Draper", died 1636

1 When he is sued for a house and 20 acres of land by James (s. of Nicholas) Leveson, S.H.C. XVIII, p. 150.
2 For amplification see Wolverhampton Antiquary, Vol. I, p. 170.
3 S.H.C. N.S. IV, p. 114.
4 Of Oldfallings Hall, a supporter of Charles I.

Sir Richard Pipe of Bilston who served the office of Lord Mayor of London in 1587 was a member of the Draper's Company.

The merchants most probably had a guildhall where they could attend to their corporate business and this was perhaps the building which stood on the north side of old Lichfield Street and on the site of what is now the fountain and gardens. Most of the building was destroyed in the 18th century but a chimney breast of the Tudor period survived until 1859.[1] This was revealed when adjoining buildings were demolished and on it was a coat of arms. Four shields of arms were displayed. At the top was the Royal Arms of the period 1509—1603 surrounded by the Garter. Below were the arms of the Drapers' Company, the City of London and the Merchants of the Staple. Here perhaps was all that remained of the first public building (other than the church) in Wolverhampton.

During the period of the town's prosperity in the 15th century a drastic reconstruction of St. Peter's Church took place. It may be that the well-to-do families of the town, conscious of the unworthy condition of the fabric, decided that something must be done. The old church had suffered numerous alterations and additions in the previous three hundred years and at least one part, the tower, had never been completed. The new work was more in the nature of a reconstruction than a rebuilding for the old ground plan together with a great deal of the original structure was retained.

The rebuilding of the church was a long and tedious process. It began with a commission under the Great Seal 1 July 1439 to John Hampton, Thomas Swynnerton and William Leveson, Esquires, and James Leveson, John Mollesley, William Salford and Nicholas Leveson to take and provide the stone required to build the church———on the soil of John Appulton, one of the prebendaries, on reasonable terms. This quarry was probably one formerly worked near the west end of the church.

Before alteration the church consisted of the lower part of the central tower and the chancel, both in the Early English style, and a nave with aisles probably in the Decorated style. The chantry of Dean Erdington probably stood at the east end of the north aisle. The aisles extended as far as the eastern side of the tower and the whole of this part of the church was covered by three pent roofs of equal height. The position and height of these roofs is indicated by the line of stonework over the east window of the Lady Chapel and the stone string course running over the south window of this chapel indicates the original position of the wall plate of the south wall of the nave.

In the reconstruction two major changes took place, a clerestory was added to the nave and the building was converted into a cruciform church. New arcades had to be built to carry the clerestory and the roofs and outside walls of the north and south aisles were lowered to improve the external appearance of the building and to give adequate clearance for the clerestory windows.

The south transept was contrived by the erection of a west wall with an opening to the south aisle and in line with the west wall of the tower. Unfortunately in this position the wall blocked out part of the splay of the easternmost window of the south aisle. To give the new transept the appearance of projecting beyond the wall of the nave two large buttresses were built to project southwards. The west and south walls were raised above the top of the Decorated east window which was not disturbed, clerestory lights were inserted, the walls battlemented and a flat lead covered roof erected.

The north transept was not completed until about 1510 and here a major alteration took place which, if our theory is correct, involved the destruction of the Erdington

1 See article in Wolverhampton Antiquary, Vol. I, p. 15 et seq.

Photograph by permission of J. B. Baker, Esq.

William Baker of Audlem, Architect of St. John's Church

Interior of St. Peter's Church

High Green, looking down Dudley Street. 1835

Chantry then probably about 250 years old and perhaps in need of substantial repairs. The last part of the new work to be completed was the great central tower, a graceful structure in the late Perpendicular style, and this late completion no doubt accounts for the absence of any bells at the time of the Reformation. These, 3 in number, were brought here from the newly demolished abbey of Wenlock in 1540 and hung in the new tower. Many of the more important local families gave liberally to the cost of the new work and the dean, John Birmingham, who was also Treasurer of York Minster and who died in 1457 bequeathed 100s. to the rebuilding. It is thought that the most substantial benefactor at this time was Humphrey Swynnerton of Hilton and that the beautiful pulpit is his memorial.

In 1457 William Duddeley was appointed dean and his beautiful seal which has survived reminds us of his time here. It is probable that he was a supporter of the rebuilding of the church for a great deal of the work was done during this period. He was a younger son of John de Sutton, Lord Dudley K.G., a prominent figure in the Court of Henry IV and Edward IV. On 4 December 1473 he was made Dean of Windsor and in 1476 Bishop of Durham which office he held at the time of his death in 1483. He lies beneath an elaborate altar tomb in St. Nicholas Chapel in Westminster Abbey. He may have been the one through whose influence King Edward IV decided to unite the deaneries of Wolverhampton and Windsor. This important event took place on 18 February 1479 when the King appointed Richard Beauchamp, Bishop of Salisbury, as dean of the united deaneries. This union survived the Reformation and continued its creaking existence until the death of Dean Hobart in 1846 when the Wolverhampton Peculiar was dissolved.

During the time of dean Duddeley the King issued a new charter to Wolverhampton Church confirming all the privileges already granted by past charters and the following is a translation:—

EDWARD by the grace of God King of England and of France and Lord of Ireland to ALL to whom the present letters shall come greeting. We have inspected the Letters Patent of the lord Richard lately King of England the second after the Conquest made in these words:— Richard by the grace of God King of England and of France and Lord of Ireland To All to whom the present Letters shall come greeting. We have inspected the letters patent of the lord Edward lately King of England our grandfather in these words: Edward by the grace of God King of England and of France and lord of Ireland to All to whom the present letters shall come greeting. It is clear to us from an examination of the rolls of our Chancery that we have lately caused our charter to be made in these words:— Edward by the grace of God King of England lord of Ireland and duke of Aquitaine to the Archbishops, bishops, abbots, priors, earls, barons, judges, sheriffs, provosts, ministers, and all bailiffs and his faithful, greeting. We have inspected the charter of lord Edward formerly King of England in these words:—

"I Edward King greet 'Leven' (*i.e.* Leofwine, bishop of Lichfield 1053—1067) bishop and 'Leven' earl (probably meaning Eadwine, who was Earl of Mercia from 1062) and all my thegns in Staffordshire kindly. And I tell you that to my priests at Hampton—to them I have pledged my troth. Now will I that they and their minister be free, their possessions thereto rightly belonging also to be free, with sac and with soc, as full and as free as I first had it in everything. And I will give them then whatever shall rightfully belong to any of them (? ic wille giuen heom than that heom enyg man enyg on riht beoth)".

We have inspected also a certain charter of the lord William (the Conqueror) formerly King of England in these words:— "W(illiam) King of the English to L(anfranc) archbishop and G(osfrid) bishop of Coutances and P(eter) bishop (of Chester) and R( ) the Sheriff (perhaps Robert of Stafford) and the rest of his faithful of Staffordshire greeting. Know that I had given to Sampson my chaplain the church of saint Mary of Wolverhampton with the land and all other things and customs such as the aforesaid church had better in the time of king Edward. And see that he holds all this with honour since I wish it well".

We have also inspected a certain charter of lord Henry (the second) formerly King of England our ancestor, in these words:— Henry King of the English, Duke of Normandy and Aquitaine and "Comte" of Anjou to his sheriffs and ministers of Staffordshire greeting. I order that the lands and vassals which belong to the church of Wolverhampton be in peace and exempt from court attendance (placitis) and fines (querelis) both of shire and hundred and from all things except (the fines for) murder and highway robbery even as they were better off in the time of King Henry my grandfather. As witness Thomas (a' Becket) the chancellor at Westminster.

We have also inspected a certain charter of the lord Henry duke of Normandy and Aquitaine and Comte of Anjou in these words:— Henry Duke of Normandy and Aquitaine and Comte of Anjou to all archbishops, bishops, earls, barons, judges, sheriffs, and all his friends and faithful both Normans and English greeting. Know that I have granted to the church of Wolverhampton my chapel all that liberty which it had in the time of King Henry my grandfather and all that quiet in wood and field, in meadows and pastures, in waters and without, in roads and paths and in all places. And I grant to the canons of the same church the same freedom and quiet. Wherefore I demand and strictly order that the same church be my free chapel and exempt from all customs and demands with all its appurtenances and that the canons possess all their things freely and in quiet, nor shall any presume to do them harm or vex or harm them. As witness Roger earl of Hereford, Walter his brother the constable, Henry his brother, Gervase Paganell kinsman, at Dudley.

And we deeming the aforesaid gifts and grants assured and satisfactory do for us and our heirs as much as in us lies, grant and confirm to our beloved clerk John of Melbourn dean of the chapel aforesaid and to the canons of the same chapel and their successors even as the aforesaid charters reasonably bear witness. As witness these: the venerable fathers W( ) archbishop of York the primate of England, John of Ely and John of Winchester bishops: Henry earl of Lancaster, John de Warenne earl of Surrey, Roger de Mortimer, John Maltravers steward of our household and others. Given by our hand at Northampton the seventh day of May in the second year of our reign (1328).

And we do make a copy by the present writing of the aforesaid charter and all its contents at the request of our beloved clerk Richard Postell now dean of the place aforesaid, in witness of which thing we cause these our Letters to be made Patent, as I myself bear witness at Westminster the twelfth day of December in the year of our reign of England the fortyeigth but of our reign of France the thirtyfifth. And we deeming the aforesaid gifts and grants assured and satisfactory do for us and our heirs as much as in us lies accept approve ratify and to the aforesaid dean and canons of the chapel aforesaid by the tenor of these presents have granted and confirmed them as the letters aforesaid reasonably bear witness and as the same dean and canons and their predecessors have been accustomed reasonably to use and enjoy hitherto with liberty and quiet. In witness of which thing (we cause these our letters to be made Patent as witness myself)[1] at Westminster the thirtieth day of March in the second year of our reign. We moreover deeming

1 These words are indecipherable in the original.

the aforesaid letters and confirmations and all and singular that is contained in the same assured and satisfactory do accept and approve them for us and our heirs as much as in us lies and to our beloved in Christ now dean and the canons of the chapel aforesaid by the tenor of these presents do ratify and confirm as the letters and confirmations aforesaid reasonably witness.

In testimony of which thing we have caused these our letters to be made patent, as witness myself at Westminster the twentyfirst day of November in the first year of our reign, (1461).

(There follows a note of the fee paid:—) "For twenty shillings paid into the hanaper. Kirkeham".

(and below)

(Examined by) Robert Kirkeham (and clerks).
William Moreland

We close this chapter with a list of the deans of Wolverhampton before the union of the deanery with that of Windsor.

DEANS *of* WOLVERHAMPTON

∴

c.1078	Samson, afterwards Bishop of Worcester
c.1105	The Prior of Worcester
c.1112	Roger, Bishop of Salisbury
c.1139	The Bishop of Coventry and Lichfield
c.1145	The Prior of Worcester
c.1180	Peter of Blois
1203	Nicholas
1205	Henry, son of Geoffrey Earl of Essex
c.1224	Giles de Erdington
1268	Tedesius de Camilla
1295	Philip de Everdon
1303	John de Everdon
1308	Walter de Islip
1321	Geoffrey de Rudham
1326	Robert de Silkeston
1328	John de Melbourne
c.1332	Hugh Elys
1339	Philip de Weston
c.1368	John de Newnham
1369	Almiric de Shirland
1373	Richard Postell
1394	Laurence Allerthorp
1406	Thomas Stanley
1410	Robert Wolvedon
1426	William Felter
1437	John Birmingham
1457	William Duddeley
1477	Lionel Wydville
1478	Richard Beauchamp, Bishop of Salisbury

CHAPTER V

THE TOWN UNDER THE TUDORS

THE Tudor period begins on 22 August 1485 when the royal crown was picked up from a gorse-bush on Bosworth Field. At that skirmish there was present the lord of the manor of Wolverhampton, a man full of honours and the last of his line. He was Chamberlain of the Household and Chief Butler of England, styled Viscount Lovel, lord Holland Deincourt, Burnell and Grey, and K.G.[1] He subsequently fought with other zealous Yorkists at Stoke, 16 June 1487, and was last seen trying to swim the Trent on horseback. At any rate he disappeared. But in 1708 when they were making a new chimney at Minster Lovel, there was discovered a large vault or under-ground room, in which was the entire skeleton of a man, sitting at a table with book, paper and pen. There also lay a cap, all much mouldered and decayed "which the family and others judged to be this lord Lovel, whose exit hath hitherto been so uncertain".[2]

Lovel's moated mansion at Wolverhampton, which lay where the Chillington Tool manufactory is now, was with his other property forfeited. That it survived as a manor-house is possible, but being in a bleak situation, it may not have invited occupation as a headquarters for the future lords of "Stow Heath", who had dwelling-places elsewhere.

A more appropriate break in the history of Wolverhampton is to be found rather earlier, in February 1480, the time when King Edward IV united the Deaneries of Windsor and Wolverhampton. This was not an act, as Dr. Oliver sees and laments, for "promoting the interests of religion",[3] but merely so that the dean of Windsor, who was known to the King and in his favour, should have more pocket money. It had indeed the effect of saving one dean by giving another power over two distinct chapters, with separate seal and so on. For the dean, the work at Wolverhampton was almost a sinecure. There was some preaching to be done but a deputy could perform this, and the leases specified two days and three nights entertainment a year in case the dean wished to stay at Wolverhampton, which he very seldom did. He could far more often be found at Windsor, and there Wolverhampton people journeyed to meet him.

A feature of Tudor rule was the distribution of General Pardons: it may have been easier to regulate by fine (for payment was necessary, the copying alone in the long letters Patent was heavy work) than to direct wrong doers by administrative effort.

Such a pardon was granted in November 1505 to some 477 merchants of the Staple of Calais, including the mayor, for offences against the Statutes for regulating trade, and the penalties for exporting wool without bringing into the country its value in silver plate (2 marks the sack). The trade must be for England, and merchants residing at Calais (which was not yet inscribed on Mary's heart) were not allowed to buy beyond the seas merchandise of the staple—wool, wool fells, hides, lead, tin and so on.

1 C.P. sub Lovel, 225.

2 See Francis Peck, Memoirs of Oliver Cromwell, p. 87.

3 Oliver, Coll. Ch., p. 56.

The list of the guilty is a valuable one. Tenth among them is Stephen Jenyns, a man now making his way upward—there is a pardon in 1495 to a merchant of Bristol who owed him money, he being "citizen and tailor of London". One notices, too, Humphrey Suthwyke, John Nechylles, Nicholas Waryng, Richard Waryng, William Austen, William Lane, Henry Plankeney, Joan Heylyn, Nicholas Leveson, Thomas Waryng, William Salford, Christopher Rawson all connected with Wolverhampton. The quality of the goods must be maintained, and responsible packers be found: "the sworn packers inscribing their names and the nature of the wool on every sarpler (large sack), poke and pocket".

But by Tudor times the wool trade had been long established; men and families had been enriched by it, and set up their homes and prospered. After Queen Mary, Merchants of the Staple shipped to Bruges instead of Calais. On the Patent Rolls of 1 September 1560, another long list of pardons against the statute is entered. It includes John Leveson, senior, Thomas Leveson, senior, Matthew Cradock, Nicholas Leveson, Henry Planckney, Henry Offley, Edward Leveson, Margaret Kyrton, widow, Deonise Leveson, widow, Sir Richard Leveson, Sir Thomas Offley, Knt., mayor of the Staple.

Thus the masters of the craft keep their presence known; and thus do we glean a little about the occupations of some of the more prominent men of the town. Or again, we may look for evidence of the doings of Wolverhampton people—in matters more sinister perhaps—in the records of the Star Chamber. The work of the King's Council which took place there was particularly directed against such offences as riots and unlawful assemblies. It was set up early in the reign of Henry VII and was not oppressive under Henry VIII but a security against the oppression of others, the rich and powerful.

Later it became a means of rule by proclamation, and, in consequence, very unpopular. The records consist of Bills (petitions) and Answers and Depositions; but no decrees and orders have survived.[1]

The method of presenting the case was one in which great exaggeration was practiced; what reads like a bloodthirsty riot was often open to a more peaceful explanation. That so many of these cases concern Wolverhampton proves that many who lived there were of a quarrelsome disposition, especially those of the leading family of Leveson.[2]

The first case to interest us occurs some 13 years after the opening of our period.

It appeared then that on the Wednesday before Trinity Sunday 1498, Thomas Rice of Walsall in an affray got hurt, was "soore wounded and bett" and put in peril of his life. The attackers were caught and imprisoned in the Walsall gaol. Then came John Beaumont, squire of Wednesbury, Walter Leveson of Wolverhampton, Richard Foxe priest of the same, and Roger Marshall, a priest it seems of Wednesbury, with a riotous assembly of some 200 men, arrayed in manner of war, to effect a rescue. They were quelled, however, by two Justices of the peace, and further riot was abandoned; and a fair on Trinity Sunday at Willenhall was put out of bounds.

Roger Dingley, mayor of Walsall, claimed that the inhabitants of Walsall on that day kept themselves at home. Notwithstanding there came from Hampton one calling himself the "abbot of Marham" and one Walter Leveson with him with the inhabitants of Hampton to the number of four score persons in harness after the manner of war, to Willenhall to the said fair. And there was one of Wednesbury calling himself "Robyn Hood" and Richard Fox priest, and 100 persons more who riotously assembled, declaring that if any of the town of Walsall came, they would strike them down. But no man of Walsall was seen at Willenhall fair on that day.

1 Scargill-Bird, 302.

2 The cases will be found in S.H.C. vol. X (N.S.) pt. 1, vol. 1910, 1912.

The explanation is not without interest. As for the coming to the said fair of Willenhall, a participant writes: "hit hath byn of olde tymes used and accustomed on the said fere day that wyth the inhabitants of the sede townes of Hampton, Weddesbury and Walsall have comyne to the said fere with the capitanns called the Abot of Marham or Robyn Hodys to the intent to gather money with ther disportes to the profight of the chirches of the seid lordshipes", whereby great profit hath grown to the said churches in times past.[1] And the Wednesbury company came in a peaceable manner to the fair and met divers from the town of Walsall and "they made as gud chere unto them as they shuld do to ther lovyng neyburs". Walter Leveson's evidence was to the same effect.

It is an unexpected peep into the past, and Stebbing Shaw, the historian, has something to say about it 300 years later. (ii. 165, col. 1).

"Another custom was (says he) the annual procession on 9 July (the eve of the great fair) of men in antique armour, preceded by musicianse playing the Fair-tune, and followed by the steward of the deanery manor, the peace-officers and many of the principal inhabitants. Tradition says the ceremony originated at the time when Wolverhampton was a great emporium of wool, and resorted to by merchants of the staple from all parts of England. The necessity of an armed force to keep peace and order during the fair (which lasted according to the charter eight days) is not improbable. The men, twenty in number, were furnished by the proprietors of the burgage-houses (one for each burgage), who had likewise, in rotation, the annual appointment of bailiff of the staff, whose office was to preside over and receive the tolls of the market . . . . This custom of *walking the fair* (as it was called), with the armed procession, &c. was first omitted about the year 1784".

Walsall too is not out of the picture. It has to this day some of its 'Colts', clubs which were borne in procession on fair days from the remote past.[2]

From its people we turn to the town itself.

Perhaps the most extensive alteration that has taken place—and was, in fact, not entirely completed—was the rebuilding of the collegiate church already referred to. More will be said about this in due course, but, meanwhile, we may take a more general view of the town.

During the whole of the Tudor period Wolverhampton was almost entirely a place of timber and thatch. There was stone at hand for the more important buildings and this was used as a basis for the timber and wattle superstructure in the usual way. It seems evident that brick had not appeared in these parts, except in a few cases, before the reign of Elizabeth and the use of coal for brick kilns. The same applies to tiles for roofing; a flat tile is not an easy thing to make. There is no sign of stone roofing having been used in Wolverhampton. The Romans would have brought this from afar (as they did for the Pennocrucium villa) but the natives were content with a roofing of local origin, and this was thatch. It accounted for numerous fires in the town, and two conflagrations at least, due to it, are known to history.

When therefore was the Great Hall of the Leveson family built as we know it from its many pictured appearances? There is no direct evidence; but it is likely to be the work of Thomas or John Leveson his brother, and therefore before 1575. A date during the reign of Queen Mary—a time when John Leveson had consolidated his position as the town's chief inhabitant—is perhaps as near as we may guess.

1 S.H.C. x, i (N.S.) p. 81.
2 Willmore 99-1. Palmer P.C.P. 64.

Of the previous history of the Great Hall on Snow Hill and its age there is at present no evidence. Did it appear for the first time under the Tudors or did its beginnings date from Saxon times? It is possible that the spade may reveal something on this point sometime, or some document may turn up. Walter Leveson (d. 1512), John Leveson's father possessed on his death a house and land in the town which he held of Nicholas West, Dean of the royal free chapel, "but by what service the jurors are ignorant". That statement gives the appearance of antiquity and the house may have been the moated hall; but we do not know. It may be the place was wooded or else it was on a cold exposed spot—snowhill. But the ridge-way passed by it, and people from Dudley coming north could say "here is Hampton".[1]

The Elizabethan town of Wolverhampton, like others not far distant (Walsall, Dudley, Kidderminster), was divided into two districts, the town and its "foreign". The town on its hill was concentrated, and there was the church. The foreign was country and here we have the country estates:—

The Lea, the home of the Warings.
Graseley (grassy lea), home of the Ridley family.
Oxneford (*or Chapel Ash Farm*, as it was later).
Merridale the home of the Saltford family.
Newbridge—a hamlet rather than an estate.
and *Dunstall*, the old home of de Hampton; but from 1580 the Moseley family, who rebuilt it, in the Elizabethan style.

In addition, there were also the following:—
Seawall the residence of the Huntbach family.
Oldfallings, belonging to the Challenors
Nechels to the Hopes
and *Prestwood* and *Ashmores* to the Levesons.

Finally, there was *Bentley*, to be distinguished in the next century by the most popular of the Lanes.

Each has its history, each had its family ghost; but where are the houses now? How recent a date marks their fall.

In the years 1587—9 we have clear evidence of the break up of the ancient open fields and their consolidation into farms. It was a complicated process and meant much conveyancing; but the benefits to all were so evident that it was carried through by the landowners concerned without outside help. Perhaps it should be mentioned that of the common fields, on the North lay Quabbe field (later called Windmill field); on the east: Horsley Field, Wyndfield and Monmore field; on the west: Ablow or Abley field (by St. Paul's church), and Broadmeadow field (by the Park).

Returning, however, to the more immediate affairs of the town itself, an unimportant enough incident which occurred in 1534, invites our attention, giving us some otherwise undiscovered details of the place.

The manor of Wolverhampton had been from days before the memory of man divided into halves, one being of the deanery the other lay Church and King. At this time with the lords of each part distant cousins of one family, James and John Leveson, there was bound to be confusion. An example declared itself when the bell-man of the market died and each side had a candidate ready to succeed.

1 It is arguable that this enclosure was indeed the Heantun (High Town), as opposed to Dunstall in the valley, the lower town.

On 10 June 1534 being Market Day at Wolverhampton the King's subject James Leveson, merchant of the staple of Calais found Thomas Leveson of the same town, gentleman and John Leveson his brother, and some twenty others ready to make an assault upon him. Indeed Richard Foster "having a salet of steel on his head and a coat of fence upon his body, and others in harness likewise" bid fair to murder him, so he complained.

The defendants explained that Wolverhampton was a market town, within which there had always been a bell-man chosen by the whole agreement of the inhabitants whenever that office became void. John Sympson late bellman was dead, and while there were those ready to buy the place, James Leveson "of his own high mind as he is wont to do in all suchlike matters" gave the office to Robert Welbe his brother's servant. There was discontent. Thomas Leveson took the matter up and went to speak to James who kept to his house. A crowd may have collected but it was peaceful; there was no assault or riot.

Next day James Leveson "perceiving the great fury of the said defendants" went into the market to see it should not be disturbed (this was on his door step, he living then at the High Hall, the block of buildings in the Square—then High Green—which was demolished in 1841). He was in fact then the dean's lessee both of the market and half the town, and also owner of the other half of the town, the manor of Stowheath. Thomas Leveson's party were then in the Swan, which stood on the site of Lloyd's Bank, and coming forth "riotously" made assault against the said James, which the constable of the town perceiving, ordered them to keep the peace, which they refused. Next day Walter Wrottesley esquire (who was brother in law to both parties) and John Gravenour, gentleman, both magistrates, caused Thomas Leveson and his brother John to be bound in £100 to keep the peace.

As a Star Chamber case depositions were taken at Wolverhampton in October 1534. They were likely to be contradictory as there were two sides. Let us dip into the evidence and see.

Thomas Jackson, chaplain, aged 40, was drinking at the Inn called the Angel with certain persons of Penkridge, and the wife of the house showed anxiety about the growing tumult. Thereupon deponent went out and saw the defendants armed standing at James Luson's door, and he fearing the mischief that might follow went into the house and exhorted James Luson to keep his house, and with the help of James's wife he was kept in the house until Thomas Luson and his company departed. Then the said James went to the cross and caused the market bell to be rung and commanded the constable to see the King's peace kept.

William Gesselyng of Sedgley aged 25, sometime servant to Thomas Leveson, took friendly notice of his doings on that memorable 10th June and followed him from the Swan to James Luson's house. There he heard Thomas Luson say "I come not to fight nor brawl with him, but to speak with him, but the churl will not come forth".

John Howlat of Wolverhampton draper, one of the constables of the town, aged 36, said he was selling cloth in his shop, and saw the defendants armed, and he went to the said Thomas and commanded him in £100 to keep the peace, and the said Luson would not obey him. And he met his fellow the other constable John Hyggyns (butcher) and they saw the said James with a staff in his hand and others with him coming towards the market, whom they commanded to keep the peace, and he said he would with all his heart and commanded all about him to aid the constable to keep the King's peace.

Richard Waynewright of Wolverhampton shoemaker, aged 55, says Thomas Luson would have had him to have the bellmanship, "before the business began", but as James Luson said "it was now done and past".

John Hope of Nechill, husbandman, aged 33, said he saw the defendants armed before James Luson's door, and afterwards he saw the said James Luson in the market with many persons with him, some with weapons, some without, and further the said Thomas came out of the "Swan" with his followers, to the "Flesshambuls". . . . .

These were the butchers' shops, the same shown on Rowlandson's drawing of the Wolverhampton Market Place in the Art Gallery and dated 1799.

We shall hear of the bell again.

Another entry from the Church-wardens' book refers to "the Church vessells . . . . and also the brass pewter, &c. belonging to the shambles" (1559).

The shambles were in the market place at or near the Market Hall; the "vessells" were for brewing beer. The old custom of brewing *Church Ales* was a regular way of raising money for the church. It was besides great fun. "Keeping of church ales, in whiche with leapynge, daunsynge and kyssung they mayteyne the profett of their churche".[1] Such scenes were a frequent subject of the brush of Peter Breughel whose gay pictures of village life are well known. But the Puritans had different ideas and church wardens no longer brew ale but take serious thoughts about bazaars.

There were, however, well before the middle of the 16th century, signs that the market town was growing up. We may cite, for example, the appearance of Wolverhampton's market hall.

A recent discovery (Salt deed 82.11.43) is a copy of the grant made by master William Cretyng, prebendary of Fetherstone at his court held at Wolverhampton *in le Wadehall* on Monday before the feast of St. Catherine the virgin and martyr on 24th year of the reign of King Henry VIIth (20 November 1508). John Falans who held from the lord certain lands with their appurtenances in Wolvernehampton by a rent by year of 3s. 2d. has died since the last court, and there has fallen to the lord by way of heriot according to custom 6d. William Falans is his next heir. He comes in his own person in full court and claims to have and to hold these lands, to be held from the lord to him and his heirs and assigns for ever. And he gives to the lord as a "relief" 2d. and his oath was respited until he was of age.

He is the forty-shilling freeholder who appears on the Lay Subsidy Roll for the town in 1522—4,[2] and then the name leaves us.

The Wadehall was perhaps a cloth-hall (from Waed). Such a building stood once in Lichfield Street, near the fountain, and the plaster coat of arms set under its chimney, bears this out.[3] The arms were the Tudor Royal coat of arms and those of the City of London, the Draper's Company and the Merchants of the Staple.

We are told that the Wolverhampton Market Cross was built at the charge of the town in 1532.[4] From the appearance of similarly called buildings at Walsall, and Birmingham we may be sure that a large room raised on arches is meant. This is where James Leveson rang the market bell in 1537 and where the Assizes were held. And where, much later, Mrs. Siddons (Sarah Kemble) made her first public bow.

1 Quotation N.E.D. 1544.
2 W.A. 184.
3 W.A. Plate i.
4 W.A. 150.

A word may properly be said here about the holding of Assizes in 16th century Wolverhampton. In March 1547 there is a Commission to the King's Judges to deliver the gaols of Worcester Castle, Stafford County (meeting at Wolverhampton), Shrewsbury Castle (meeting at Bridgenorth) and Hereford Castle. The judge coming from Hereford could save part of his journey if he could go no further north than Bridgenorth. Robert Powell of the Park near Oswestry, sheriff for 1594, naturally preferred Shrewsbury. He writes to the bailiffs of that town 11 February 1593—4:— "I was promised from my Lord Chiffe baron's mouth if thasssizes for Stafford shier were kept at Stafford that he would kepe our Assizes at Salopp, but if he were brought to Wolverhampton then I must travaile to Bridgenoth, but whether this course doe hold or noe I know not, for I have noe perfecte Intelligence of eyther as yet".[1]

Very few men of Wolverhampton were appointed Sheriffs in the old days. This is partly accounted for by the frequent times the office fell to a member of the Wrottesley and Gifford families, and to them may be added the name Vernon.

James Leveson was the first Wolverhampton man who was so appointed and he was Sheriff in the last year of his life, 1546—7. He was J.P. 1536.

John Leveson served this office in 1562, and died in 1575. His son Thomas Leveson (who died 1594) in 1592.

There were thus many who for reasons of convenience would not look amiss at Wolverhampton as an Assize town. But Stafford was aggrieved.

Queen Elizabeth made her famous progress through the Midland Counties in 1575 without visiting Wolverhampton. From Lichfield she went to Chartley where she stayed ten days. On the 8th August she came to Stafford where an elaborate welcome awaited her. Asking the cause of the decay of the town, she was answered that the decline in cap-making was one, and that the Assizes were taken away from the town was another "To the which her Majesty most lovingly answered that she would renew and establish better the said Statute for Cappinge and for the Assizes she gave her promise that the same should ever after be kept at Stafford. And so after many most sweete and graciouse wordes to the great comfort of the Poore Inhabitants of Stafford she passed . . . to Stafford Castle where she stayed to dinner and sopted there".[2]

On her way to Worcester she stayed one night at Chillington, the Tudor mansion there having not long been completed. The next move was to Dudley castle where she had lunch, and the night was spent at Hartlebury Castle. Her silver and pale blue velvet saddle is still treasured by the Dudley family of the elder line.

While in Staffordshire the Queen had learnt how many of the Roman Catholics of the county had ceased to attend their parish churches, and at Dudley her secretaries summoned the leading Roman Catholics, including John Gifford her late host, to appear before the Privy Council and answer for their neglect, and long years of fine or imprisonment awaited them. The Pope had struck, but Elizabeth had her answer.

The historian Shaw has preserved a curious tradition about the days of Assizes at Wolverhampton "in Queen Elizabeth's time".[3] There were on the South West side of the church, and "still to be seen" handsome and spacious rooms or vaults, about 30 feet square, with strong and massy groins meeting in the centre at the top, the whole unmutilated and very perfect stonework. These, he continues, might have formed part of the base-story of a building of considerable magnitude. The walls are of great thickness, near three yards (!)

1 Vide Shrops. Arch. Soc. Trans. 2nd. series Vol. IV. p. 295. On 26th Aug. 1594 the Assizes were at Shrewsbury.
2 Cherry 72
3 Shaw ii, 161-2.

in which are still visible the remains of door-ways or passages . . . Here then were kept the felons awaiting trial at the town-hall near by.

It seems very possible that here was the cellarage of Archbishop Hubert Walter's proposed monastery, a project that failed on the archbishop's death in 1205 after about one year's work thereon.

I understand something of this nature was laid bare at the time when Mr. F. T. Beck's frontage (by the war memorial) was built and it seems a pity it did not receive a rather different treatment at that time.

We may easily overlook the fact that during the second half of this period a marked improvement was noticeable in the roads and highways of Wolverhampton—a matter of private endeavour long before it became a public burden. Sir Stephen Jenyns left in his will (1522)[1] a sum of ten pounds "toward the reparation and amending of the foule broken and noyous high wayes where most nede shalbe nere London". Nearer home Walter Leveson, 1551, left £40 "towards the amending of the evil highways *at the wirges* and between Tetnall and Wolverhampton with Tipton Lane in co. Stafford".[2]

Conspicuous however is the gift "with all plain Truth set down" on the List of Benefactors, of John Nechells, Sir Stephen's son-in-law "a Merchant of the staple borne in this Parish"[3] who "Gave towards ye continual repaire of the Pavements of this Township certain Lands and rents in Bushbury called Green fields now (1728) of the yearly value of £61 13s. 4d. . . . Mr. Nechells died in 1531.

It is possible to get another view of this gift from certain manorial lists of Chief Rents which survive from an early date, the land having always been subject to this payment.

In June 1526 there was payable as a "rent of assize" to Rose Cleyton, widow, lady of the manor of Bushbury, "from Lawrence Pendulbury for the Grenefeldes per ann. iii s"

In 1555 (to Walter Gravenour, lord of the manor) "From John Bradney for Greenfildes—iii s".

In 1573 (to the same) "From Thomas Eggenton for certain lands and meadows called grenefyldes now in the tenure of Richard Graunger . . . iii s. xi d."

In 1597 (to Jonas Grosvenor, esq.) "Of Mr. Huntbache for Greene fildes xviii d." (half year).

Then we have the "rare example" of master John Ligh, an aged priest, one of the vicars choral of St. Peter's[4] who, as Holinshed noticed in 1577, bore stone for the highways of the town and contributed £20 thereto out of his meagre resources. He is still annually remembered in the church-wardens' book of Doles.

Finally, John Leveson, junior, (d. 1605) left in his will 20s. towards repairing the pavements of the town.

THE LEVESON FAMILIES[5]

THE Tudor period showed the rise of two families in the town bearing the name Leveson or Luson (as it was pronounced and sometimes written). They were distant cousins and their lines separated in the long past; but they were both of the Wolverhampton neighbourhood and it is not easy to identify individuals who often bore the same Christian name. By the 16th century James Leveson and his brother Nicholas of the younger line became

1 School History, 355.
2 P.C.C. 25 Tashe.
3 Oliver op. cit. 181.
4 W.A. 86.
5 The Leveson pedigree is fully set-out in Shaw II, p. 169

prominent as new men, educated and capable. It was a time of the greatest pomp and circumstance. They procured a new coat of arms and crest (quarterings of a somewhat fictitious character though the heralds did their best); their cousins however had borne arms since 1380 at least, when they are entered on a Roll of Arms. Namely: Quarterly azure and gules, three sinister hands couped at the wrist argent. (Being then entered as Richard Lewson's arms.)[1]

Though new men, James and Nicholas Leveson were wealthy and successful and very much a local power. The difficulties of finding land to purchase with their profits was considerably eased by the release of land through the sale of the Monasteries and of this they were considerable buyers. When he made his will (April 1545) James Leveson makes bequests to no less than 58 parishes from Wellington to Halesowen and Cannock to Enville, to pray for his soul. And did he not have the chancel stalls removed from Lilleshall Abbey to Wolverhampton in 1546, fragments of which remain.[2]

In 1533 the brothers contributed handsomely towards the High Altar, Nicholas giving £40 towards the gilding and 40s. to the altar. "Jamys" gave £3 6s. 8d. to the altar, which cost £95; in all, an immense sum as then reckoned (about £2,000). Nicholas Leveson also gave a chalice in 1529. And why? Because the church had been robbed. Detection then being in its infancy, we learn that "the church wardens went to a wiseman". It was discovered that "pooles robbed the church, and the wardens went to Beaudley to the Lady Blunt for an answere for the Church goods". They received £10 12s. 6d. "for the Church plate that they had at Beaudley"[3] which though satisfactory does not explain a very cryptic action, and who was Pooles? Some long lost document may eventually explain.

On 23 June 1547, at the beginning of a new Reign, the lists for General Pardons were again thrown open. Candidates were offered until 28 January 1548 to avail themselves of this benefit. James Leveson now receives his, and he is styled . . . "or Luson of Lylleshall, Salop, esquire, Merchant of the Staple of Calais, mayor of the said Staple, Sheriff of Staffordshire, *alias* late of Wolverhampton and London, mercer".[4]

So both brothers were members of the Mercer Company.

James was the younger, and the crescent observable on the bronze shield of arms accompanying his descendant Sir Richard's statue in St. Peter's Church is the mark for a younger son.

Thomas Leveson (c. 1498—1563), the elder brother of John Leveson, appears mostly before us until succeeded by his brother as a landlord, business man, and gatherer of rents. Copyhold, the tenure of most of the land near Wolverhampton at that time had many surprises in rents and dues called Herriots paid according to the custom of the manor: the best beast in the field is taken, the best ornament in the house is due, it may be, on the death of a tenant. There are dealings of apparent harshness which are brought before the courts. Several grievances caused the Petition of the Inhabitants 1537. The people complained that they the King's subjects are daily oppressed by one Thomas Leveson of Wolverhampton, gentleman,[5] and others his adherents, as in taking their goods in the name of heriots not due, and in wasting and destroying their corn and herbage with his cattle and many times taking some of the cattle of your said subjects out of the commons and impounding them . . . and setting persons to take men's cattle out of the common

1 S.H.C. iii, 25.
2 W.A. 272.
3 W.A. 271.
4 Cal. Pat. Rolls, 1 & 2 Edw. VI, ii, 145.
5 S.H.C. 1912, p. 71.

lanes and put them in his ground . . . and threatening the officers of the law and causing the peace to be broken. Also poor men plough their grounds and the said Thomas Leveson sows the said grounds and carries away the corn alleging them to be his. It was a matter for enquiry by "indifferent gentlemen" of the county.

The open field system had much to answer for. There was need for give and take. Thus a tenant in Horseley Field[1] next the land of Thomas Leveson "falced, sturryd and mukkyd" it; but when the crop appeared Thomas Leveson took it. Moreover he tethered his horses on adjacent land, saying he would make amends "but ther ys non to be gooten of hym but evull words and ongraciose". On another occasion[2] Nycolas Smyth found Thomas Leveson's beasts in his master's corn, and would have driven them away had not "Copes servant of Thomas Leveson" come and thrown stones at him.

Robert Cut had a lease of lands in Wyndfield (near Blakenhall) and would have made hay; but the night before it was ready Thomas Leveson "soopyd" it away.

In parochial matters the name of James Leveson appears from the beginning of the old account book (1519). He had by then taken the wise step of marrying Alice, one of the sixteen children of Richard Wrottesley, esquire, and Dorothy Dudley his wife whose incised marble grave cover, dated 1521, reminded "every Christian mon, to prey for our soules that bin gon".[3]

His three sons, Sir Richard Leveson of Lilleshall, Edward Leveson of Perton and Walter Leveson of London came from that marriage; but Alice Leveson died in 1525.

James' second wife was Margaret Offley a widow of Thomas Michell of London, ironmonger (a Staffordshire man) who was reputed "one of the richest commoners in the city of London", who died without issue, leaving a great substance to his wife of goods, money and lands. Sir Thomas Offley her brother advised the marriage with James Leveson, and there were two daughters.

The elder, says an almost contemporary account, was married to Walter Aston, son and heir of Sir Edward Aston of Tixall, "a famous Knight and mighty in livings, rents and services. The marriage was solemnized at Wolverhampton (c. 1544) where for a fortnight's space great provision was made for all kinds of meat, beer, ale, wine and meats most plentiful. In all the inns and victualling houses, with cooks in every inn, and tents set up in the fields, not only for the town and country adjacent, but for all strangers and passengers that journeyed through the town (being a great market and thoroughfare to the town of Shrewsbury, Wales and the city of West Chester) and all such were liberally received with wholesome and delicate fare, frank and free, with horse meat and man's meat, without payment of any money, and so well all travellers entertained during that time, such a solemn frank and free marriage was never heard of". He was the builder of Tixall gatehouse.

The other daughter made also an important marriage, but we are not told where nor who were entertained. Joyce Leveson married John Giffard in 1551. He was born in 1533 and his grandfather, Sir John, of marksman fame, was still alive. They were the parents of eight sons and six daughters. She died in 1608 (14 March) and appears on an altar tomb in Brewood church. He died 28 August 1613. Their son Richard Giffard, a marked man during the Babington conspiracy (against Mary Queen of Scots) subsequently lived and died at the Lea, Wolverhampton.

1 Ib. 114.
2 Ib. 115.
3 Wrott. Hist., p. 256.

Finally, there is Nicholas Leveson. Though closely connected with Wolverhampton in his younger days, Nicholas Leveson's interests tended to keep him rather in London and S.E. England (Kent) as a married man. His will makes him a citizen and Mercer of London and merchant of the Staple at Calais (will 7 November 1536) and was a parishioner of St. Andrew's Undershaft, where a large brass to him and some armorial glass remains. He had goods and chattels "beyond the sea". He served the office of sheriff of London in 1534, but did not live to be Lord Mayor.

He left his brother James £100 and a gold ring; made provision for prayers for his soul and those of his parents for ten years; gave £20 towards scholarships at Oxford and Cambridge. "To three servants of my brother James Leveson, a black gown each". There is much besides.

He was direct ancestor of the Dukes of Sutherland, and by failure of his brother James's heirs with the vice Admiral (1605) his family succeeded to the Staffordshire estates of Trentham, Lilleshall and Wolverhampton, the half manor of Stowheath being shared with the Giffard family of Chillington. This family were in the height of their power.[1]

A grant exists which explains their interest here. The great Sir John Giffard had obtained from the King, when Gentleman Usher of the Chamber, the Office of Joint Bailiff of the Manor of Wolverhampton, forfeited by the attainder of Lord Lovell (18 June 1512). This was not the lordship itself but the collector of the rents of the lordship. It may be, therefore, that it was through the marriage of James Leveson's youngest daughter Joyce to the grandson John Giffard (1533—1613) in 1551 (after her father's death) that the grant of this manor is owed.

Before concluding our remarks on the Levesons of Wolverhampton, a word should be said about the tomb of John, who lies buried in the South transept of the Collegiate Church. Joyce Ashfield who married John Leveson and appears with him on the tomb, came from what the pedigrees call "Eythorpe", Oxfordshire, but known to us as Heythrop. John Ashfield, the father, died too young in 1522 to know of this marriage; but he mentions his daughters Joyce and Dorothy ("£150 each"). To this day in the chancel of the church of St. Nicholas in Heythrop (the old church) before the image of our Lady his tomb exists; and he bequeathed £3 6s. 8d. to make a window on the south side of the chancel. It should still be there. His altar tomb gives his effigy in rather crude brass. The clause in his will which reads: "I bequeath to my son Humfrey my best horse, 1,000 sheep, 8 oxen for the plough, six horses and six kine", shows the nature of his interests.[2]

John Leveson's alabaster tomb has come down to us in a very battered condition. This was occasioned by the Civil War. It was fortunate that at the time of the Restoration there were direct descendants of John Leveson still active in the town, and so it was put together instead of being broken up, as were several other tombs.

But it is not in its original position nor even in a good position. The date is earlier and the workman-ship better than Thomas Lane's tomb in the north transept; but the Burton alabaster carver's hand is there, as is seen by the flattened goggle of the eyes.

He carries a sword and wears armour. His coat of arms associated with that of *Ashfield* is mediaeval; but his Crest was a recent grant (6 November 1562 by Laur-Dalton, Norroy) and is here seen on the helmet: "an arm embowed in armour argent, holding in the gauntlet a battle-axe".[3]

1 The pedigree of the Leveson family is set out in Shaw, vol. 2, p. 169.
2 P.C.C. 20 Maynwarying.
3 S.H.C. iii (II), 106.

The effigies on the side of the tomb with their shields record the children's marriages with the Brooke and Stamford families. The son, Thomas Leveson, married Mary, daughter of Chief Justice Sir Robert Brooke whose splendid tomb (with a representation of her on it) can be seen in Claverley church.[1] The other, Anne, the only daughter, married on 15 November 1562, Robert Stamford of Perry Hall, a house which his father Sir William Stamford, chief justice, in need of a country estate had acquired. Robert was one of the 300 knighted at King James's coronation on 23 July 1603. The other effigy commemorates John Leveson the fourth but second surviving son, who was buried at Wolverhampton 30 July 1605. He lived in the district and as a bachelor uncle of many nieces and nephews played his part, if only by will, as such uncles should.

That John Leveson, senior, was one of the first of this locality to direct his attention to iron-making is shown by a licence to him by Letters Patent dated 30 March 1563,[2] to fell and "Ymploye to cole or other fuell for the making of yron" or otherwise for 12 years timber of oak, beech and ash in Chestlyn Hay belonging to Ambrose Earl of Warwick. There is a letter of John Leveson's thanking the earl for his good will in buying wood in "Chestelyn haye" even though it was at Leveson's loss.[3] This estate remained with his descendants until 1699.[4]

John Leveson's will mentions his gift of the Stretton rent which he had obtained with the Chapel and glebe there at the Reformation. This he conveyed to the church-wardens in 1558 and the income is still forthcoming.[5] He mentions his coal mines, which he gives to his son John. Servants benefit as is usual "for suerlie they are all good seruaunts painfull and true".

For the history of St. Peter's during the Reformation we are fortunate in possessing some pages of NOTES taken towards the close of the 17th century by the local antiquary, John Huntbach of Fetherstone, from the old church-wardens' Book which seems now to be lost for ever. S. Shaw drew upon this information and prints some if it in a haphazard way in Vol. II (p. 161). But a much more complete account from the original MS. will be found in the Wolverhampton Antiquary. The notes cover nearly 100 years.

On this slender evidence we must rely almost entirely for the names of former chapels in the church. Two were in the "chancels" or transepts, St. Catherine's in the North and Our Lady's in the South. St. Catherine's may have been of quite recent date owing to the re-building of that part of the church about the year 1500.[6] William Wilkes J.P. was buried there in 1505 and generations of his descendants followed him. He was an important and almost the sole magistrate of our early period.

There were also the chapels of St. George, St. Nicholas, and St. Loe. The former which was sold at the Reformation to John Leveson for 10s. may probably have been in the South Transept. St. Loe's (the saint of metalworkers) was at the upper end of the S. Aisle. There were also the St. George's and the Bachelors' Guilds about which we know nothing, together with that of our Lady.[7] Pyper's chapel, as it was called, has a history of its own; it seems to have been connected with John Pippard, a priest who served the hospital for the aged poor.

It was customary at this period for the Deans of Wolverhampton to pay 40s. at the time of their installation (and prebendaries 20s.) thus Dr. Clarke pays the amount in 1522, Dr. Sampson in 1525 and William Franklin in 1537.

1 See W.A.
2 Cal. P.R. 5 Eliz. I, p. 478.
3 Printed W.A. 176-7.
4 W.A. ii, 38.
5 W.A. ii, 34,
6 W.A. 34.
7 Shaw ii, 160.

Queen Anne House, 19, Bilston Street,

Old Hall from Bilston Street, 1835

There is an Inventory of the Church goods compiled by Michael Brooke and Raphe Grafton, church wardens in 1541.[1] It is interesting for showing that the Wolverhampton church was not one that could make any startling parade of wealth. There are numerous candlesticks large and small of "mastlen" (pewter) and other vessels of the same metal. There were several gilt chalices but that was to be expected, and one silver cross weighing 44 ounces. The poverty of the church is very marked. True, St. Catherine's 'shough' were of silver, but they were sold to Harman Beyne, the foreigner admitted to residence (denizen) and agent for wool, for 16d.

Among the relics was "one image of sylver, and over gilt, with a glass therein, and a thorne, weying 5 ounces and a quarter". Also "a cross of wood, with sylver thereabouts, not weyed, which was called parcell of the wholly cross". Then there was a silver box "wherein it is said should be inclosed a peece of the wholly candle, not weyed", and "another box of sylver, like a salt, with birral (*i.e.* beryl or crystal) not weyed". These were in the hands of the sacristan, but they do not represent the rich hoard that might have been expected in a church of such antiquity and honour.

The wealth from the wool trade had only made itself felt in the last hundred years. The "bederole" (a list of those specially to be prayed for) to which we are introduced under the year 1537, gives only two names (surely a poor record) Mr. Toll and Sir Stephen Jennings; and Mr. John Toll who made his will in 1517 was a Bilston man.

The Inventory of Church Goods for the Hundred of Seisdon Staffordshire was ordered on 6th October 1552 (6 Edw. vi) by Walter Viscount Hereford (Lord Ferrers of Chartley) Sir Thomas Gifford, Kt., and Walter Wrottesley, esq., but was taken during April and May 1553.[2] Its intention was to turn to the King's use what had survived after years of private plunder and speculation. It shows only the remnant of the church goods left over from previous sales on the King's behalf, when official prices may have not ruled very high.

The Puritans and fanatics now had their chance to do all the harm and destruction they were able against the beauty and craftsmanship of centuries. Wolverhampton was a conservative place given to the old ways of life; but this offered little protection against the march of events.

At this time (April 1553) the church goods at Wolverhampton were mainly Copes of every description:—[3]

> Two of white silk; one of black velvet; two of green silk; one of red silk, tinselled; one of green velvet; another of black silk; one cope of cloth of Venice gold; another of blue silk; two of white damask; two of white fustian; one of white satin; one chequered cope of white silk and green.

Bilston at this late date had nothing except 4 small bells; the chalice and other ornaments had been sold 1 August 1548 to Richard Forsett the King's Surveyor, and a receipt given.

At Tettenhall there had also been a sale, where most of the profits went to the repairs of the church; but it too was rich in vestments which had not yet been dispersed.

Willenhall was not unworthily endowed with goods; but these too had gone to the King's Surveyor.

At Penkridge, which is comparable with Wolverhampton, they sold a bell and spent the money "partly in plucking down of the altars and defacing of the church"; but provision was made for a young man "to tech wrytynge scole and the reste we have bestoed on iij lame creatures whoe are not able to goe abrod".

1 Shaw ii, 160.
2 S.H.C. 1915, 405.
3 S.H.C., N.S. VI, i, 188.

There were also at Wolverhampton two chalices and patens of silver, one cross of copper and gilt, one cross of wood with an image of copper, and seven bells whereof two were small bells. So at this date the church had its complement of bells which were to last until 1698.

The extant Staffordshire chantry certificates and returns are very incomplete. Wolverhampton suffered particularly in this respect. The chantries at the chapels of Bilston, Willenhall, Pelsall with their values &c., are returned; but for the mother church we are referred to Berkshire (Windsor), and, of course, Windsor knew nothing of it. On the other hand they realized that they had lost Wolverhampton, and that the revenue of the dean of St. Georges was so much the worse. The dean was a careful man in matters of money, and taking a dim view of the Act of I Edward VI for the dissolution of colleges, had protected himself so far as possible. He contrived to take the income of the late chapel of Wolverhampton from Easter 2 Edw. VI "by colour of a late provisoe in the Act of I Edw. VI". He was pardoned for this and allowed such income as did not exceed £40 yearly. Meanwhile he was granted the rectory of Donstable Houghton, and the vicarage of Dunstable, Bedfordshire, late of St. Alban's monastery with a value of £41. William Franklyn, the dean, therefore came comfortably through the crises.

Sir Walter Mildmay "general surveyor" of the new court of Augmentations and his assistant Robert Kelway found the church of the late College of St. Peter of Wolverhampton was a parish Church, and that there was "no parson nor vicar endowed in the same for the discharge of the Cure there, a thing that was very nedefull", as well as an assistant to act as Curate. They found too that the "late Chauntrye of Pelsall" was in the parish as a Chapel of ease "distaunt four miles" where it was necessary to continue to administer divine service and the sacraments. The commissioners therefore on 20 July 1548 declared the Collegiate Church should continue to be a parish church with two of the late prebendaries, William Sale of Wobaston, and Thomas Sadler of Willenhall, to be vicar and curate together. There was provision also for Pelsall, but the document is in a torn and tattered state and does not say what.[1]

William Sale's tenure as first vicar of Wolverhampton was short; but he continued Prebendary there under Queen Mary, then was master of St. John's Hospital, Lichfield, under Queen Elizabeth and was a Resident Canon of the Cathedral when he died in July 1588. The dean (Boleyn) witnessed his will and received a "spurre ryall" (a gold coin) as a bequest. Well to do, Sale left several benefactions of money to poor artificers, each to enjoy it for four years and then make repayment, "and so to continue for ever". But this Wolverhampton charity has long been "lost", though at Stafford it exists in another form.[2]

On 2 March 1553 John (Dudley) Duke of Northumberland and lady Jane his wife received a grant of much land,[3] including:— the college of Wolverhampton and the manor, prebend and rectory of Wolverhampton, and also the prebends of Hatherton, Wyllnall, Fetherston, Halton *alias* Hulton, Monmore, Stonewall *alias* Kinwaston and Wobaston, Staffordshire, and all other possessions late of the said college. These were to be held "in chief by the service of one Knight's fee" and an annual payment for the lands of Wolverhampton college of £10 16s. 4d. Doubtless the intention here was to make some provision for a cure of souls.

At any rate it was clear that the King's Free Chapel of Wolverhampton had ceased for the time being.

1 Augmentation. Particulars for Grants for Schools, Bdle 1, No. 24.
2 W.A. 65-9.
3 Pat. Edw. VI., vol. 5 p. 179.

Ultimately, the seizure of the Duke of Northumberland's lands brought his Wolverhampton possessions more or less intact into the Queen's hands and on 26 December 1553 she was moved to establish the "college, free chapel or deanery" which (in the view of her advisers) her "progenitors, Kings of England" had anciently founded. Her letters patent describe the appropriation of this deanery by patent, 21 February, 19 Edw. IV (1480) to the deanery of the royal free chapel of St. George in Windsor Castle, which made the dean of Windsor also dean of Wolverhampton and its first prebendary, with power to collate the seven other prebendaries and officers (of which that of the sacristan or 'sextenshipp' is mentioned). It is also recited that the Act of Parliament which transferred the lands of dissolved chantries, colleges and free chapels in I Edw. VI (1547) to the crown, though exempting the said Chapel of St. George and its possessions, was held by the Officers of the Court of Augmentations to apply equally to the college of Wolverhampton and its possessions, which therefore came into the King's hands. Thereupon by patent, 2 March 7 Edw. VI. (1553) all its lands were granted to John, duke of Northumberland and his heirs; but now that he had been attainted his estates in the said lands had come into the Queen's hands. The Queen not unmindful of the great love of her father and all her progenitors from the time of Edward III towards the dean and canons of the said chapel of St. George, and also that there her father lies buried and the Order of the Garter is installed; desiring also that the possessions of the chapel should rather be increased and that there should be no alteration of the grant of Edward IV; wills that the College of Wolverhampton with its prebends and offices should be as they were and that it should have such perpetual endowment as it had before the said act.

The College within the parish church of Wolverhampton is therefore restored. William Francklyn, clerk, present dean of the chapel of St. George, Windsor, is restored as dean of Wolverhampton and prebendary of the first (Wolverhampton) prebend. The others appointed were as follows:—

2nd	Kynvaston	prebend,	Adam Broke.
3rd	Federston	„	Thomas Cresswall.
4th	Hilton	„	Thomas Asten.
5th	Wylnall	„	Humfrey Horton, clerk.
6th	Monmore	„	William Lynde, clerk.
7th	Wobaston	„	William Sale, clerk.
8th	Hatherton	„	John Leveson.

and the sexton John Wallowes, clerk; all for life. They were to have a perpetual succession, to be able in law to answer and be answered in all courts, and to have a common seal. The lands, etc., were reckoned at a yearly value of £1,131 13s. 0¼d. The tenure was as of old that of frank almoign. The college of Wolverhampton was to be reputed as a member of the free chapel of St. George, Windsor. Taxes of "first fruits" and "tenths" were released by the crown both now and hereafter.

The needs of Windsor and the quick fall of the Duke of Northumberland thus helped to reverse a wrong committed to the church of Wolverhampton during the wreckage and spoilation of a Reformation. Had it been otherwise there can be little doubt that the lands and manors attached to the church would have been re-granted as rewards to government officials, or have been purchased (as in the case of Tettenhall, to look no farther) by the local landowner.

The charter prebendaries to some extent, like the dean, had been known to the old regime. Humfrey Horton, William Lynde (until his death in 1555, vicar of Wombourne) and William Sale had held their prebends in 1548, and so had Thomas Creswell, "esquire", while John Wallowes, the sacrist, had been Morrow Mass priest. The new appointments were lay and apparently a sop to the landed interest, indeed Adam Broke was only a child of about 14 at this date (but a son of the Recorder of the City of London a chief Justice to be)[1] William Francklyn was shortly to resign his post, in consequence, it is said, of complaints against him for alienating some of the revenues of his church;[2] but old age may have helped him in his decision. He was succeeded by Dr. Owen Oglethorpe, a canon of Windsor, on 8 February 1554,[3] who as bishop of Carlisle crowned Queen Elizabeth.

During this reign Wolverhampton was visited by a cardinal of the Roman church, an event that was not to be repeated until the coming of Cardinal Wiseman in 1855.[4]

Finally, it is not perhaps out of place to mention here the numerous leases made during the period of the Wolverhampton Deanery.

No leases appear to occur before the uniting of the Deaneries and possibly this was the cause, a matter of convenience for an owner living at a distance.

The earliest known example is of 1516[5] (8 Hen. VIII) when John Vescey, dean of Windsor and Wolverhampton, leases to Richard Wrottesley esq. and James Leveson, gent. his manor and lordship of Wolverhampton, for ten years, paying £38 1s. per ann. (James was Wrottesley's son-in-law).

There was found and copied from the old church chest a lease from dean George Carew, dated 31 August 1566. It is fragmentary in parts but had been drawn up on what had become stereotyped lines, and the beneficiary was John Wrottesley, esquire, the years to run 99 and the rent £38.

One of those exploratory Chancery suits of 1584 (Chancery Proceedings Series II. Bundle 213 no. 15. Walter Leveson of Lilleshall co. Salop, esq. Plaintiff v. Raphe Grafton of Wolverhampton, yeoman, defendant. Bill dated 13 October 1584) gives us an interesting account of the manner in which all this came about.

On the death of Sir Richard Leveson at Lilleshall in 1561 his brother Edward Leveson of Perton acted as his executor, and a lease of the deanery of Wolverhampton was found among his property. There seems to have been a doubt whether the lease continued after his death, and the dean, George Carew, having received offers for it from certain persons of honour, asked the executor to go and see him on the matter.

With Edward Leveson went Raphe Grafton "yeoman", his man of business. And this is his explanation, given in his Answer. "Mr. Care (Carey) then Dean of Windsor, being at Poplar not far from London": they went to Poplar, and the Dean declared he would rather grant a fresh lease to Edward, because his predecessor had received great sums of money from Sir Richard for it; and instead of the £100 he had been offered he would only take £40 from him. It was kindly proposed and thankfully received. The Dean then asked him to get the Earl of Leicester to write him on his behalf "So that he might better satisfy the other persons who had applied for the same"; and this Edward did, though in favour of John Wrottesley, Esq. (a relative of the Earl) who should hold it in trust for his nephew, Walter Leveson, then under age, "and expressed his good opinion of his honesty and good will".

And after the new lease was drawn up in the name of the said John, the said Edward and the defendant (Grafton) travelled to Windsor where the Dean sealed the same. Grafton then paid the Dean's wife the £40 mentioned on behalf of Edward, and so far as he

1 As to whom and an illustration of Adam Broke in effigy, see W.A., p. 289.
2 Cooper's Ath. Cant. I, 141, where there is a sketch of his career.
3 Cal. Pat. Rolls, Phil. & Mary, p. 220.
4 He stayed at Moseley Court with Mr. Francis Whitgreave.
5 Huntbach M.S.

remembered Edward had the lease afterwards. Edward Leveson died 21 August 1569; the lease was mislaid and these proceedings in Chancery instituted in 1584 by Walter Leveson to find it. It might very well have got into John Wrottesley's hand. Later it found its way into the Church chest, and here Huntbach probably saw and copied it. It has now disappeared for good.

The immediate result of this lease seems to have been the appointment by Edward Leveson of George Upton to the office of Belmanship of the church and market. It was an office to which many fees, profits, and advantages belonged, and the inhabitants claimed it as of their appointment. On 12 June 1567 the inhabitants headed by Henry Vernon, John Leveson, Thomas Leveson, John Pype, William Howe, Michael Brooke, John Creswell and others filed their Bill. They tell us the market is greatly decayed and the people resorting there much troubled by the contention and strife between the parties. That the gift of the office ought to belong to the parishioners. But the death of the defendant probably brought this suit to an end.[1]

THE FINDING OF THE SAXON CHARTER

An event which clearly aroused some excitement in Wolverhampton and which occurred during the last 30 years of our period may be allowed to divert our attention from the more serious history of the town.

A suit in Chancery was often used as a means to obtain information which is withheld in the ordinary course. The process was for a plaintiff to make quite a gross and unfounded charge in his Petition or Bill and receive the information required in the Answer. As a source of facts, these suits are often of the greatest use to historians, recounting as they do documents that are gone and lost for ever.

William Grene described as of Wolverhampton, gentleman, whose neat hand and signature is known to us on legal documents, was Register(*i.e.* Registrar) or Chapter Clerk of the Dean and Chapter, and looked after, though we might think in rather a casual way, the muniments of the Collegiate church. He antagonized John Leveson, principal inhabitant of the town as he most assuredly was, who in May 1572 presented his grievance to the courts. John, as owner of the rents lately belonging to the prebends of the church, was alarmed that "certain writings" concerning the same had got into William Grene's hand, who having "craftily got" one blank sealed by the Dean and Chapter to engross therein at leisure certain "good orders and constitutions" agreed upon by them to be had in the church, had misused his position by conveying to himself certain secret estates in the lands which defrauded the plaintiff of his rights and inheritance.

The defendant took the view that the Collegiate church had never been dissolved because it had been annexed to St. George's at Windsor, and that John Leveson had obtained a grant by crafty means. It was true that the King's surveyor, Richard Forest, had come to Wolverhampton and surveyed the church's lands and took them into the King's hands; but the Dean and prebendaries took another view and "stood in law" with the King in the Court of Augmentation concerning the college and prebends, and while the matter was still uncertain, John Leveson persuaded them to grant him the lands in Fee Farm, promising in the defendant's presence that if by any means divine service could be maintained at Wolverhampton he would give up all rights granted to him to them and their successors again. Upon this promise certain grants were made to him. Afterwards the

1 S.H.C. 1938, 139.

prebends were dissolved and the prebendaries "put to their pensions" but the dean's own right was so effectual that it could not be dissolved by law, and to induce him to give up his right willingly, he was given in exchange a parsonage called Dunstable Houghton.

The King transferred the prebends to John (Dudley) Duke of Northumberland, whose officers recovered the rents thereof without any gainsaying by John Leveson. But these fell to the Queen on his attainder. Under the new foundation John Leveson "by colour of the said grants" re-entered into the lands belonging to the prebends and the prebendaries "being poor men not certain of their continuance" did not withstand him. He was bound to pay certain rents to certain prebendaries, and a sufficient stipend to every curate and to as many vicars choral as were accustomed to serve such prebends; but this he refused to do, so that whereas eight ministers used at one time to serve in the church now there are only three for lack of sufficient stipend. To reform this and other church matters (we are told), at a Chapter held at Wolverhampton divers good orders were agreed upon, which one of the prebendaries wrote in a little paper book. So that the same should remain in force, they agreed to put their Chapter seal to a piece of blank parchment and gave it to William Grene to engross the same, which he accordingly did, "this being the blank parchment mentioned in the bill". The plaintiff seeing he would have to pay, made agreement with certain of the prebendaries in order that his former promises might be forgotten. It all seems very irregular. Moreover we have light thrown on how John Leveson himself became prebendary of Wobaston. William Grene had himself obtained (from the dean, presumably) a grant of the next appointment to this prebend. He was ready to let John Leveson have it in exchange for that of the next presentation to Penn, which was in his possession.

The end of this document is in bad condition but it lasts long enough to come to this tremendous conclusion. We are told that "an old priest called Sir John Lye delivered to the defendant for safe keeping an old writing in Saxon, by which it is declared that a woman called Wylfrome gave divers lands, now belonging to the church in Hampton, by a deed dated the third Olympial of the reign of King Ethelred; which since that time and by that woman hath been called Wylfrome Hampton".

This was our foundation charter, which had recently been discovered in the rubble of a wall, lapped in a sheet of lead.[1] (Dotatio et confirmatio literis Saxonicis in pergameno conscripta, in ruderibus muri reperta est, lamina plumbea inclusa, circa annum Domini millesimum quingentesimum sexagesimum).

Thus the removal of an alter or some such structural alteration has yielded its long-held secret. The news was welcomed by the new and growing band of chroniclers and archivists. It made some little stir: a document in the hand of a notary of King Ethelred is still a surprise.

A manuscript History of the Church of Lichfield written in Latin in 1565 recounts its discovery (p. 37). Though too late for Leland, it was seen and fully reported by Holinshed (1577), who found therein a new meaning, Wulfrun's Hampton, to explain the origin of the town (known in 13th century but long forgotten, apparently). Sir Henry Spelman (d. 1641) made a copy of it. Dugdale at Windsor in 1640 made a copy of it.

Leland's *Itinerary* did not take him past Wolverhampton. He visited Lichfield, going from Gloucester *via* Hereford and Ludlow to Shrewsbury; then by Bridgnorth to Worcester and through Birmingham to Lichfield, and so to Coventry . . .

1 W.A. 194.

CONCLUSION.

The Earl of Essex, Queen Elizabeth's Essex, was beheaded 25 February 1601.

An informer's List of the "Names of those gentlemen which met at Wolverhampton 10th September last (1601)" was bound to give food for thought.

They were:—

Edward Devereux of Castle Bromwich, Warwickshire, uncle to the said late Earl of Essex, and his son and heir, with other of that name.

Sir Edward Littleton Kt. (d. 1610) whose lady is also a Devereux.

Roger Fowke, esq. lately made a justice of the peace (26 November 1597, of Brewood) by the procurement of the said late Earl, who lay in London all the last winter until the said Earl's insurrection, and often frequented Essex house, a man very unfit to have that authority in the country for many oppressions of poor men: . . . . (as can be proved). John Lane, William Cumberforde, John Fowke of Gunston, Richard Gifford of Ashmores, John Leveson (d. 1605) and Walter Leveson, esquires, with many others. (1 page Hist. Man. Com. *Salisbury Manuscripts* XI p. 387).

At this time, says the informer, "those false rumours and misreports were spread in the country of your Honour (Lord Salisbury) the Lord Cobham and Sir Walter Raleigh".

The succession to the throne was much in doubt. There was a plot to put Arabella Stuart on the throne, as an alternative to her cousin James VI. This was espoused by Cobham and Raleigh. Richard Gifford was an old Babbington plotter.

CHAPTER VI

WOLVERHAMPTON IN THE EARLY SEVENTEENTH CENTURY

THE CARRY FORWARD

THE beginning of the seventeenth century in Wolverhampton includes, of necessity, the tail end of the sixteenth.

Queen Elizabeth died upon the last day of the official year of 1602. Her gallant sea-captain, vice-admiral Sir Richard Leveson, was buried at Wolverhampton on 2 September 1605, having died in London.[1]

Thomas Maddoxe, M.A., headmaster of the Grammar School, after a long and successful career, ended his days in July 1605.

Mrs. Margaret Moseley, of Dunstall, a great and possibly fearsome lady, who had recently received a general pardon under the great seal for all her civil misdeeds,[2] died 'full of virtue full of years', on 19 December 1606.[3]

Joan Spooner, says the Parish Register, 'was kylled by the fallinge downe of Prestwood Hall' and died in the burning of it, May 1612. This marks the end of the house built by Henry de Prestwood, forester of Cannock, who died just three hundred years before. He was the founder of a chantry chapel in St. Peter's in 1311.[4]

The town of Wolverhampton, which was built of timber, plaster, and thatch, was accustomed to these burnings. The Swan Inn in the Market Place had been burnt down in 1515 (or soon before);[5] the Cock Inn in Cock Street (for its sign gave its name to Tunwell Street) was consumed in the fire of 22 April 1590;[6] yet not the old timber house on the opposite side of the street which still stands, nor the Old Barrel Inn, also of timber, a little lower down.[7] Possibly an open stream of running water from Snowhill, which crossed the road here,[8] gave welcome help. But towards and in Salop, or Barn Street, 104 houses were burnt, 694 men, women and children 'impoverished by the fire', and thirty stacks of hay, corn and straw destroyed.

On 11 October 1607, there was baptized at Wolverhampton, William, son of Thomas Perry, of Bilston. What he did on his way from school, and how the bishop of Lichfield

1 The date and place are given on his monumental brass: 4to. nonas Sextil. an 1605, e vita pie, discessit Londini (i.e. 2 August). *Shaw*, II, p. 158. This may be deceptive. At his funeral there was a *Sermon* preached by Samuel Page (S.T.C. 19094).
2 The original has found its way into the writer's possession. This shows that the Dunstall Deeds have been dispersed.
3 In her epitaph, *Shaw*, II, p. 159, she was called a 'pearle of lustre bright'.
4 *Shaw*, II, p. 150; *S.H.C.*, 1911, p. 308, for Inquisition. The Leveson family, of Wolverhampton, later Leveson-Gower, quarter the arms of *Prestwood*.
5 Sir Richard Paget's *Oldfallings deeds*, No. 26A.
6 *Shaw*, II, p. 163, citing Huntbach MS, in W. Salt Library, Stafford, which is here quoted. The Cock Inn burning is mentioned in a Chancery Suit (*Leveson* v. *Haynes*), 1630.
7 Photographs of this in its latest very quaint state of the year 1870 are known. Part of the Grammar School nearby was burnt (*School History*, p. 45).
8 It was crossed by a bridge (? foot only) as late as the eighteenth century (Constables' Accounts, October 1719). The stretch of road here is called Boblake. The name is comparable with Bablake at Coventry, which is explained (P.N.Warw. p. 161) as '*Baba's* stream'.

and Coventry triumphed over him (an uneven contest), will be found in that scarce booklet *The Boy of Bilson* (*sic*), printed in 1628.[1]

There were other changes.

At *Merridale* the Saltford family which had occupied the house, now a modernized fragment of the later wing of the old building[2] standing at the corner of the Grammar School field, had released its hold of three centuries. A new man, William Normansell, a mercer, now owned it. His son, also William, became a magistrate during the Commonwealth, and was one of the nine local voters for the Barebones Parliament, 1653.[3]

At *Graseley* (I prefer the correct spelling), the fifteenth-century home of the Ridley family, there were also changes, John Ridley, the last male, died in 1608. The Parish Register shows that his daughter Rachel married, in 1603, John Rotten, of Moseley, Birmingham. The wild life of their son Walter ended this line[4]; but some cousins in the eighteenth century came to live at Oxley Manor. When one notes on the map of the town ROTTEN'S ROW, a name that appears in the Register in 1639, one might call this family to mind for explanation.

At *the Lea*, another moated homestead (for the cattle if not the people needed protection, when such houses were planned), there was an interregnum.[5] Richard Giffard, who died here in April 1606, was 'of the Lea Esquier'. Of his family more anon.

RECUSANCY: THE LEVESON AND GIFFARD FAMILIES

THE history of Wolverhampton from 1600 illustrates the unsettled state of religious belief. The King started his reign with an open mind, and he had schemes for furthering the union of all Christian Churches and was not intolerant of the Roman Catholics. The poor spiritual quality of the ministers of religion after the Reformation encouraged nonconformity. The Low Church party, the Puritans, men of small pleasure except in attack, intransigent in council, did not make for unity. They called, in 1604, the curates of St. Peter's notorious drunkards and dissolute men'.[6] The sacrist, Thomas Meeke, who died in 1610, must then have been elderly, for he seems to have occupied that position at Penkridge in 1548[7]; he was certainly at Wolverhampton in 1565.[8] He marked time with one foot in the past.

Richard Lee, who succeeded Joseph Hall, Dean of Worcester, in his prebend of Willenhall in 1623, was an able preacher but outspoken. He promised the town (in his rare printed sermon of 1624[9]) a 'Spirituall Spring' and endeared himself to members of the old faith, of which there were locally twenty families of importance, by remarking: 'I never knew any part of this Kingdom, where Rome's snakie brood roosted and rested themselves more warmer and safer, and with greater countenance'. However, Archbishop Laud had a rod in pickle for him.

The Recusants, as members of the old faith were called, existed in an uneasy alliance with the Protestant religion, barred from public offices, penalized if they did not go to church. Of these families the two which concern us particularly are those of Giffard and Leveson. They furnished lords for the two manors. On the other hand the Lane family was Protestant.

1 Short Title Cat. No. 1185. The Cambridge University Library and Bodleian seem to be without copies in 1926. It was the occasion for writing a forty-eight page 'Discourse concerning Popish Exorcizing' by Rich. Baddeley, and the story was popular in anti-papal controversy. Arthur Wilson, in his *History of the Reign of James I* (1653), devotes several pages to it. It delighted Dr. Plot. The incident took place in 1620.

2 The north wing, of timber and wattle, was certainly Tudor. It was demolished about 1925.

3 MS. in W.S.L.

4 *Shaw*, II, p. ★172.

5 The history of this place is given very fully in the *Wolverhampton Antiquary*, vol. I.

6 *S.H.C.*, 1915, p. 350. 7 *Ibid.*, p. 204. 8 Chancery Suit; *S.H.C.*, 1926, pp. 148–9. 9 S.T.C. 15354. Copy in W.S.L., Stafford.

Richard Giffard of the Lea had married Elizabeth, sister of Sir Walter Leveson, of the Great Hall on Snow Hill. Of the juvenile family he left to his widow were Edward Giffard, Edward Giffard, S.J., John Giffard, Knight of Malta, and Mary, who in 1611 married Francis Purcell of Little Bloxwich. The fact that this marriage was registered at the Collegiate Church is remarkable. It is probably their grandson, rather than son, Mr. Richard Purcell, who 'died here and was buried at Black-Ladies', on 6 August 1706.

The widow, Elizabeth Giffard, had been marked down as a Recusant, and in 1608 had trouble with the law, as the following document bears witness[1] (*literatim*):

> Whereas Elizabeth Gifford late of the parishe of St Andrewe in Holborne in the countye of Middlesex widowe was Indicted at the Sessions of gaole Deliuerye here holden for the said countye of Middlesex the twentithe daie of June last past 1608 for not cominge to Churche: And for that yt appeareth by a certificate vnder the hands of James Burton one of the prebendaryes of the Collegiall Churche of Wolnerhampton in Staffs. and Walter Cowper curat there: that the said Elizabeth Gifford was borne, and the most parte of her life resyant in their parishe, and frequented Devine Service in their Churche, (Except lf late hundered by meanes of her husband's sicknes, and other extra-ordinarye causes)[2]: And that vpon the xvjth Daye of September last 1608 she came into their Churche voluntarilye to heare Divine service, and there in verye reverent manner continued vnto the end thereof, As by the said Certificate amonngest other things appeareth. It is therefore ordered by the Courte that the said Elizabeth Gifford shalbe Discharged of the said Indictmente of Recusancye and all proceedings thervpon against the said Elizabeth from henceforth to be staid.

The shortage of Protestants of suitable rank had the curious effect that there were no resident magistrates at Wolverhampton. A Wrottesley, a Littleton, a Leigh (from Rushall) and others from farther afield might and certainly did attend, for there was much work to be done. The Recusants were unqualified. In any case the list was very restricted at this date.

Nevertheless, Sir Walter Leveson managed to have all his children baptized at the Collegiate Church. One, Catherine (1612), married Andrew, fifth son of Walter Giffard, of Chillington. They lived in Cock Street, and had sons: Thomas, d. 1707, papist; Augustine, d. 1721, papist; Andrew, 1644—1714, priest; and, most remarkable, Bishop Bonaventure Giffard, 1642—1733, President of Magdalen, Oxford, 1687, and first Bishop Apostolic in England. The brothers were educated at Douay College, where Bishop Bonaventure bequeathed his heart. He was buried at St. Pancras, London, and his tomb (and that of his brother Andrew) exists.

The magistrates of Staffordshire are known to have been slack in dealing with cases of recusancy, and there were times when they had to be sharply reminded of their duties in this respect. It is known that there were houses tucked away here and there (Boscobel and Moseley, for example) which could harbour priests with fair safety.

The Privy Council took notice of these in 1635. There was a school kept at the house of a Mrs. Vaux, called Stanley Grange, Derbyshire, 'where sons of persons of quality were brought up under the tutorage of the Jesuits'. In July the Council sent a messenger to arrest the Jesuits 'and bring them to be examined, with all such children as he shall find there', or, if they were dispersed, to discover whose sons they were, how long they were there, and where they now remain; 'as also to seize upon all books, papers and massing stuff'. This draft order in the State Papers (Domestic) of Charles I, 1635,[3] bears a memorandum in secretary Coke's handwriting which implies that this form was subsequently used when the house of 'Mr. Leuson, within two miles of Wolverhampton' was searched on a similar account.

1 In the writer's possession. It appears to be a registered contemporary copy of the Certificate, cut from the register.
2 This reminds us of the Wolverhampton Grammar School master in 1648, who never absented himself from services except 'when it pleased God by sickness or his physitian by remedy to detayne him'. *School History*, p. 137.
3 *Calendar*, p. 303.

This house was Ashmores, and its remoteness can be judged from the fact that in 1665 ravens chose to nest there in the trees by the house, much wondered at (by Dr. Plot) because they were hatched near Christmas day.[1]

It is easy to see that this school grew up through the needs of the Roman Catholic gentry of the Wolverhampton neighbourhood. It was more convenient than sending them abroad. The Privy Council papers mention only three pupils, who were taken into custody by their messenger.

1. John Stanford, son of William Stanford, of Perry Hall, Handsworth, who, being grandson of Sir John Fitzherbert, of Norbury, was put by the Council in his custody until further order (9 December).

2. John Bloomfield, a youth of fourteen, who was put into the hands of Sir Ralph Done, of Dutton, co. Chester, on Sir Ralph's promise to see him brought up to the liking of the Lords, or else that he remain with him as a servant.

3. Richard Wakeman, son of Edward Wakeman, of Beckford, co. Gloucester, being about fifteen or sixteen years of age. On Sir Christopher Nevill, of Newton St. Loe, co. of Somerset, promising to place him in the University of Oxford (he is not found there), the Council put him in Sir Christopher's hands, 'expecting a good account of his undertaking him'.[2]

There appears also Thomas Leveson, for whom (18 March 1635—6) there is a warrant to the Keeper of the Marshalsea to set him at liberty. It is not quite clear what he was doing there, nor is his identity—uncle or nephew—certain. But if he was Thomas, Sir Walter Leveson's son, he was owner of, and responsible for, Ashmore Hall in virtue of his lease of the Deanery of Wolverhampton, it being a country residence belonging to that manor. He had, moreover, lately fallen behind with his rent, and, while he was under age, had come under the wing of the Master of the Court of Wards and Liveries and continued to take shelter there. Now the new dean of Windsor and Wolverhampton, Dr. Christopher Wren, protests and petitions against this, Thomas Leveson being upwards of twenty-four years of age.[3] 'To suit out one's livery' (as it was called) from the Court of Wards involved expensive payments, and that may have been the trouble. During his minority the manorial business (as is shown by the Court Rolls) had been done in his uncle Thomas Leveson's name, which the dean said was irregular as it was done without his consent; but nevertheless it had continued for fifteen years.

GUNPOWDER PLOT

THE year 1606 found Wolverhampton drawn into the politics of the kingdom. On a memorable date, 5 November 1605, Guy Fawkes failed to blow up the House of Lords, and the conspirators forthwith fled towards their homes in the West Midlands. It is only one of the backwaters of the Plot which concerns us here, but one that is usually overlooked.

The pursuit was actively prosecuted until the chase ended at Holbeach House, Himley, the home of Stephen Littleton (the name is variously spelled), where four of the principal actors were killed and others taken. But in the hurly-burly Stephen Littleton and Robert Winter escaped and fled to the house of Christopher White at Rowley Regis, who hid them in his barn, where they stayed a great while, 'but with very poor and slender fare'. Meanwhile, much rumour blazed abroad, and, White becoming suspect, the refugees

1 *Wolverhampton Antiquary*, I, p. 327.
2 *Cal. S.P. Dom.*, 608 (31 December 1635).
3 *S.P. Dom., Chas. I*, 1635–6, p. 69, 302.

were passed on from hand to hand, being able to pay for help, it seems, to saviours of shifty and uncertain loyalty. Such were Thomas Smart and John Holyhead, of Rowley, who brought them 'to a barley-mow in his barn, a place to be least suspected', where they continued for nine days, sustained by 'Peck', his man and maid of Hagley. Finally, Humphrey Littleton, of Hagley House (commonly called Red Humphrey, because there was another Humphrey Littleton), gave them shelter, their appearance one night being known only to John Fynes, alias Jobber, 'Cook to Mrs. Littleton'. But that was one too many, for the cook next morning (Thursday, 9 January) told the village, and they were seized, when attempting an escape, in the courtyard. They were sent to London and executed in St. Paul's Church-yard, on 30 January 1606.

Red Humphrey was found at Prestwood, near Kinver, Staffordshire, his old home; but with Peck (or Perkes), his man and his maid, was sent to Worcester for trial, and on 27 January they were found guilty of High Treason and ordered to be drawn, hanged and quartered, except the woman, who was sentenced to be burnt.

The record of this part of the business has escaped the State Papers (Domestic), a Calendar of which, 1603—10, was printed, incorporating the special Gunpowder Plot collection. Fortunately, two other sources exist, apart from the scarce printed booklet (S.T.C. 24916) by 'T. W.' who confirms the executions at Worcester and 'Wolnerhampton' without giving particulars.[1] Of first importance is Harleian MS. 38B., p.102,[2] in the British Museum: 'A true declaration of the flight & escape of Robert Winter, esq. and Stephen Littleton, gent. . . .', a long abstract of which Stebbing Shaw buries deep in his *History*, II, pp. 227—8. Dean Lyttleton's MS. account of 'The Parochial Antiquities of Hagley, Clent, Arley, &c.', which contained (as might be expected) local and traditional information not to be found elsewhere, Shaw also used. For instance, Peck's house and barn at Hagley, which hid the refugees, were in 1760 'both standing opposite the blacksmith's shop and pound, in the right [of the] road from Hagley to Pedmore'.

Holyhead and Smart were duly discovered and brought to Wolverhampton, where a special assize was held under Sir Richard Lewknor, who was summoned from Ludlow for that purpose, and they were indicted and convicted without delay, and received the usual sentence: to be drawn, hanged and quartered. It is likely that such was carried out in High Green before a closely packed audience.

The judge reported to the Privy Council as follows:

Jan. 27. 1605–6.

Itt may Please your honorable Lordships to be advertised that I together with Mr Richard Barker Mr Richard Barker Mr George Wylde Mr Pagott Mr Trentham & Mr Chevington[3] dydd execute the commission of Oier & terminer to us directed for the tryall of suche as had beene receyvors aydors or releevers of Robert Wynter and Stephen Lyttleton in Staffordshere where only Thomas Smarte & John Hollingshead weare found gyltie and receyved judgement & are executed wee fynding no sutche cause to repryve Smarte (as itt seemed your honorable Lordships had beene by the Sherriff informed) although it be true that once he made shewe of an intencion of discovery, butt dydd itt nott, but defased not only for feare but for corrupcion & hope of greater gaine as itt fell oute before us, neyther dydd he stande uppon it that feare was the cause of his not discovery neyther was that stoode uppon or urged for him, he the said Smarte being playnely proved to be the greater offender of the two & the drawer of Holingsheadd alias Hollyhedd into the action togather with three brothers named Whyte (whoe are all escaped) and nott being yett ap-

1 The title-page is illustrated in my *Early Wolverhampton Books and Printers* (1922), where it forms a frontispiece, and I had considered it to be the only copy known to the S.T.C. (which is marked as being in a private collection). But recently Mr. H. E. Palfrey, F.S.A., in the Worcestershire Archæol. Society's transactions, has claimed it for his copy, and two other copies have since appeared in book sales at high prices.

2 This reference is misleading. Robert Dent and Joseph Hill, in their *Historic Staffordshire* (1896), p. 222, use this account independent (it seems) of Shaw's, which they must have overlooked. Their reference is B.M. Ayscough's Collection 4160, 138.

3 Barker and Wylde are Worcestershire men. Mr. (Walter) Bagot, Mr. (Francis) Trentham, and Mr. (William) Skevington were Staffordshire magistrates at this time.

prehended. In Worcestershere I with Sir William Walshe [the sherriff] Sir Edward Pitt Mr Barker Mr George Wylde & Mr Francis Dyngley proceeded against Humfrey Lyttleton John Parcks Margaret Parcks sister to the saide John, and Thomas Burford his seruaunte, whoe weare all founde gyltie and hadd judgment . . . Mr Fleete being a Justice of peace . . . hath nott only taken great pains and done verry good service att thease tryalls both in Staffordsheare & Worcestersheare but also hath beene a paynefull traveller & examyner thereof from the begynnyng. And so hasting to Ludlowe wheare the proceedinge this terme staye untyll my retorne thyther . . .

R. Lewkenor

To his Majestyes privie Council.

[British Museum, Additional MS. 6178, ff. 697–9.]

There is another paper in the same collection: 'The manner of the discrying & apprehension of Robert Winter & Stephen Lyttleton', which amplifies the details. It shows that there was conflict between the executives of the two counties, Staffordshire and Worcestershire. Staffordshire was slow to anger where papists were concerned. Sir Thomas Lawley, writing to the Earl of Salisbury from Prestwood on 14 November 1605 about the Holbeach affair, which he attended with the sheriff of Worcestershire (8 November), 'and with all the small power I was able (upon a sudden) to make', declared that the sheriff of Staffordshire 'was not at that service nor any gentleman of Staffordshire but my self'. Following this, the Privy Council addressed a 'Minute to the Gentlemen of Staffordshire for the taking of Wintour and Littleton' (29 December 1605), particularly leaving the arrest to them, having heard (they tactfully say) of their 'more than ordinary zeale and discretion'.[1]

So when Humphrey Lyttleton was apprehended at Prestwood, there were Staffordshire men assembled to keep him within their jurisdiction. Those of Worcestershire having a different opinion, 'there was lykelihood of a great affray amongst them.' On the way to Worcester 'one Sir Thomas Whorwood Knight of [Compton in Kinver] Staffordshire overtoke them with a good Companie of men well appointed, and said he would have the Prisoners from them . . . but the Worcestershiere men . . . brought them to Worcester where they delivered them to the under sheriff. . .'[2] Sir Walter Leveson, of Wolverhampton, was a little shy about this business. It was but three years since he was knighted, an honour without precedent among his ancestors and descendants. It was reported that he and three other Justices of the Peace for Staffordshire were at Wolverhampton 'within four miles of Holbache' on the day of the taking of the rebels, upon business of the King's (as they said), and, notwithstanding notice given to them before our [the Worcestershire men's] coming to the house, they never came nor sent till all was done. 'This Sir Walter married one William Colles his daughter a Worcestershire man, a most obstinate papist.'[3] It was a difficult position, and may account for Sir Walter's name being removed from the list of magistrates about this time, never to be restored.[4]

In March 1624 one John Brent, of Chillington, near Wolverhampton, was prosecuted by the Mayor of Evesham, and taken to Oxford, charged with uttering scandalous speeches against Queen Elizabeth and the Church of England. He had been apprehended at the time of the Powder Plot, but set free, was an 'obstinate papist' of forty years' standing, and

1 *Ibid.*, ff. 677–8. 2 *Ibid.*, ff, 743–5.
3 *S.P. Dom., James I*, vol. 216. William Colles was of Leigh, Worcestershire, and died, heavily in debt, in September 1615 (Chancery Proc. James I. L. Bundle 16, No. 70, *Leveson* v. *Skinner*).
4 The Quarter Sessions Rolls (*S.H.C.*, 1940, p. 31) give him acting as a magistrate at Wolverhampton in September 1603 (being then a Knight), and at Ashmores 30 September 1604 (*ibid.* 177). He also occurs 31 March 1606, but is not on the Calendar for June.

carrier of letters between recusants who were his friends.[1] His complaint against the Church of England was that its ministers were 'Parliament ministers, not called of God', and could do no miracles.

The sheriff of Staffordshire, too, seems not to have been free from criticism. The office was filled in 1604—5 by Sir William Whorwood, of Sandwell Hall, West Bromwich. He served again in the following year, an unusual proceeding, but nevertheless so. His conduct of the business of the arrest of Winter and Littleton in November, led to some complaint, and Sir Gilbert Wakering is found acting in his place early in the new year.[2]

MANORIAL: PIEPOWDER

Two important and continuous sources of original information begin in 1603: the Wolverhampton Parish Registers (of baptisms, marriages and burials), which are printed and indexed up to 1660; and the Registers of Court Rolls of the Deanery Manor.[3] We are not quite restricted to these, for notes of an earlier Parish Register, beginning in 1538, are available, and there exists a number of grants of copyhold dating from the fourteenth century.

The Deanery Courts were held once a month by the steward of the manor, who was a lawyer. Much of the business related to small debts and trespasses (County Court work), and a great deal of the record is of little interest. We find that tanning and the sale of leather was one of the town's trades in those days. In this pie there are occasional plums. We come upon, for instance, the

COURT OF PIEPOWDER

This valuable piece of evidence is fortuitous and takes the form of a loose scrap of paper. This gives a list of twelve jurors of whom six were sworn. It is shown by its heading to have belonged to a Court of Piepowder (it is actually marked 'de le Pypepouder') held on 13 February 7 James (1609).

A Court of Piepowder was normally attached to fairs, being a court of summary jurisdiction dealing with contracts for goods bought or sold; with fights, disturbances, and words to the slander of wares in the market. It is said to derive its name from the dusty shoes (*pieds poudrés*), [but surely not in February?] of the litigants. That it did not operate with undue dispatch at Wolverhampton this single incident will show.

On 13 February 1609, then, the jurors with one accord prayed for a day to deliver their verdict, namely 28 February next to come, under a penalty for each one who shall be in default. A further adjournment is made to 7 March.

1 *S.P. Dom., James I*, CLX 73 [Calendar].
The Calendar reference has been turned up. This is *S.P. Dom., James I*, 14/16, No. 54, *P.R.O.* It appears to be a document, compiled and signed by Sir Edward Leigh and Sir Gilbert Wakering, Staffordshire magistrates, after a conference with the sheriff, Sir William Whorwood, undated in itself and msplaced under 12 November 1605. They were concerned with 'the takinge of Winter and Littleton by virtewe of a Letter brought by the same Mr. Sheriffe ffrom the Lords of his Majestes honorable privie Counsell'. This was evidently the 'Minute' mentioned on page 14. The sheriff made four suggestions or 'mocions': firstly that 200 men should be raised and charged upon 'the Contrey'. This was thought 'unreasonable because we knowe the Contrey sufficient to effect a much greater Service with lesser Chardge by much'. Secondly, he would have 'Holliheade' set at liberty for the taking of them, and so he (the sheriff) should not be suspected, the gaol should be 'broken' to allow for an escape. The others thought this 'daungerous, Hollyheade beinge committed by the Lord Dudley for Treason for harboringe or Keepinge them Tenn daies'. Thirdly, the sheriff 'moved' that Smart should be set free because he was used to catch Winter and Littleton. But the two magistrates thought this 'daungerous and suspicious' because of his commitment, and in that he had told the sheriff of his and Hollyhead's entertaining them three weeks before their escape. Lastly, the sheriff proposed 'that the watches shoulde be dischardged' (the hunt should end), and it should be given out that Winter and Littleton had been seen to pass over the Trent towards Yorkshire, where Winter had land or good friends. It is not surprising that this 'increesed oure suspicion' and the magistrates 'thought good to strengthen the said watches'. A change of sheriffs followed.
I have greatly benefited by Miss D. Leech's work in this research.

2 I am much obliged to Mr. S. A. H. Burne for checking the sheriff's names in the Sessions Rolls at Stafford, and for the reference to the complaint in *Cal. S.P. Dom.*, 1605, p. 253. Sir William Whorwood died in 1614 (M.I. in *Shaw*, II, p. 132).

3 These volumes are at present on deposit at W.S.L.

At that date, Hugh Tomkes and Richard Sothwicke appeared 'about the fourth hour', the others, 'solemnly exacted', did not come, and forfeited 10s. each.

On 13 March 1609, they all six turned up and found that the piece of leather sold by Robert Maunsell to Thomas Pemerton was 'not searched & sealed according to the statute'. It was therefore a dispute about the quality of leather.

At a Court of 11 December 1604 the constable, Robert Bryndley, produced 8 lb. of nails, a dagger, and two trinket boxes belonging to Richard Hyndley. Richard had assaulted William Pierson and drawn blood, and was fined 6s. 8d. He did not pay the fine, so the goods (mentioned) were taken and are now priced in court by two of the tenants of the manor to the use of the lord: the nails 2s. 4d., the dagger at 6d. and the little boxes (*pixides*) at 2d. He now owes 3s. 8d.

At a Court of 9 July 1605, Francis Wood, the constable, produced a sword and a dagger of the goods of William Grene because he assaulted William Buckle and drew blood. The sword and dagger are priced at 3s. 4d. by Henry Glover and Robert Sherwyn.

There is another small loose sheet of paper, dated 1 July 1605, which from its appearance is another transaction of Piepowder. There is the steward, Gervase Hall's list of tenants, of which six are sworn, who are willed and required to make their personal appearance presently before him in the town hall to inquire upon such articles as upon his Majesty's behalf shall be ministered according to the Statute touching Shoemakers, and they must fail not thereof. Dating the ixth of July 1605.

It appears that four pairs of shoes were seized on 29 July, 'whereof one pair of Bellamys of Birmingham, price vjd., And one other pair of Thomas Taylers of Pattingham price xd.,' are found insufficient, etc., and remain in the custody of Hugh Sambroke (bailiff).

At a Court held 16 January 1621 (18 James) came Henry Fareley, bailiff of Codsall, who presented that William Underwood, 'on 29th December last past,' assaulted John Sawyer and gave him a wound with a knife, of which he died. Underwood for this was committed to Stafford gaol. When he did the act, he was possessed of 'one Lome, one Round Kymnel, one Chelece [?], one little wheele, one Coffer, one little Barrell, a little Ricke of Haye, a yoke nager & a sythe', which, if he be convicted, are forfeited to the lord of the manor. (But if convicted he would have no further use for a yoke nager.)[1]

On a little separate piece of paper addressed to the steward, *c.* 1626:

> Mr Hall, our neighbour Tho: Ellyettes hath bene with Mr Leveson & tould him what advise you have geven him for the recoveringe of his cowe and he lyketh well of yt. And he hath left with me 40s. for a paune to save him & the Courte harmeles and would have you to help him to his Cowe . . .
>
> yours Jo: Fyrchild
>
> [Lord's bauliff, who died March 1642–3.]

TAXATION: KNIGHTHOOD AND SHIP-MONEY

I WILL now touch upon two forms of taxation which the town shared at this time: Fines for Knighthood and Ship-money—both forced upon a needy executive, and soon to be abandoned.

King Charles had dissolved Parliament in 1629, and fell back upon the old feudal system for filling his Exchequer. It was the rule that freeholders worth £40 per annum were due for Knighthood, or must compound with a fine, which was usually £10. There were few freeholders at Wolverhampton, most of the land being copyhold. But there was a small array of potential Knights in the lists of August to June 1630—1.

1 Lome=Loom, an open vessel; nager=auger.

Here they are:[1]

		Fine
	Alexander Wightwick of Wightwick, gent.	£10
	John Huntbach of Sewall gent.	£10
	Thomas Moseley of Bilston, Esqr.	£12
	Thomas Lane of Bentley, Esqr.	£17 10s.
(Attorney)	Richard Barnfield of Wolverhampton,, gent.	£10
	Walter Pipe of Bilston, gent.	£10
(Attorney)	Gervis Hall of Wolverhampton, gent.	£10
	Thomas Creswell of Wolverhampton, gent.	£10
(Mercer)	William Normansell of Wolverhampton, gent.	£10
(Tanner)	George Birch of Wolverhampton, gent.	£10
(Draper)	Henry Gough of Wolverhampton, gent.	£10

It does not appear that any choice was offered (one paid the fine and remained a gentleman).

Wolverhampton paid Ship-money from 1635—9. The scheme itself was above reproach. It was argued that of old, the English nation defended the high seas and had ceased to do so, and the British seamen were suffering great violence and hardship from the unspeakable Turk. 'The charge of defence which concerneth all men ought to be supported by all.' A Navy cost money. Ship-money raised some £200,000 for five years; but no naval successes followed to make it popular. The legal question, tested by John Hampden, whether it was constitutional, was decided against him. But this was after the money had been collected.

Walsall is in almost a unique position in having preserved (which the Public Record Office has not) papers which show how the assessment was made and how the collection was organized and from whom.[2] This town is not so fortunate; but it came under the same warrant.

There is first the writ to the sheriff, addressed to fit men (*probi homines*) in the various towns, boroughs, and the city of Lichfield and among these Wolverhampton is mentioned. The sheriff imposed the assessment upon the different county divisions; first on the hundreds, then among groups of parishes or constablewicks (each contributing £36). We find Willenhall, £8 12s. 10d., and Wednesfield, £9 7s. 2d. (which are in Offlow hundred like Walsall), grouped with Tipton, Darlaston and Bentley. Walsall's payment is £35 and Walsall 'foreign' £20. I think Wolverhampton's share would have been about the same, the town paying with its outlying chapelries two units of £36, i.e. £72.

Next these divisions are apportioned amongst the richer inhabitants, who pay from 12d. to 6s. 8d., not a very heavy imposition.

In all, the County paid £2,840; the corporate towns, Stafford, Walsall, Newcastle and Lichfield, £236 (a total of £3,076). What the Lichfield Close paid the sheriff did not know. Nobody knows.

A somewhat comparable assessment made in September 1604 by Sir Edward Leigh and Sir Walter Leveson on the townships of South Staffordshire, 'for the relief of the poor in Typton township infected with the plague, payable weekly for 3 weeks', may be noticed in this respect.[3]

1 *S.H.C.*, II, ii, pp. 13–21.
2 See my account in *S.H.C.*, 1931, pp. 103–20.
3 *S.H.C.*, 1940, p. 176 (Quarter Sessions Rolls).

"*Old Barrel*" Inn, Worcester Street

St. Peter's Church, 1838 *By R. Noyes.*

CHURCH NOTES

A NOTE or two about the Church of St. Peter can find a place here.

There is evidence that the women at Wolverhampton sat separate from the men. That may not have been unusual in the churches of past times (in Parliament they used to put them behind a grill or grid). Our information comes from a scrap of paper found among Mr. Vernon of Hilton's documents, which purports to be an abstract from the long-lost Wolverhampton 'Overseers & Ch: wardens accounts 1637', dealing with the seating accommodation. It shows where the Lady Vernon, of Hilton, could sit, if she tackled the 'four large miles distant' from Hilton that this seat was set, instead of going to Shareshill, lying within half a mile.

It gives a list of 'The women placed in ye south side [of the nave?]', taking the first four rows.

The first for Mrs Pipe[1] & Mrs East.
The second for Mrs Marshall, Mrs Adams.
The third for ye Lady Vernon of Hilton.[2]
The fourth for Mrs Richards,[3] Lettice Hanbury.[4]

That and no more. But we may conclude that the women flocked together in an orderly manner when attending the church services. The men doubtless took the benches to the left. Proprietary seat-taking was rampant at this time: we are told that the first pews in this church were no earlier than 1558.[5]

I apprehend that the custom of dividing the sexes was a Protestant one.

Of Jacobean work in the church there were the tombs of Margaret Moseley, and Nicholas Barnesley, Grocer and Citizen of London, 1608. The latter was said to have been well carved;[6] but both have entirely disappeared (during the Civil War) and their destruction can be regretted.

Most of the Grammar School gallery, by the wood-worker H.E., [7] still stands in good order. This was erected in 1610 as a sop to appease the townsfolk by the Merchant Taylors. The name of Randulf Woolley, then a Warden of the Company, but once a schoolboy here (and a boarder) is seen thereon. The town was pleased with the result: 'There was never any work so much tended to your glory as this', they wrote the Merchant Taylors, 'being so publique a spectacle to all men, who with admiration behold the orderly sitting of the schollers and their reverent hearing of God's word.'[8]

Jacobean also was the Communion Table, of which more anon. The painted wooden tablet commemorating William Walker, organist,[9] is also of this period.

1 Elizabeth, daughter of John Wrottesley, buried 11 May 1642.

2 Margaret, only daughter and heiress of Henry Vernon, of Hilton. She was born 1592. married Sir Edward Vernon, of Sudbury, 1613, and died 3 January 1655-6.

3 ? Wife of Walter Richards, married 3 July 1637.

4 Wife of Robert Hanbury, died January 1638–9.

5 *Wolverhampton Antiquary*, I p. 273. Dr. Cox, in his book on *Churchwarden Accounts*, p. 188, shows that the fashion arose from giving seats for the old, firstly to women. Wills show the owners were often buried by their pews.

6 *Shaw*, II, p. 159. 'Their effigies being very well cut in a praying posture'.

7 A joiner or carpenter with these initials is to be sought. The parish register produces a Humphrey Edge, who died in 1612. His trade is not given, but there was a Richard Edge, carpenter, in 1626, and a John Edge, 'joyner', in 1656. It was evidently the family trade.

8 *School History*, p. 85.

9 Stated to have 'served childe of the Chappell of St. George [Windsor Castle] 7 yeares to Queen Elizabeth, and six yeares to King James'. He died 18 January 1634(5), aged 52, so could not have been William Walker, Shakespeare's godson. Nothing can be found of him as a child actor. He kept to music throughout his life (as other choristers have done). His 'coat-of-arms' (on the tablet) show him flamboyant.

THE DEANERY LEASE AND CHARTER

THE Court Rolls throw some light on another matter, that of the Deanery lease. It is somewhat remarkable that the annual rent reserved on this property remained constant at £38 per annum from the time of Henry VIII until the last lease fell in in 1891. The first known lease was in 1510 for ten years. How this sum of £38 was made up is seen in the *Valor Ecclesiasticus* of 1535.

The lands £10
Chief Rents £20
Profits of his court £8. Total £38.

This rent was probably a very true value then (when a gallon of beer cost 1d. One should therefore multiply by something like 64=(say) £2,500. How different now!).

The *Fine* which the Dean, as lessor, exacted, as was usual before making a new lease (key money, a form of extortion), made up or regulated what was lacking in the annual income; but only the luckier Deans had the opportunity to 'fine'. In our period there was a renewal of the lease, which covered the greater part of Wolverhampton, in 1610. The manor rolls give the procedure. It coincided with the ceremony of the installation of the new Dean, Giles Thomson (famous as one of the translators of the Bible, Authorized Version), by proxy.

The Court Roll of 27 March 1610 describes how one Gregory Baker, 'servant of Giles Thomson Professor of sacred theology and Dean of the free royal chapel of St. George in the Castle of Windsor', appeared at Wolverhampton and showed there in the Common Hall before Gervase Hall, steward of the manorial court, and before the suitors there, a certain writing sealed by the said Dean, dated 20 March, by which he was appointed the Dean's attorney 'to enter in his name into the prebend of Wolverhampton and into the manor of Wolverhampton and into all lands, tithes, mines [etc.] thereto belonging, and to take full and peaceful possession thereof in the dean's name'. Apparently Sir Walter Leveson had at that time forfeited the lease for non-payment of the reserved rent.

On the previous day Gregory Baker 'entered into a certain parcel of land called Deanes Croft' within the manor according to his directions. So the Dean became landowner. Afterwards, on 3 April 1610, the said Gregory Baker, servant of Giles Thomson, together with Robert Watson and James Burton, two of the prebendaries of Wolverhampton, and Thomas Meeke, sacristan there, went to the Chapter house and produced the Chapter seal of Wolverhampton, and then and there sealed a lease ('a certain indenture of demise' they call it) dated on the previous day, 2 April, made between the Dean and Walter Leveson, Knight, and his assigns of the Manor or Deanery of Wolverhampton for the term of the lives of Edward Leveson, his son, aged two, Anne (*recte* Mary) Leveson, his daughter, aged sixteen months and of John Giffard, son of Elizabeth Giffard, widow, of Ellenhall (*sic*),[1] who was Sir Walter's sister.

There was also a deed appointing Gervase Hall steward for life, dated 28 March; and afterwards Gregory Baker and Silvester Hayes (bailiff of the manor), by virtue of letters of attorney made to them by the Dean, delivered to Sir Walter Leveson full and peaceful possession in the site or manor house ('*in scitu sive domo manerii predicti*') which presumably was the Deanery Hall. It was all cut and dried.

1 I suspect 'Willenhall' is the correct reading: where her brother Thomas Leveson, a Papist, lived. Edward Leveson was baptized 28 September 1607, and buried 28 April 1611. Mary was baptized 1 December 1608.

After this date[1] the Deanery Courts are held in the name of Sir Walter Leveson until his death on 10 January 1620—1, before Gervase Hall, the steward, a solicitor of experience, who died in 1633.

The reserved rent of £38 was continued; but it is not known what 'fine' the Dean received. He had stolen a march over his successors, for no further advantage of this kind could be expected for many years to come. It was all a gamble, a sort of tontine. Who could have foretold that the first 'life', baby Edward Leveson, would have fallen in so soon, or that John Giffard, Knight of Malta (the third 'life') would have survived until 17 March 1672, aged seventy-five?[2] His tomb was once to be seen on the north side of the chancel in St. Peter's Church-yard; for a Roman Catholic this position may have been necessary.

Dr. Giles Thomson did not long survive, for he died on 14 June 1612, and was succeeded by Dr. Anthony Maxey, who died on 3 May 1618. It was during this Dean's tenure of office that two of the prebendaries, Dr. Joseph Hall and Christopher Cragg, took courage to question in Chancery Sir Walter Leveson's title to much of the former deanery property. This had come into lay hands and been alienated in the time of Edward VI, when the Deanery of Wolverhampton had been suppressed. What these estates were they did not know: they groped in the dark. Dr. Hall, then Dean of Worcester, gives an account of this enterprise. He had received the free collation of the prebend of Willenhall, without seeking it:

'It was not the value of the place (which was but nine nobles a year) that we aimed at,' he writes,[3] 'but the freedom of a goodly church . . . completely endowed, and many thousand souls lamentably swallowed up by wilful recusants in a pretended fee farm for ever . . . . We knew not wherein to insist, nor where to ground our complaint; only we knew that a goodly patrimony was, by sacrilegious conveyance, detained from the church.' But by good fortune much of a suspicious nature was discovered, such as 'a counterfeit seal found in the ashes of that burned house of a false register [register=registrar, probably William Grene, the Elizabethan "register"[4] who died in 1603] . . . erasures, interpolations and misdates'. Dean Hall continues a lively account of it all, and finally Lord Chancellor Ellesmere gave judgement on 11 November 1615.[5]

What the law was, was not at all clear; that was a matter for bringing an action in the High Court; but it was evident that somehow the church had been robbed, and Sir Walter Leveson must refund. The defendant then decided to compromise. He made, it is true, 'some flourish of trying his title at law' and caused several actions to be brought, but never received any verdict on any of them. Now he agreed to pay each prebendary £30 and Hall's prebend £40;[6] 'the then Dean Master Antonius de Dominis, Archbishop of Spalata gave both way and furtherance to the dispatch, all [writes Hall] had been most happily ended' when Sir Walter Leveson died, leaving his 'young orphan' ward to the King. 'All our hopes were now blown up.' But the Master of the Wards decreed that the orphan could have no more, no other right than the father, so all was well, and Hall in pity of the destitution of so many thousand souls at Wolverhampton, resigned his prebend in favour of Mr. Richard Lee (another Calvanist) 'who should constantly reside there, and painfully instruct that great and long neglected people'.

1 I have not a note of the lords of the Deanery Manor between Admiral Leveson and this time.
2 The new long lease was not before 21 May 1677.
3 *Autobiography*.
4 *S.H.C.*, 1926, pp. 148–9.
5 Chancery Decrees and Orders, 1615A, ff. 243–4.
6 Chancery Suit: *Wren and Callendrine* v. *Leveson* (1661–2); Bridges 40. 71. Also suit of 1705.

In this turmoil King James thought it well to confirm the church's Charter. These Letters Patent, dated 3 July 1620, have gone the way of other of the town's documents and have been lost or destroyed. Failing an income, it may have given his strange bearded protégé, the Italian Archbishop of Spalata (Spalato, now Split, in Dalmatia), Mark Antonio de Dominis, now Dean of Windsor and Master of the Savoy, some comfort and a vision of better things to come. Doubts also concerning the ownership of the property might be settled or allayed.

The prebendaries appointed on this occasion were (citing *Shaw*, II, p. 154):

Kinvaston	William Bailey, M.A. [also the Official]
Fetherston	Samuel Burton, B.D., Archdeacon of Gloucester.
Hilton	Thomas Goad, D.D., chantor of St. Paul's.
Willenhall	Joseph Hall, D.D., dean of Worcester.
Monmore	John Fox, D.D., prebendary of Westminster.
Wybaston (alias Blossoms)	Thomas Gurrey, M.A.
Hatherton	Godfrey Goodman, D.D., prebendary of Windsor, and John Skinner, clerk, sacrist.

William Bailey, who was vicar of Pattingham, seems to have been the only man both of the locality and resident, although Samuel Burton was Wolverhampton-born.[1]

Obviously, the Dean knew nothing of these men, and the Crown stepped in to make the appointments. But it did not matter. The mission de Dominis had set himself, to unite all Christian churches, had not gone well; and in January 1621—2 he wrote a sudden letter of farewell to the King, complaining of old age, the sharpness of the cold air of this country, his great want of friends who could look after him. He was led to believe the Pope wanted his return. So 'Farewell [he ends] the glory and ornament of Princes'.[2] James, distrusting, let him go reluctantly. He returned to Rome, was imprisoned by the Inquisition and died. His book defending the Church of England could have helped him little; he was, moreover, by general agreement thought dishonest.

But he made one appointment when Dean of Wolverhampton. Prebendary Godfrey Goodman resigned (he later became a papist), and Cesar Callendrine, S.T.B., a German and a Puritanical theologist, was appointed in his stead.[3]

THE NEW ALTAR

IT was not the low church but the high that brought the town notoriety. If a stand was to be made against the Puritans, here surely was the spot.

Two Deans, Matthew Wren (1628—34—5) and his brother Christopher Wren (April 1635—58), father of the greater Christopher, were of the same opinion as Archbishop Laud, and thought something better could be made of Wolverhampton church. In 1634 Matthew Wren made some 'very good orders and Chapter Acts' to regulate the services, and then resigned the deanery in favour of his brother. The Archbishop considered it a good time to 'visit' the church and college of Wolverhampton, and of this Metropolitan Visitation the Deans (forgetting precedents to the contrary) approved. The month of May suited his vicar-general, who was 'visiting' Lichfield and Shrewsbury. 'I am informed', the Archbishop wrote him, 'that Wolverhampton is but 12 miles from Lichfield and not out of the way to Shrewsbury' (so it was made easy for him). Laud remembered also Mr.

1 Hall's *Life; School History*, pp. 97–8. I have his signature in a folio volume of Persius' *Satires* (Paris, 1523), which he got when at Oxford (though it is an early Cambridge binding). John Sprint, minister of Thornbury, addresses his book *Cassander Anglicanus* (on the Necessity of Conformity) to him, 1618, being 'drawn by your private lenity and kindness'.
2 *M. Ant. de Dominis . . . his Shiftings in Religion*. 1624, p. 6.
3 *S.H.C.*, 1915, p. 341.

Lee's low-church views and how he was 'schismatical and seditious'. 'If', he added, 'you can fasten upon anything whereby he may justly be censured, pray see it be done.' Mr. Latham, of Lichfield, could give details of offence: but one of the things that so shocked the Archbishop was Mr. Lee's 'causing a bellman in open market to make proclamation for a sermon'. (Tch!) In the end, Mr. Lee was suspended.[1] (This action was thought harsh and held against the Archbishop at his trial.)[2]

The powers that be, the Dean and chapter, seem to have chosen an elaboration of the choir service, like the Cathedrals. It was the Dedication of the new altar, a Laudian altar, that so distinguished the town, and made Puritans seize their pens.

The three authors who felt strongly about it were forced to do so anonymously through a foreign press. William Prynne prints at Amsterdam, 1637: *A Quench-coal: or a briefe inquirie in what place of the Church the Lord's Table ought to be placed. By a well-wisher to the Truth of God.*[3] Robert Baillie prints first at Edinburgh, then at Amsterdam: *The Canterburians self-conviction.*[4] And Henry Burton writes in prison his *For God and the King* (two sermons), 1636, which was printed at Middleburg, Holland.[5]

But these are hard come by, and a full account of the ceremony can be found in *Hierurgia Anglicana*, 1848 edition, p. 394. Whether Prynne was present or whether Mr. Lee supplied him with the account, who can tell?

Tradition says (and again who can tell?) that the oak altar table in the Lady-chapel is the original table dedicated at this time. It can be said in support of this view that its style is that of the period of Charles I.[6]

Upon Saturday, being the 10th of October, 1635, Master Edward Latham, one of the Proctors of Lichfield, and surrogate of Wolverhampton, accompanied with some twenty or thirty persons, men, women, and choristers, came to the town, many of the inhabitants, but chiefly the clergy, going to meet him.

It was a gala day, and the Dedication of the Communion Table 'to be an altar' and the consecrating certain altar-cloths 'to the glory of God' was his intent and purpose. The table was new, being 1½ yds. in length,

exquisitively wrought and inlaid . . . and the rail before it was made to open in the middle, and not at one side, the middle where the ministers tread being matted with a very fair mat.

Upon the Table was placed a fair Communion Book, covered with cloth-of-gold, and bossed with great silver bosses, together with a fair cushion of damask with a carpet of the same.

On each side of the Table hangs two pieces of white calico, and betwixt them the Ten Commandments, written in a fair table with gilded letters . . . There are needlework pictures of St. Peter, St. Paul and St. George and the dragon.

The next day, being the Lord's Day, as soon as the priests (for so they would be called . . .) came to the church; each of them made a low congie apiece at their first entering in at the great church door, and another congie apiece at the aisle door, and after that, three congies apiece towards the altar (before its dedication); and so they went into the chancel, where a basin of water and a towel was provided for the priests to wash in ['It seems they came to church with polluted hands and stinking souls', W. Prynne comments] where was incense burned which perfumed the whole church. And then they returned back making three congies apiece, and went to service, which was solemnly performed, the organs blowing, great singing not heard of in this church before, which kind of service lasted two hours at least.

Service being finished, there was a sermon preached by one Master Jeffery, Archdeacon of Salop, whom the Surrogate brought with him . . . His sermon lasted an hour.[7] After sermon they went to the *Dedication*, or rather, as the preacher styled it, *Renovation* of the Altar: and in the bell-house [under the tower] four of them put on the rich broidered copes, and every one of them had a paper in his hand . . . reading it as they went. . . .

1 *W. Antiquary*, I, 307. 2 *Canterbury's Doom*, 1645 edition, p. 380.
3 S.T.C., 20474. 4 S.T.C , 1205 and 1206. 5 S.T.C., 4141. There were two printings.
6 But its measurements, 65 in. by 30 in., do not tally with the description. The word 'altar' had a shocking effect upon good churchgoers.
7 St. John x, 22, 23.

As they went they made three congies apiece, and when they came to the altar, they kneeled down and prayed over the cloth and the other consecrated things, the organs blowing all the while; this solemnity lasted almost half-an-hour.

After all this was performed there was a Communion, and one was appointed to stand with a basin to receive the Offertory: divers gave money, and it was thought it had been given to the poor, but the man that held the basin gave it to the surrogate (the sum gathered being reputed about 40s.); he calling the church-wardens gave them, as he said, ten shillings; the remainder, he told them, he would bestow on other pious uses, but the ten shillings being counted, proved to want six. . . .

None gave the Communion but the four that had copes. . . . These copes and silver basins were brought from Lichfield.

The Communion and Dedication ended, they went to dinner, and in the afternoon they come to church again [and heard another sermon . . . .] Which being finished, they went to prayer, which was very solemnly performed, the organs blowing, and divers anthems and responds being sung at that time:[1] which done, they departed from the church to their lodging, where they were very merry.

The account ends with invective. On Monday those of Lichfield returned, some very drunk, 'defiling themselves with this swinish sin like so many filthy brute beasts, to make the altar more holy and venerable, and themselves more apt to nod and congy to it . . . with all which I here conclude my rude discourse and Quench-coal'.

On the whole it had been a success.

The Royal Commission on Ritual noticed this ceremony on 28 November 1867.

THE NEW ORGANS: MR. LATHAM

THE organs that pealed so successfully on this occasion had a history which is found among the state papers of the realm. It provides also an example of how hard is the lot of a treasurer in Wolverhampton.

Before the Rev. William Bailey, M.A., vicar of Pattingham, Prebendary of Kinvaston and Official of the Collegiate Church, died in September 1633, he realized that the old organ (or pair of organs) was very much decayed, and Emmuel Creswell, organ-maker (and for a short time one of the curates) certified that it was past repair. A happy recollection that Sir Stephen Jenyns, founder of the Grammar School, had given these organs, made him write to the Merchant Taylors' Company, as it was thought they might like, as trustees of the school, to make a contribution. This they did, 'out of their pious inclination' to the extent of £10, the bearer being Mr. Thomas Tomkis, a lawyer of Wolverhampton and friend of the school.[2]

The Rev. Andrew Bailey, William's son, one of the curates, and an old Grammar School boy, was thereupon sent to the Dean of Windsor, Dr. Matthew Wren (afterwards Bishop of Norwich), to acquaint him with this difficulty, and he 'condescended' that a new organ should be erected, and told Andrew Bailey to use his (the Dean's) name to the chiefest of the parish so as to obtain their help. It was agreed that Creswell should erect a new organ for £140. He began to work upon the organ but needed money to buy materials. Henry Gough furnished £100 and John Hawkins £30, and the Rev. Andrew Bailey was bound responsible for repayment. There was only the collection to be made. But before the organ was finished, Mr. Bailey senior died, and his son had only collected £41 10s., and found himself without remedy to collect the residue 'in regard that divers refused to pay'. Meanwhile, he endeavoured to pay the interest on the £130, but was sued for the principal in the summer of 1636, and judgment was given against him, which forced him to mortgage his land for £200. So he took courage and petitioned

1 Prynne (or Lee) could be appreciative; he was not always driven to scorn.
2 *School History*, pp. 118–9. He was educated at Shrewsbury, and may have gone to Trinity College, Cambridge and if so was the playwright.

Archbishop Laud,[1] who did what he could, for he handed the paper to Sir John Lambe, Chancellor to the Queen, who endorsed it: 'I wrote to Mr. Latham, 11th. February 1637—8'. And so it got round to the Dean's commissary, who drew the attention of the church-wardens to a proper view of their responsibilities, and by 1640 they had agreed that the petitioner, Andrew Bailey, should have about £100 for his disbursements (which were, he says, 'above £200'), and had gone far in collecting the money; but lately had 'desisted in its collection', and had not paid the petitioner anything. So he besought again Sir John Lambe to renew Mr. Latham's admonitions so they might pay him what they had and collect the rest.[2]

Mr. Edward Latham, LL.B., could be unpleasant. The Puritans disliked him: he could, and doubtless did, excommunicate them, a sanction which still had some force in the Church of England. There exists an abusive letter written to him by a Mr. Tarte, of Wolverhampton, from the safe distance of New England.[3] As invective the letter, which came before the High Commission Court, is worth reading.

The sad thing was that within three or four years the new organ was to be swept away (and how many have followed it?),[4] and the Rev. Andrew Bailey was lodged in Stafford gaol for debt to the great distress of himself, his wife and numerous family.[5]

And what of Edward Latham under these changed conditions? There is one significant clue.

There was, in fact, a sequel which occurred at the surrender of Bridgnorth, 26 April 1646.

Many refugees congregated in these strongholds (Dudley, Bridgnorth, Shrewsbury, Lichfield . . .) for safety, while their country houses were seized or went to wrack and ruin. Chiefly they were the wives and families of those in arms for the King; clergy who were pronounced malignant; Roman Catholics who were always in danger of challenge.

The Articles[6] agreed upon at Bridgnorth were favourable and gentlemanly, and those besieged marched out at 7 a.m. next day in good array. But there was one ominous exception. The last Article, No. XX, is as follows: 'That Mr. Edward Latham be delivered to the mercy of the Parliament'.

When Worcester surrendered later, Sir William Russell was also excepted from the terms of the Capitulation, and it was required that he should be given up unconditionally. The Royalists protested, saying it would be as much as consenting to his murder. (But he lived another twenty-four years.)

The fate of Mr. Edward Latham leaves an uncertain pen.[7]

1 *S.P. Dom., Chas. I,* vol. 381, No. 85.
2 *Ibid.,* vol. 451, No. 107.
3 *W. Antiquary,* I, pp. 219–20.
4 Owen and Blakeway, *History of Shrewsbury,* II, p. 191, record a tradition that the organ at St. Chad's, Shrewsbury, replaced in 1716, went to Wolverhampton.
5 Chancery Suit: *Bailye* v. *Hackett,* C.8, 101, 13 (1646).
6 G. Bellett, *Hist. Bridgnorth,* p. 229.
7 Gaol fever (natural causes) seems to have been his main danger (and the most obscure).

CHAPTER VII

WOLVERHAMPTON: 1640 to 1660

THIS is a period of turmoil.

In the last chapter we saw the people separating into irreconcilable extremes, both active, but with the usual large unthinking centre, meeting troubles as they came.

Propaganda confuses the issue. The King fought for the Protestant Religion, the Laws of England and a Free Parliament, while Parliament was prepared to go into battle for the King (though they considered him a misguided King). They were not above putting the King's well-known portrait on their pamphlets, however crudely drawn. The idea of a republic did not enter their minds. Differences of religion played their parts, but the choice of sides was curiously uncertain. So many did not want to fight; few knew how to, and the method adopted was not one that gave results. Each landowner wished to save his hearth and home, but few were successful, and the war starting with both sides quite unprepared, dragged on.

For hostilities in Staffordshire, Wolverhampton provided two of the principal actors, Captain John Lane and Colonel Thomas Leveson, while Colonel Edward Leigh of Rushall, and Sir Walter Wrottesley of Wrottesley, were protagonists on the flanks, so the town is well in the picture, and there is more in the story than has hitherto appeared. But there is something besides warfare, and through the smoke and politics bits of the town peep out from passing events.

The Lord Lieutenant of Staffordshire at this time (1612—46) was Robert Devereux, Earl of Essex, whose home was Chartley. (His father, Queen Elizabeth's favourite, died on Tower Hill on 25 February, 1600—1). The son, restored in blood and honours in 1604, commanded the expedition against Cadiz in 1625, and was appointed Lieutenant General of the Army in 1639, a token of his position in the world and not of his skill or experience in battle. When, after the Short Parliament in 1640, the King found it necessary to resist the Scotch Covenanters—they had objected to his bishops and the Prayer Book—a Muster of an army was ordered.

The army was on a local basis, worked through the Lords Lieutenants and their Deputies by means of the high constables of the Hundreds and the petty constables of the Townships. So were raised the rough and unready trainbands, buttressed by an equal number of pressed men—a real but inefficient force.

The deputy lieutenants who acted on this occasion were Sir Hervey Bagot, Bt., Walter Wrottesley, and Thomas Crompton, who later took different paths. It is due to Walter Wrottesley that the details of the Staffordshire Muster have been preserved, which show[1] that 400 trained and 300 impressed men, 50 horses for ammunition carriages, with 17 impressed carters, besides light and heavy horse to the number of 100, raised on a mediaeval basis were duly handed over to their commander at Uttoxeter in July.

1 S.H.C. **XV**, 201 et seq.

Wolverhampton's share (with Bilston, as part of Seisdon Hundred) consisted of 10 "trained" and 7 pressed men. There was no glory in this enterprise, which cannot be said to have disturbed the Scots; but at Uttoxeter, north of the county, there was rioting, an omen which did not prophesy success. It was a rehearsal for the next trial of strength.

The King left London in January 1642, was rebuffed at Hull in April, and set up his standard at Nottingham on 22nd August. With him were the young princes, Charles aged 12 and James 9½; with him too were his nephews Prince Rupert and Prince Maurice, who had gained military experience on the Continent. The intention was to collect an army to march on London.

From Staffordshire the King gained a rich quota of volunteers, but the forces under the Lord Lieutenant fell to the share of the Parliament. It has been said that with the exercise of a little tact Essex would have sided with the King. The violence of the Parliament caused a reaction among the moderates, and many threw in their lot with the King. Of such was Walter Wrottesley, who in August 1642 became a Baronet, and the poorer by the sacrifice of the greater part of his silver plate. For the Roman Catholics there was only one side and one fate, and Astley of Patshull, Giffard of Chillington and Thomas Leveson of Wolverhampton and others were to see their houses battered by the Roundheads. Conspicuous among the Protestants was the family of Lane of Bentley.

An order of Parliament for the seizure of the arms of the Roman Catholic Recusants brought strife within the town. Mr. Thomas Leveson, recognized as "an active and dangerous recusant" could not get delivery of his arms from John Tanner, armourer in Wolverhampton. Mr. Leveson (9 April) went in person to his shop. "Sirrah", he said, "why did you not send me my arms? Who were these deputy-lieutenants who prevented delivery?" And John Tanner replied "Mr. Crompton, Mr. Wrottesley and others. Thereupon Mr. Leveson, in a violent passion, said that Mr. Wrottesley was a fool and a knave and he (meaning John Tanner) was a stinking rogue, and with these words, with a cane which he had in his hand, stroke him two or three blows, one whereof hit him on the head, and made a great knob in the skin thereof". In this manner the Peace was broken at Wolverhampton.

The King reached Stafford (from Derby) on 18 September; he was at Wellington with 4,000 horse and about the same number of foot on 19th and entered Shrewsbury on Tuesday 20th. Problems of supply are met with at the start.

The Church-wardens' Accounts at Stafford mention the provision of 10,000 loaves of bread, and a messenger sent to Lichfield to obtain it; likewise "paid John Clarke for goinge to Penkridge and Wolverhampton to speak for bread, 2s. 6d." "Paid W. Harding for going twice to Hampton, himself and his horse, being forth 5 daies and 3 nights when the Earl of Chesterfield and his forces were there, 11s. 0d." "Paid Mr. Braddock for going twice to Wolverhampton, 5s. 0d." "Given unto the Prince's Trumpeters, 10s. 0d." "Paid for beare and spice, bestowed upon Capts. Lane and Fowke, 1s. 6d."[1]

The Earl of Chesterfield[2] had been commissioned in November to raise a regiment of dragoons, and established himself at Lichfield with about 300 men charged with hope but unsupported by experience. Essex, who was now "General of the Army of the Parliament" took up a position between the King and London. When a convoy set out from Oxford with the college plate for the Shrewsbury mint, he attempted to cut it off. Prince Rupert at Leicester was ordered to its relief, and he passed through Wolverhampton at night on

1 "Stafford in Olden Times", J. L. Cherry, 1890, p. 22.
2 Philip Stanhope, 1584–1656.

the way to Worcester. He was just in time to fall upon the enemy at Powicke bridge (22 September) and the convoy reached Shrewsbury safely on 26th. King Charles left Shrewsbury for London on 12 October 1642, taking the way of Bridgnorth, Wolverhampton, Birmingham. Prince Rupert with his brother left two days earlier, Monday 10 October, and passing by Shifnal reached Wolverhampton on Tuesday and there spent the next day. Some accounts of the Mayor of Walsall, John Walton, show that Walsall too was visited, perhaps for saddlery or bridles. The expenses may not have been sustained without some benefit in return.

"The Last of October 1642.

A note of money Recd and Paid by mee John Walton as followeth concerninge the Towne.

	£	s.	d.
Recd. of my Sister Heynes for which Mr. Henry Sheapherd and my selfe have given Bond for it ..	30	0	0
Payd for Wyne and Bottles presented to Prince Roberte & otherwise for beere in all ..		17	0
Geven Prince Roberts Secretarie ..	2	2	0
Geven Prince Roberte in Gould, And a Purse withe it ..	20	0	0
Pd to my Sister Heynes for a nagge which was geven Prince Maurice ..	7	6	8
Pd for Charges at Hampton ..		3	6
Pd for Wyne and beere wch was spent on the Captines at Sherwyns ..		9	0
geven Captine Selbye ..	1	0	0
pd to Captine Major Button ..	1	14	0
pd for beere att Henry Woods when Sr John Beomonte was there ..		6	0

"Sister Heynes" was Cicely Haynes, landlady of the Cock, Wolverhampton.

Prince Rupert then proceeded to Mr. Moseley's at Enville, and, Friday 14th to Mr. Foley's at Stourbridge, which points to armaments; thence to Birmingham when he joined the King.

Charles's arrival at Wolverhampton on Saturday 15 October made unprecedented stir. It is difficult to see how he fitted in with his forces new to discipline and drill. There were too, the headquarters' staff and noncombatants; the princes Charles and James, and the Lord Chief Justice Heath who held an Assize.[1] Two documents exist which proclaim the King's visit on this occasion, one of the milestones in local history. The first is a commission to Colonel Richard Herbert, governor of the town of Bridgnorth, to be captain of a troop of four score horse to be levied voluntarily "for the defence of our person, the two houses of Parliament, the Protestant religion, the laws of the land, the liberty and property of the subject and the privileges of Parliament" (it is the usual formula) and for the better defence "against any attempts that may be made by the traitorous proceedings of the Earl of Essex and his adherents". It was signed by the King and dated at Wolverhampton (Monday) 17 October, 1642. The other is a summons to the "trusty and welbeloved" inhabitants of Lichfield to bring all their arms, without concealment, to their Town-hall for despatch "to our Royall Standard", and further that they contribute in money or plate towards the King's "extraordinary visible necessity". It too was signed and "Given att Our Court att Wolverhampton this 17th day of October, 1642."

The town was then a garden city set on top of a hill. Few houses were here built otherwise than of "half-timber", and many were thatched; the majority were only of two storeys high. Survivals tell us this. The streets were narrow. The Market Place on the *High Green* in the centre of the town showed special congestion, being blocked by a large three-storey building of early-Tudor origin, known as the *High Hall* (it was only removed

1 S.H.C. 1941, 137 for letter of Secy. Nicholas, 16 Octr.

in 1841), and also the Town Hall and market cross, and another independent building of antiquity called the Roundabout. The throng of Market days also blocked it and of necessity invaded the adjoining streets, and the annual Fair increased the pressure till 1885.

Aloof, outside the town on Snow Hill, on the Road to Dudley, was the Great Hall, a Tudor mansion of brick, surrounded by a moat and garden wall, not a fortress but a place as ready to resist light attacks as its owner, Thomas Leveson, was to defend it. He had married young, at about the age of 17, Frances, daughter of Sir William Paulet, Kt., a Protestant. He was now 27, and was contemplating sending his son to France "to breed him up in Popery";[1] but the war prevented this, and he (Robert Leveson) grew up a member of the Established Church. It may be that his mother continued to live at the Hall. She had married secondly a Mr. John Potts, who as "husband to ye Lady Leveson" was buried at Wolverhampton 17 December 1643.

The position between Thomas Leveson and his wife was strained. According to a statement that she made later she had found him brought up in the Popish religion, "and she and her friends by persuasion did get him to go to church, to prayer and sermons, for several years, and so long as he continued going to church he used her with loving respects, but for near three years before the late war (he) was again drawn to Popery by persuasion of his Popish friends, and from that time he used her disrespectively and harshly"; but he had settled £200 a year on her to maintain her and her daughter.

So it was then that St. Peter's Church, Wolverhampton, though it sheltered the tomb of his ancestor, was not his church, and loyalty to his King overcame sentiment. In October 1642 he considered the church a useful lodging for the soldiers, and so for five devastating days it was arranged; but not without protest. For John Richardson, an apothecary, with others, tried to persuade him to remove the soldiers and send no more. But Mr. Leveson, the Colonel to be, was obdurate and sent an answer "after a space" by a Major Mole regretting his inability to please them. His actual words, which are on record, were "God dam me we will have a garrison for our own ends and not yours in spite of all your hearts".

Much wreckage is done by soldiers in their idle moments or in search of plunder. Here the church chest was broken open and rifled, and many records and papers are known to have disappeared; tombs were destroyed, brasses ripped from their matrices. The bronze statue of Admiral Leveson, which had been erected barely ten years, and was taken away to be cast into a gun, was rescued by his family and lodged at Lilleshall Church, to be restored only in 1714 by Lord Gower. Thus here the royalists did Cromwell's work. We learn[2] that Thomas Bradney, one of the soldiers, took advantage of his being billetted there to prosecute a private quarrel[3] he had with his landlord by disarranging his title deeds, a very damaging performance. Some survivals were copied by John Huntbach later in the century; but the bulk of the Wolverhampton muniments were scattered and lost to posterity.

The historian Huntbach reminds us that during the war the chancel was wrecked by the lead being taken from the roof, and that Silvester Pierson "one of the clerks of this church in the late times of confusion" assisted in this and other sacrilege.[4] Indeed "so kind were the people of those times unto him, that they never questioned him for it, but rather pitied him by reason of some hurt he received when he endeavoured to make his escape by leaping from the battlements of the church upon the North porch." He was buried.

1 Wrott. 315.
2 W.A. 310–11.
3 Lee v. Bradney.
4 Shaw, ii. 155.

The house which the King occupied during his first stay at Wolverhampton stood on the site of the present Star and Garter Hotel. The hotel itself was a piece of 19th century enterprise on the part of a popular host after the European War (1815) and more lavishly after 1836, when the place was rebuilt. The view of the old building, or rather of that side of it facing the street, painted by Robert Noyes at this date, shows chiefly an extremely ancient portico of timber, and a very unimpressive range of stunted timber building, a most unlikely residence for royalty to all appearance. But there is no doubt some substance in the sturdy tradition attached to this site, and we are left to suppose that an entrance from the road led into an inner court-yard where stood a hall and buildings of a more palatial nature. It was in 1642 a private house owned, it is said, by a "Madam St. Andrew, who was either sister or aunt to Mr. Henry Gough"[1] and was hostess to the King, while Mr. Gough "ventured to accommodate their royal highnesses Charles Prince of Wales and James Duke of York", presumably in his own house, wherever that may have been. "An ancient tenement still remains at Wolverhampton, which is part of the house where these princely guests resided" says our chronicle (Shaw in 1800), thus confusing the issue but in any case it has all been swept away. One can add that John Gough, the first, in his Will dated 1596, mentions his "newly built house" in the town, and that Henry Gough his son, though he subsequently bought Oldfallings, still lived, perhaps always lived, in the town.

The inhabitants are said cheerfully to have contributed to the King's appeal for funds for the royal cause, "but the most ample supply was expected from Mr. Gough," whose loyalty was as eminent as his fortune was superior, when, to the great surprise and disappointment of everyone" (we read) "he refused any assistance, though strongly urged by the King's commissioners".

Mr. Gough was now over 80 years old, and with hardening arteries liked to do things in his own way. At night therefore "putting on his hat and cloak" he went secretly to the King, and having with some difficulty obtained admission to the royal presence he then drew from his cloak a purse containing a large sum of money and presenting it with due respect, said, "may it please your majesty to accept this, it is all the cash I have by me or I would have brought more". The gift was said to have been £1,200, (enough alone to make Mr. Gough somewhat cautious as to his movements and explanations on a dark night in times of upheaval). But the gesture found favour and an offer of Knighthood was made him; but he declined the honour.

His grandson (not then born)[2] who became (we are told) "one of the finest gentlemen of his time" reversed this decision, and on being introduced to the Court of Charles II, received the accolade on 7 April 1678.[3]

Henry Gough, the grandfather, was a draper. It is said that emphasis was given to the affluence of the family by the children in the street following him *or his father* saying:

Here's old justice Gough
who has money enough.

The story must however belong to the grandson, Sir Henry.

The *Itur Carolinum* says the King 'rested' three nights at Wolverhampton; "and on to Bremicham, to Sir Thomas Holt's." This means that he left on Tuesday the 18th October. Money to pay the soldiers is said not to have been ready until Thursday 20th.

1 Shaw, ii. 188.
2 Born: 3 Jan. 49.
3 Shaw ii. 190.

The King's movements are shown in a letter of Basil Waring of Shrewsbury (Shrop. Arch. Soc. 2nd Series VII (1895) p. 248) "we hear his Majesty on Tuesday last, with his army, were at Birmingham, Prince Rupert demanding 2,000 pounds, or he would plunder the town; but most of the inhabitants were fled to Coventry. Upon Thursday he marched to Meriden, three miles off Coventry, and intends . . . . to march towards Bambury . . . ." (October 18th 1642).

To get to Edgehill, via Birmingham, meant some 60 miles of marching, and the fight took place on Sunday 23rd October. It seems likely that Wolverhampton was clear of troops by Thursday 20th. Before this they should have received their pay, or enough to encourage them considerably (and the townsmen too) for the Shrewsbury mint had been busy. Thomas Bushell, esquire, "farmer of the Mines royall in Wales" had set up this mint at Aberystwyth in 1637, and it was moved to Shrewsbury, on its way to Oxford (and finally to Lundy Island) in October 1642, where it continued until January to mint coinage from plate contributed to the royal cause by the gentry of Shropshire and Wales, the two Universities, and other well-disposed persons. The pieces struck were in silver of 20s., 10s., 5s., and 2s. 6d. denomination and bore the date 1642, showing on the obverse the King on horseback and on the reverse, in abbreviated Latin:—

RELIG. PROT. LEG. ANG. LIBER. PAR.

(The Protestant Religion. The Laws of England. The Liberties of Parliament) and, round the side:—

EXVRGAT DEVS DISSIPENTVR INIMICI.

(Let God arise and let his enemies be scattered).[1]

The highest value was paid to the colonels, the lowest to the private soldiers. Examples are now very rare.

There is an estimate which shows that a soldier was paid in 1644 8d. a day, and with beer at $\frac{1}{2}$d. a pint it was not without effect.[2]

There is evidence that after the King left Wolverhampton, the town remained for a time a headquarters. A royal letter from Reading, dated 7 November 1642, mentions the employment of Daniel Lambert and John Morgan "two yeomen of our Guard from our Towne of Wolverhampton to Shrewsbury to fetch from thence divers Armes and other provisions for war . . . ." [3]

It was indeed important to keep open communications with Shrewsbury and Wales (which meant cattle) and the Trent Valley to Newark, the gateway to the North. Parliament had active forces in Cheshire, Coventry and Birmingham (Edgbaston). Wolverhampton and Stafford could be stepping stones for either side.

Orlando Bridgeman writes from Chester, Wednesday 3 o'clock, January 25th (1642—3) to Sir Francis Ottley, Governor of Shrewsbury:

"It were well if forces lye at Wolverhampton that some now and then would meet with the pacquett betwixt Lichfield and Stone." And many 'pacquetts' were met, and the royalist leaders of these parts got the names of "rob-carrier". Eccleshall Castle e.g. had been garrisoned "by the great cow-stealers, the lord Capell his forces . . . . (and) their fellow rob-carrier, colonell Hastings."[4]

1 Owen & Blakeway, i. 423–5 and plate facing, p. 427.
2 Shaw, i. 67.
3 Harl. MS. 6851, fol. 220.
4 Shaw, i. 60.

The question of arms and ordnance was a problem for both sides. It rested with the ironmasters and those who controlled them. Sir Henry Hastings writing 9 February 1642—3 from Ashby de la Zouch (after having been attached by the Moorlanders north of Stafford) to Prince Rupert, asks for arms: "400 muskets and some quantity of match and powder, and two pieces, which we conceive may be brought safe to Wolverhampton by Worcester, and from there we will convey it; we are now beginning a hopeful foundation on which we are resolved to lay our lives and fortunes to serve his Majesty."[1]

The problem of ordnance was one which faced both parties. South Staffordshire could supply both sides.

Edward, lord Dudley had a patent from King James in 1620 (22 February 1621 for 14 years; V.C.H. Worc. ii. 267) for making iron with pit-coal (an invention of his son's Dud Dudley) Dud (or "my son Dudley" as his father called him) had come down from Balliol College, Oxford, to manage his father's ironworks on Pensnett Chase.[2]

About a year later his brother-in-law Richard Parkes or Parkshouse "esquire", had a fowling gun made of Pit-coal Iron, with his name on it; "which Gun was taken from him by Colonel Levison Governor of Dudley Castle, and never restored."[3]

The invention provoked much opposition from other ironmasters and hardship for the patentee; nevertheless he succeeded in getting a further patent, 2 May 1638, in which were united (as a safequard) certain influential men, including "Roger Foulke, Esquire, a Counsellour of the Temple, and an Ingenious Man, and also an Iron Master, my Neighbour, (he lived at the Lea, S.W. of Wolverhampton) and one who did well know my former Sufferings, and what I had done . . ."[4]

All seemed favourable to him, when the Civil War broke out and shattered his prospects. Dudley was an ardent Royalist and lost all his estate and money in the war, having been twice imprisoned and making two escapes.[5]

A rival was Mr. Richard Foley of Stourbridge who died in 1657 at the age of 80. He founded a family upon whom fortune smiled. He married a Brindley of Willenhall, as did his father Edward Foley, on a second marriage. He is then, 31 October 1621, described as "of Bristol",[6] which points to activities in the Forest of Dean.

Richard Foley made a considerable fortune during the war as an ironmaster, drawn doubtless from both sides, for Stourbridge was usually within the Parliamentary area.

The amateur garrison which defended Lichfield was overcome by the first serious attack. It is true that the Parliamentarian General, Robert Lord Brook, was killed in the fight (2nd March), but the defenders surrendered to Sir John Gell on March the 5th 1643, and were made prisoners. The Earl of Chesterfield was soon to make his peace with Parliament and dropped out of the war, dying in 1656. He was ancestor of another Philip Stanhope famous for his odd letters of advice to his son, and Dr. Johnson's comment: "a wit among the lords and a lord among the wits."

And the taking of this fortress by the rebels stirred the Royalists to immediate action; Prince Rupert who hovered about Stratford-on-Avon and Henley-in-Arden was sent to reduce it. At Birmingham on his way, there was an unfortunate incident, for he was halted by a barricade which was soon overpowered. His men however got out of hand and punished the town by burnings and plunder, a move that the inhabitants considered harsh[7] (and out of keeping with their minor gesture of opposition. If they had been

1 W.S.L. auto. 550.
2 Metallum Martis (reprint) 1665 (1851), p. 5.
3 ibid. 7.
4 ib. 17.
5 See S.H.C. 1920 for Dudley.
V.C.H. Worcs. ii. 268, citing Cal. S. P. Dom. 1660–1, p. 202.
6 Wolverhampton Register.
7 " . . . . an act not becoming a gentleman, a Christian, or Englishman, much less a Prince", said Col. Russell, defender of Lichfield.

playing at war, it was now brought home to them in all its violence. The "Prince of Plunderers" as he was called moved on, and a newly raised rabble army followed to support him).

The constables of the townships had indeed been busy, and there were three or four hundred "proper fellowes from Walsal, who came with bills and hooks to serve the King."[1] Sir Henry Hastings' order to the Constable and bellman of Wolverhampton summoned all the townsmen between the ages of 16 and 60 to take up arms in like manner under pain of hanging, drawing and quartering. It is certain many of the inhabitants chose the lesser evil. The action of John Gough, son of old Mr. Henry Gough on this occasion is well testified, as it was brought up against him when he was making his peace by compounding for his estates in 1651.

In the depositions Edward Elliott, a butcher, said he saw Mr. Gough among his neighbours with a sword; John Allin, tanner, saw him at Lichfield "with a short sword or hanger by his side". William Cotton, tailor, went to Lichfield to fetch two of his sister's children to safety and saw Mr. Gough there "and heard him called Captain Gough". Two labourers, William Cartlech and Thomas Fleming, went towards Lichfield as far as Pelsall "and then returned home" and saw Gough on horseback with a sword. Walter Huntbach, gentleman, who was then Constable of Wolverhampton, deposed that he went with Gough and others to Lichfield.

The force was overpowering; Prince Rupert arrived before the Close on 10th April, and Colonel Russell, the governor, surrendered on 21st. Lichfield remained the King's until his cause was lost.

Parliament answered by taking Stafford.

There had already been thrusts in this direction. The battle of Hopton Heath, just north of the town, had taken place 19th March with indecisive results. There is a letter which the Royalist generals, Lord Northampton (junior) and Sir Henry Hastings, wrote from Chillington on 27th March 1643 to Prince Rupert commending Wolverhampton as a place likely to help him, Stafford being unfit for his army "the Countrey beinge poore and provision for men and horse all spent".[2] But on Monday 15th May, Colonel Sir William Brereton with his troopers of horse and dragooners assembled secretly near Audley on the county border, and joining with "Colonel Ridgeway" (Simon Rugeley) whose companies lay at Newcastle and Leek, on Tuesday morning by three o'clock almost peaceably entered Stafford Town (the people being still abed) and the whole surrendered without loss. Some 400 prisoners were taken, including many gentlemen of worth. There was a report that Colonel John Lane, the governor, was slain; but he escaped. There was only one slight check. Old Lady Stafford in the Castle toughly resisted; they parleyed, but she stood firm. "Wee spent much time in this treatie,"[3] writes Brereton to the Earl of Essex, "but it was vain and fruitlesse; we conceave her heart was hardened by the pernicious councell of some preists jesuites, or other incendiaries about her, who delight in nothinge but fire and sworde . . ."

The fall of Stafford was an "unhappy surprise" for Sir Richard Leveson of Lilleshall, for he feared his own house would be made unsafe;[4] so he took steps immediately to send two wagon loads of household stuff for safe keeping at Shrewsbury, where he had with foresight reserved a room for just such a purpose.

1 Willmore 309.
2 Salt A. L. 568, printed S.H.C. 1941, 139.
3 Shaw, i. 55.
4 Letter to Sir Fra. Ottley, 16 May, 1643. Shrops. Arch. Soc. 2nd series VII (1895) p. 318. Owen & Blakeway, . 444.

Sir William Brereton (the Parliamentarian) decided to pursue his success. He must have known that Wolverhampton could now be had for the marching, and march he did. He writes: "lieutenant Collonell Hopkins, and captaine Jackson, tooke out my troupe of horse, and three companyes of my dragoones, and went towards Wolverhampton, which towne wee entered about three of the clocke in the morninge, without any opposition or resistance, the greatest malignants were fled, those that remained were summoned and appeared, and theire armes, whereof wee brought two or three cart-loades, and some cannon bulletts, from Mr. Folies forges; and the moulds which made these bulletts, which were intended for Lichfield, all which were brought into Stafford; reservinge the ransome and compositione of that towne for some more reasonable opportunity, when the greate and rich men were returned."

These reverses and fear of further reverses prompted the King to address a warning to the gentlemen of South Staffordshire, his "right trusty and well-beloved the Lord Dudley, Sir Walter Wrottesley, Sir Edward Seebright, Mr. Ashley, Mr. Peters, Mr. Grosvenor, Mr. Gray, Mr. Whitwicke, and Mr. Lane." It told them little they did not know already to their cost. The King found "to our great displeasure that few places in that our county of Stafford, of any consideration (besides the Castle of Dudley), but are possessed and held by those now in actuall rebellion against us". He observed that their estates lay near the same, and might be much prejudiced by it. They should therefore give all support to Colonel Leveson, and therein "doe us acceptable service, the which we shall reteyne in our memory. And so wee bid you heartily farewell. Given at our Court at Oxford, this 14th of June, 1643."

Leveson who had lost his moated Hall at Wolverhampton, was now appointed Governor in Dudley Castle. Such a post may not have been possible with the old lord in possession, for he had assured the King in 1639 of his boundless loyalty and complete absence of funds, but had centuries of "goodwill" behind him.[1] The new owner, lady Dudley, had letters on Leveson's behalf, and Leveson was empowered to raise money and provisions to support the garrison from the Staffordshire hundreds of Cuttleston and Seisdon, and to seize the estates and profits of these in rebellion against the King. This warrant, signed by the King, was dated 2nd July 1643.[2]

The method employed may be shown by quoting one of the warrants to the Constable of Wrottesley sent from Nether Penn the 21st November, 1643 by the high constable Francis Cartwright. "Seisdon Hundred.

"According to a warrant from colonell Leveson to mee directed, these are, in his majestie's name, to charge and command you to levie and gather within your constable weeke, your ratable parte of three hundred pounds, in this hundred, for and towards the paying of a greater number of souldiers then formerly; now lately raysed, for the defence of the castle of Dudley, and country adjacent; and that you make payment of the same unto the said colonell, or his lawfull deputie, at the said castle of Dudley, at or before the thirteenth day of December next ensuing the date hereof; and that you returne the names of such as neglect or refuse to paye their ratable proportion of the aforesaid payment. Hereof fail not at your perills."[3]

For example, seven score beds, and 140 feather beds together with sheets, blankets and bolsters and other furniture had to be found for Mark Davies quarter-master of the colonel's regiment of Foot in Dudley Castle, at the end of the year.[4]

1 S.H.C. IX, ii, 112.
2 Shaw, ii, 145.
3 Shaw, i, 60.
4 ibid.

Brief, or Appeal for Funds after Fire, 1696

Giffard House

Photograph by Margaret Roper

Old Grammar School, John Street

Still later,[1] Seisdon was required to provide 300 workmen or pioneers with tools and materials for fortification, Wrottesley's quota being 37 men.

To give the colonel wider scope for his authority the King had appointed him high-sheriff of Staffordshire for 1644 (an appointment absent from the official list; but the original letter was printed by S. Shaw *Hist*. II. 145) "you may and ought to take the posse comitatus upon all occasions to assist you" he is told. If those under his command are insufficient, he is required, being sheriff, to supply such addition from out of the county, and cause them to be armed so that their presence should not be fruitless. They should not serve, unless they wished, beyond the county, and none should have just cause for complaint; rather the King should be thanked for ordering it and the sheriff for putting it into execution, as he was bound to do. It is dated 4th January 1643—4, and we have Colonel Leveson's letter to the King in reply. The 'posse' was raised and found too raw to use.

Most sacred Sir.[2]

I thought myself bound to yield you an account of what success I have had in raising the Country for your service . . . . Upon my first summons the Country came in very freely and willingly but unprovided of arms, and for the most part people of a mean condition unable to buy them: upon which consideration I dismissed them requiring a second appearance of the better sort of men such as were fit to buy arms and be trusted with them. But before the day appointed for their appearance my Lord of Loughborough having not only discharged them of their attendance but commanding me to summon them no more, and on the other side the Rebels, sending forth their warrants to forbid any obedience to be given to mine, hath proved very disadvantageous to your Majesty's service. And I dare confidently say hath deprived you at the least of 1,000 men and arms which otherwise you had had. For the opposition I received from the Rebels I did not much value, and I believe the country as little; but when they saw the Rebel's warrants sent from Stafford and other places seconded by his Lordship's and Colonel Bagot's commands, I then found a general failing in them and received many expressions of their sorrow to be deprived of so good an occasion to shew their loyalties and affections to your Majesty.

Most sacred Sir, I shall pass much under silence, it being not my nature to complain of any, having no other intention but to inform your Majesty how I have discharge that trust and those commands you have imposed upon me, most humbly beseeching you, if you would have me proceed in the execution of them, I may receive your Majesty's further direction: which shall be no sooner sent than readily obeyed by your Majesty's Most loyal and most faithful subject and servant T. Leveson.

Dudley Castle 8 February 1643(—4).

For the King's most sacred Majesty."

A garrison can have its weary moments and the following order of Prince Rupert's points to a drift towards home.

"To the Constable of Wrottesley.

"wee doe hereby strictly charge and command you and every of you, that immediately upon sighte or recepte hereof you doe make diligent search and inquiry in your towne and neighbourhood, for all the souldiers of or belonging to colonell Leveson, governor of Dudley castle; and them having founde, to returne unto theire garrison at Dudley. And that you suffer them not, at any time hereafter, without speciall command to the contrary, to come into, or abide, or lodge, in any of your townes or hamletts whatsoever, as you

1 13 May 1644. Shaw i, 61.
2 This account is here modernized by the author.

will answere the contrary at the uttermost perills, and the confiscation of your goods. Given at Salop, the eighth day of March, 1643(—4).[1]

We turn now to neglected news of the Queen who had early in the year landed from Holland and was raising an army in Yorkshire. At the end of June she advanced southwards, via Newark and Ashby-de-la-Zouch. At Burton she had such success against the enemy that she was delayed at Walsall, resting, because (as she wrote the King) the soldiers had "got so much plunder that they could not well march with their bundles".[2] Meanwhile Lord Capell, a devoted supporter of the royal cause and Lieut. General of Shropshire, Cheshire, and North Wales, waited for her at Wolverhampton.[3]

While at Wolverhampton, he reports twice to Sir Francis Ottley, governor of Shrewsbury.[4]

Sr

Att Wolverhampton (where we now are) the news of her Majesties advance to Ashby, and that of the success in the North is confirmed: Att Oxford the Prince hath beaten the Rebbells: conditions are proposed by (the Parliament) which are considered by his Majestie, and returned, what they are, or how farre accepted is not knowne: Eccleshall Castle is yett besieged, but the Rebell party there will find other business (I believe) upon the next motion of his Majesties Armye, and of theis with (. . .) I rest

yr Affectionate freind
ARTHUR CAPELL.

Wolverhampton
5to Julii : 1643

The least of our Strength here is 1,000 horse 1,000 foote.

(Ffor my worthy frend Sr ffra:
Ottley Kt Governr of Shrewsbury these)

And the other letter:—[5]

Sr I am yett att Woolverhampton attending the Queens Commands, the Forces of her Guard have yesterday taken Burton upon Trent, where there was hott service, a greate part of towne burnt, and a part of the Church blowne up by the rebells themselves; many prisoners taken, the Governor and others: . . . Brereton is runne from Stafford to his ould Burrow Nantwych, and hath left Stafford very slenderlye Guarded, and hath withdrawne his forces from Eccleshall Castle:

Sr, the Queen's safe comeing soe farre as she is advanced, with those successes which attend her, and are happened by God's goodness to his Majestie in these parts, deserve a publique Solemnety. I shall therefore desire you to give command that the Bells be rung in every Church in the Towne of Shrewsbury this night, and that Bonfires be made in every Street in the Towne, and that you signify these occurances to the Gentlemen with you: I rest

your very Affectionate
freind, ARTHUR CAPELL

Woolverhampton
7^{0} Julii 1643

1 Shaw i, 61.
2 From Walsall 8 July. Willmore, p. 311.
3 See Burke, Complete Peerage.
4 Ottley papers, Letter CLXX, Shrop. Arch. Soc. 2nd series VII, p. 343.
5 ibid. CLXXII.

That was Friday. The Queen left Walsall on Monday 10th, avoided Birmingham, and met Prince Rupert at Stratford on the day following. And where did she stay? She was billetted on Mrs. Hall, Shakespeare's daughter, at New Place for three days. "Witty above her sex" she was, and she may well have "set herselfe to chere",[1] if only "with comforts cordiall" her majesty who normally spoke French. Yet the King had a Shakespeare annotated in his royal hand.[2]

Dudley Castle was a reservoir from which troops could be drawn to support strong points in South Staffordshire and other places not too distant. William Dugdale tells us in his Diary:[3] "Colonel Leveson put in 40 muskettiers into Sir Thomas Holt's house at Aston juxta Bermicham, at the desire of Sir Thomas 18 December 1643." on the 26th the Rebels 1,200 strong, assaulted it, and the day following. On the 28th they took it, killed 12 and made the rest prisoners, though with the loss of 60 of themselves.

At this attack died Richard Gough son of Henry Gough, whose baptism appears in the parish register on 1st June 1613.[4]

Chillington fell after two days hammering, 11th August 1643; Colonel Leveson regained it in September. The King, writing to him, regarded it as "a place of much importance for our service in those parts" and Leveson is told "to place a sufficient number of souldiers there in garrison under such a commander as you shall conceive fitt". Sir Walter Wrottesley claimed to have supplied horses and cattle for its garrison that summer; but in the end it was given up as indefensible.[5]

Stourton castle and Himley Hall (moated) were outposts of the castle. It was probable that Wrottesley was drawn on to supply Stourton, for Shaw says there were many warrants for the constable there relating to Stourton castle in 1644 of which Captain Ashton was governor, but he hid not quote them, and they must now have been burnt in the Wrottesley Hall fire.

We cannot enter upon the siege of Dudley Castle in June 1644, without the battle of Tipton Green. There was a considerable concentration against it. "my Lord Denbigh" was at Wolverhampton, and Waller and Brereton were ready to join in.[6] The actual fighting did not amount to much; but Colonel Leveson blew up St. Edmund's Church lest it should serve as a lodgement for the enemy (as at Eccleshall) and so destroyed a chapel of William Dudley, 15th c. dean of Wolverhampton.[7]

We come to the case of Rushall Hall.

Rushall Hall, near Walsall, was a fortified manor house dating from the wars of the Roses. It was held feudally of the manor of Bushbury by the payment annually of a pair of gilt spurs (a payment kept up till the eighteenth century when it was found that 1s. 9d. would meet the case).

At this time its owner was Edward Leigh, M.P. for Stafford in the Long Parliament. His connection with Wolverhampton began in his wilder days arising from a curious action which he brought against the Mayor of Walsall. 18th June 1629, for false imprisonment. His fault was that of "playing at bowls in an open green at Bloxwich, by means whereof divers poor men were drawn thither". But after trial at the Assizes held at Wolverhampton on 18th March 1630, upon full evidence, the plaintiff was non-suited, the Judge holding that nothing was done that could be justified by the Statute 33 Henry VIII against unlawful games.[8] Let us never play at bowls at Bloxwich.

1 Tombstone, 1649,
2 Gosse.
3 Printed 1827, p. 57.
4 Gough pedigree, Shaw ii, 188.
5 S.H.C. 1941, 138–9.
6 Letter 17 June, Perf. Occur. Parl. no. 26, Willmore 319.
7 Ashmole.
8 Walsall Cal. of Deeds, 216.

Later Edward Leigh became known as a learned writer, and his book *Critica Sacra* (on the Hebrew and Greek works in the Old and New Testaments) became a standard work of reference among scholars and divines.

His attachment to the Presbyterian cause brought him on the side against the King, and his house was garrisoned as a fortress for Parliament. It stood in a useful position for flank attacks on travellers to Lichfield, and the interruption of trade convoys passing through the county. Unfortunately Colonel Leigh, as he became, was away when the Royalists under Colonel Hastings presented themselves in March 1643, and though his wife put up a brave fight with her men and maids, they were overpowered. Soon after Colonel Lane of Bentley, who had been driven out of Stafford, assumed the command. So troublesome was he that[1] the rebels made a special effort to remove him, and on 25th May 1644 the Earl of Denbigh with a large force set out from Stafford, taking with him "two drakes, two sakers, and the Stafford great piece, and ammunition proportionable."[2] On Wednesday 29th May, after first taking the church held by Captain Gravenor (Grosvenor of Bushbury) by shooting down the steeple and the battlements, they pounded the fortifications. Later, after much parley, Colonel Lane surrendered on easy terms, and joined the royalists at Lichfield. He there faced a court-martial. There was much booty at Rushall, including 113 rolls of tobacco. (A cannon ball has been found there weighing 12 lbs. But 32 pounders have been found at Dudley).

On its capture, the new garrison was given as from 3rd August the "weekly pay" or levy from Wolverhampton to support it, amounting to £7 14s. 4d. To this was added that of Pattingham, £4 12s. 8d., and Tettenhall £3 18s. 0d. and the pay of Wednesfield and Willenhall (not stated) already allotted to Colonel Leigh's officers and men.

THE CASE OF FRANCIS PITT

TAX paying is seldom an amusement; but to Mr. Francis Pitt it was a tragedy, as it started the course of events which brought him to the gallows.

Pitt was a prosperous farmer at Wednesfield aged 65, who had paid attention to the ministry of the Rev. Richard Lee of Wolverhampton, and had obtained "a good repute amongst the godly (ministers and people) in those parts." He had gone twice to Rushall Hall, once to pay his contribution—money and again to redeem some cattle of his neighbours. Colonel Leveson, whose tenant he was, took notice of this and sent for him to propound a scheme he had in mind for the retaking of Rushall. Knowing its strength and unwilling to waste lives in an organized attack, he thought Captain Robert Tuthill the governor might be bribed. "I would fain purchase that garrison" said Leveson, "I will give two thousand pound for it."[3]

Much intercommunication and bargaining followed; the settlement of such terms of surrender was a delicate matter—Captain Tuthill gave his own account of his treachery in full.[4]

In the end it was decided that Pitt should take £200 on account on Friday, and that Tuthill should deliver up Rushall Hall on Monday night 9th September, between the hours of 11 and 12. But it turned out otherwise. When Friday came Pitt was seized, together with an agitated Popish Priest who came with him and the royalists were met on Monday with the contents of Captain Tuthill's pistols and the discharge of his cannons.

1 On one occasion he fell upon Sir Wm. Brereton's "luggage", crossing Cannock Chase and took 9 men 60 horses and 55 packs, and good store of powder and match. Capt. Wagstaffe, with a good horse under him, escaped, and a rescue party lost its way. (W's. Rushall, p. 57).
2 Rushall, p. 60, (Denbigh's account).
3 Rushall, p. 63. See also "Relation . . ", p. 9.
4 Willmore, p. 67 et seq.

Pitt afterwards confessed deep sorrow for what he considered his blindness. It was not, he thought, covetousness that misled him. Captain Tuthill had indeed offered him 100 pounds of the money, and Leveson promised that it would be "as good as seven years Rent". But Pitt was not uninfluenced by the grievance that an intrusive rival garrison forced upon the countryside the "sore burden" of paying double taxation.

Pitt was very soon aware that he had made an awful exchange. The conduct of the garrison in which he found himself shocked him in the extreme.

"I never heard more swearing, nor saw more drunkennesse, and prophanenesse, then I saw in the Garrison at *Rushall*, (he declared) . . . The Martial he did swear and blaspheme, as if he would cause the stones to flie out of the Wals; and after I fell into his hands, he stript me and abused me, and used me more like a Jew, then a Christian." Clearly the rules of the Committee at Stafford were neglected in this household, for they laid down that an officer should be fined 12d. an oath, and that a soldier for the third offence should be bored through the tongue and cashiered. (1644).

Pitt was soon sent to London for trial, brought before a court martial sitting at the Guildhall and condemned to death (Tuesday 8 October). His friends did what they could for him, and the Lord Mayor, Sir John Wollaston, who had been born at Tettenhall, and had probably been at school with him (Pitt in his last speech called him "a merciful man, a charitable man; he is good to poor and rich")[1] no doubt helped. His parson friends, Ithiel Smart (Sir John Wollaston's nominee at Wombourne) and Edward Archer from Kinver (and two others unnamed) shocked at the part Pitt had taken, stuck to him to the last. At first in the condemned cell they found him "sad and stupid", but were able so to work upon him, that on the morning of the execution they "found him very ready and willing to undergo the sentence of death, as having hopes of a better life" and he said "he was never more cheerful in his dayes."

At the scaffold where he had to wait his turn (which he did apart in prayer) his minister friends took down everything he said till the end, and hurried off to the press, so that others who think they stand might take heed lest they fall. Thus we get the pamphlet:

A more Exact and Perfect

RELATION / OF THE

Treachery, Apprehension, Conviction,

Condemnation, Confession, and Execution, / OF

Francis Pitt, Aged 65.

who was Executed in Smithfield on Saturday, / October the 12. 1644. For endeavouring to betray / the Garrison of *RUSHALL-HALL* in the / County of *Stafford*, to the Enemy.

Published by { *Ithiel Smart* and / *Edward Archer*, } two Ministers.

who were acquainted with him in his life, / and present with him at his death. (Printed 18 October 1644).

1645 was the King's fateful year. It saw the end of the small garrisons in Staffordshire, which were taken without difficulty. The "popish" garrison at Patshull fell in the usual manner, by a happy surprise. It was the work of Captain Stone, the governor of Eccleshall Castle under Sir William Brereton, who with a small party marched against it. The old hall was in a low situation "Strongly fortified and moated about"; but taking the oppor-

1 Relation, p. 12.

tunity of the drawbridge being let down, he surprised the guard and fell in amongst the defenders, fighting them in the house.[1] The governor, Mr. Astley the owner, was taken, as well as ten others of quality and about 60 soldiers. There were also found two priests, an item of information always regarded with great satisfaction in these accounts.

The loss of Shrewsbury, 12 March 1644—5, again by surprise, was a severe blow to the King's hold on the west.

The King's forces left Oxford on the 7 May to march to Leicester. On 14th he held a meeting of the governors of the Royalist garrisons, including Dudley, at Cofton Hackett and marched to Himley "from 4 in the morning till 6 sans rest" says Captain Symonds, the diarist. "This night the King lay at Himley Hall . . . where now the lord Ward lives . . . an old house moated.

"Friday May 16th 1645. The rendezvous was near the King's quarters began after 4 of the clock in the morning here: one soldier was hanged for mutiny.[2]

The Prince's headquarter was at Wolverhampton, a handsome town, one fair church in it. The King lay at Bisbury (Bushbury) a private sweet village where Squire Grosvenor (as they call him) lives . . . .

Saturday 17 May 1645. His Majesty marched from hence by Tong in the county of Salop: a fair church, the windows much broken . . ." But Captain Stone fell upon the rere of the King's army at Wolverhampton, and again upon their quarters at Newport next day and killed many". [3] Doubtless the "souldier of Collonell Baggots" who was buried at Wolverhampton 16th May 1645, was one of these.

Leicester was taken by the King on 31st May, but his defeat at Naseby on 14th June shattered his cause, and he became a fugitive. The King spent that night at Ashby-de-la-Zouch; next day, Sunday, he went to Lichfield, and that night lay in the Close. On Monday 16th June his Majesty marched to Wolverhampton, and Tuesday 17th to Bewdley.

At Wolverhampton he slept, as the *Itur* informs us, at "Mrs. Barnford's a widow". This is sufficient evidence for the identification of Mrs. Barnfield whose husband Richard Barnfield, and once a prosperous attorney in Wolverhampton, had died 29th September 1643. The war had gone far to ruin him, but an Inventory of his goods shows a large, well furnished dwelling house, three storeys high, in Cock Street. It seems clear, if this was the same house as the large house for which his son Thomas Barnfield paid Hearth Tax in 1666, that it stood on the West side of the street and not near the present "Star and Garter." Mrs. St. Andrew his former hostess was dead.

The town's last part in hostilities came after the fall of Chester, when Parliament decided to employ the forces thus liberated against Lichfield and other fortresses. For this purpose Wolverhampton was chosen as the meeting-place of some 1,800 foot and 1,200 horse on 18th February 1645—6.[4] Sir William Brereton is appointed to command there, and Colonel Sanderson's "regiment of Reformadoes" joined him. We leave them shadowing Sir Jacob Astley who led the last royal army in the field.

Up to 1645 Sir Walter Wrottesley of Wrottesley had been looked upon as a royalist. He had contributed abundantly to their armies:[5] Lord Capell on his march to Wolverhampton had driven the park and taken 37 horses for the King's use worth £300; but he had resisted putting into Wrottesley Hall (a garrison mansion with a gatehouse of which a bird's eye view, dated 1633, is known).[6] The rebels too had drawn their share. But

1 Shaw i. 70, Letter Fri. 14 Feb. 1644–5.
2 Camden Soc.
3 Willmore 330.
4 Cal. S.P. Chas. I. 1645–7, p. 342.
5 Wrottesley History, 325.
6 ib., p. 301.

now the cause of the King was hopeless, Sir Walter handed over the custody of his house to the Parliamentarians, hoping by this step to save his estate from sequestration. He failed, for Parliament recognised no neutrality, and his enmity with Colonel Leveson still a power was of long standing. As a rebel garrison Wrottesley had some successes against the royalists.[1] This was too much for Dudley Castle, whose forces descended upon it burnt the stables, barns and granaries which lay outside the defences of the house, and cut down the timber. "All which his sufferings, debts and advance money he reckoned amounts to £6,219 or thereabouts." Neutrality did not pay.[2]

The second Civil War did not trouble Staffordshire; but the Scots in 1651 marched through the county.

Starting from Stirling and travelling via Carlisle, Warrington, Whitchurch, Newport, Wolverhampton, Kidderminster, to Worcester, they met with small encouragement on the way.

Colonel Danvers, governor of Stafford, fell upon some and gave alarm to the whole army. They were in a poor way, many unarmed, and many sick, besides "not one in a hundred can tell what they say." They camped upon Tong heath. (Account from Stafford 22nd August 1651).

Worcester fight was lost on 3rd September 1651. The King was last seen giving his officers his last order "Shift for yourselves, gentlemen, shift for yourselves." Newspaper accounts then became vague as to his movements. It is likely that, he was seen at Stourbridge going north; but darkness blots him out.

The King was in safe hands: rumours there must have been; but they did not produce him. An iron curtain closed around him. Yet Mr. Humphrey Ironmonger, a Roman Catholic of Wolverhampton knew something: his civilian marriage took place there 30th April 1655. Years later when Father Ireland alias Ironmonger was being tried for his life, Humphrey Ironmonger's help towards the King was put forward in his favour; but it is not stated what Humphrey Ironmonger did.

Authority printed proclamations:—

"A Proclamation for the Discovery and Apprehending of CHARLS[sic.] STUART, and other Traytors his Adherents and Abbettors." .... "whereas *Charls* STUART son of the late Tyrant .... (has) lately in a Trayterous and hostile manner with an Army invaded this Nation, which by the Blessing of God upon the Forces of this Commonwealth have been defeated, and many of the chief Actors therein slain and taken prisoners; but the said Charls Stuart is escaped:" .... all are charged "to make diligent seach & enquiry for the said Charls Stuart" .... and "Whosoever shall apprehend the person of the said Charls Stuart, and shall bring or cause him to be brought to the Parliament or Council of State" (shall have £1,000 reward).

Dated 10 September 1651.

Just before dawn on this day 10 September 1651, a small cavalcade set out from Bentley Manor, consisting of two men mounted with ladies behind them, and young man on horseback. They took the London Road.

How interested the wakening town of Wolverhampton would have been, had they been wider awake, for among them was the King, making his way to safety and a refuge in France.

1 ib., p. 322.
2 ib., p. 325.

The Civil War did very little damage to those in official positions in the town. The headmaster of the Grammar School, Daniel Rawlet, appointed in 1631, continued undisturbed till his death in 1658. The townsmen seem to have been united, High Church and Low, in supporting the school. The usher or second master, Francis Storr, was however ejected in June 1643[1]—it is not clear why, but he complained of "the great oppression of the souldiers there"—and his livelihood was made uneasy until he was restored in 1651.[2]

Mr. Samuel Crosse who had taken his place, was in a short time himself ejected on account of his 'scandalous' behaviour. One of his faults lay in becoming chaplain to the Earl of Newcastle, a royalist power in the North who had met and escorted the Queen. He had been recommended by the famous headmaster-printer of the Merchant Taylors' School, William Dugard, who was also a royalist, and a visit by him to the school (he reported May 1648) found the boys "very good proficients in learning; but we saw not above Forty scholars there", many owing to the distracted times being at home with their friends.

The building of a house for the usher belongs to this time.

During the Commonwealth the school received its only undergraduate headmaster, John Coles of New College, from which he had been ejected, 15 May 1648, for non-submission to the Cromwellian visitors. He became first undermaster at the Merchant Taylors' School and translated three parts of that endless French Romance, Cle'opatre, before coming to Wolverhampton. There he produced a very unusual school book, 1666, and many bursts of Latin and English prose and verse. His latin verses to Sir Samuel Morland (as one old Winchester to another) on the invention of his speaking trumpet, which he had printed on a single sheet, have recently been reprinted in the "Wulfrunian".

The Puritans' attack upon Merry England is shown by attempts to suppress a band of 16 Morris Dancers and a lively group of young people with a Maypole.

The former, of 1st July, 1652,[3] seems to have been restricted to the Tailors' craft, and they, rather drunken, provided a case for the Quarter Sessions when they were 'bound over'.

The latter aroused action at Whitehall. As we see it, the affair seems vague and not so alarming as the Puritans found it; but they knew better the young men of their day. The information takes the form of a rather bold Petition, written on one folio sheet bearing date 7th May 1653, and signed by Jonas "Grosvenear" gentleman and 28 other youths of Wolverhampton. (The next are: George Turnpenny, John Hawkins, John Tomkys, Will 'Persehowse gent'. Thomas Davis . . . . but many of the names are illiterate and hard to read, and they are little guide to their politics). It is directed to the "worthily renowned" Lord General Cromwell.

On "the happy tidings of that most glorious and never-to-be-forgotten achievement of dissolving the late Parliament",[4] we did, on May 2 last, erect a May-pole, being an ancient custom, for no purpose but to express our great joy for that most noble performance of the army. But this action was distasted by our ministers, two most rigid and malicious presbyters, whose private consultation and purchase and storing of arms may be more dangerous than our inoffensive solace. These men say that the cause we allege for setting up the pole "was rather matter of humiliation than congratulation", and have so highly incensed the justices of the peace of the county that we were summoned before them.

1 School History, 126.
2 ib., p. 138.
3 W.A. ii, 39–40.
4 S. P. Dom. 1652–3, p. 313 (paraphrase).

Nothing of misdemeanor was proved against us, and then they urged us extremely to take an oath to answer certain questions. We refused this, fearing a trap, and then they issued warrants to apprehend us.

We beg not to be ruined to satisfy their thirst of revenge, nor exposed to the tyranny of those whom nothing will satisfy but a power of regulating all men by the square of their own private fancies.

We will ever serve you with life and fortune, and pray for the prosperity of your noble and worthy enterprises.

The Council of State had other information and ordered Quarter-master General Grosvenor[1] to go there with all speed, and after consulting the magistrates try to quiet and dismiss the people; but in case of opposition to send for such troops as are quartered in those parts, and use them for suppressing the tumult, and seizing the leaders, that they may be examined and proceeded against according to law."

We hear no more, but the trouble was in the air. In August 1653 there have been riots and unlawful assemblies at Walsall.[2]

Next year, 16 August, the Council learn of "meetings of Papists, Jesuits, and ill-affected persons at Wolverhampton, and ask Sir John Worley, (sic) and Capt. John Stone to inquire into the matter, prevent such meetings, apprehend dangerous persons, and proceed against priests and Jesuits according to law."

Dangerously select is the "Freehoulders Booke"[3] compiled by Robert Ducy, high Sheriff of the county of Stafford in 1653. It was, it is believed, prepared for the election that resulted in the "Barebones" Parliament, summoned 20 June 1653 and dissolving itself by Resolution, 12 December 1653. Only two of the 140 persons summoned were from Staffordshire, and Wolverhampton's voters numbered nine, *viz:*—William Normansell, William Hayes, John Allen, Richard Tompkis, Edward Carye, John Granger, Thomas Bradney, Adam Parkeshowse and Thomas Loxdale.

THE CHURCH

THE Dean of Wolverhampton had been abolished by Act of Parliament of 8th June 1649. The estate was taken over by the Committee for Plundered Ministers with a clear conscience, for the tenant, Colonel Leveson, now in exile, had been a papist in arms against the Parliament. There were many claimants for its funds.

Mr. Richard Lee, a godly and orthodox divine, one of the prebendaries and a constant, diligent and faithful preacher at the parish church (until silenced by the archbishop) was one of the first to benefit, and for the last two years of his life had received £100 instead of £40. Mr. Ambrose Sparry, a godly and orthodox divine, was chosen to succeed him and William Kimberley was made his assistant at £50 per annum, who should have the house and yard "commonly called the Sexton's House."

The Minister of Wednesbury was also to have a bite at this plum, and the parishes of Hilton and Featherston "anciently belonging to the Cathedral Church of Wolverhampton"[4] were united with Shareshill, and the poor sixteen nobles a year were brought up to £100. It was reckoned as being "four large miles distant."

There was difficulty in giving effect to these grants, and petitions for payment are the rule of the day.

1 2 June, 1653.
2 S. P. Dom. 1653–4, p. 111.
3 W.S.L. Shaw Collections, bundle 28.
4 Miles Corbett (the regicide) signed this minute, 29 May 1647.

Ambrose Sparry and Richard Cleyton who supplied the collegiate church and its chapels were specially affected, the amount reserved for the clergy from the rents being only £30. The death of Colonel Leveson in September 1652 meant the sequestration was removed so poverty and confusion alone remained. They were even asked to refund the amount received between September 1653 and "this instant Aprill" (1654).

"Lastly (say they) your Petitioners humbly represent, that the state of this miserable Towne is so much the more sad in regard it swarmes with Papists (and thence is by many stiled little Rome) there being besides many of inferior ranke, above 20 families of Recusants of the ranke of the Gentry by whom many are drawne to Popery, and some of them were so turbulent the last Summer and guiltie of such high Ryots that could not be suppressed by the Justices at their monthly meeting, or a smaller partie of souldiers without further assistance from a whole Troop of horse.

Your Petitioners therefore humbly pray, that this Honourable Committee would lay to heart the sad condition of this towne and parish for the future: and allow the payment of what was due till 25 of March last: that soe however we suffer for want of Competent Maintenance for the future, yet we may have, keep and enjoy what we have laboured for for the time past.

Ambrose Sparry,
Richard Cleyton."[1]

This was closely copied in a Petition to the Protector dated 31st January 1655—6, by the "well-affected inhabitants of Wolverhampton". Theirs is a market town, and the largest in the county . . . . the parish has 4,000 communicants, and 3 chapels, one 5 miles from the town. The only church property is tithes, fee farm rents, and some cottages, of a total value of £144 2s. 6d., less by £31 17s. 6d. than formerly allowed. They beg a grant thereof.

The "well-affected" numbering only 13, are:—

William Normansell
William Hayes
Michael Turton
William Rudge
Edward Sheldon
John Leigh
John Hanbury
Walter Lane
John Ebbe
Robert Coxe
John Russell
John Granger, Thomas Gibbons } Church Wardens

The great need was to discover the value of the Church property, and to do this a Survey of the Deanery and Prebends was made in March 1652—3. (B.M. Addl. MS. Ga. I.A. fo. 46—77b.).

It is a long and detailed account, a mass of small rents and payments.

We find that the Deanery House is occupied by two or more families, two rooms on the East end being one tenement and three rooms "being the West part of the Mansion House" and the little croft at the back, with two small garden plots to the east, equal to one acre one rood.

There is a Court Baron held for the said Deanery, prebend and manor at the Town Hall of Wolverhampton every three weeks. A Court Leet also "at the usual times". Tenants perform suit of court (but the quit-rents from freeholders are only £2 5s. od.); copyholders pay a fine equal to double quit-rent upon descent, but upon alienation a fine according to the will of the lord and custom of the manor. Tenants dying pay a heriot in Kind, the best beast or best goods by the custom thereof. The lease of 2nd April 1610 is given, and:

1 Committee for Compounding G. vol. 100, No. 417.

"we have certain information that the said John Gifford (one of the lives) is living, but no certain information of the being of the other life".

All that plott or parcel of ground whereupon the Grist mills called Damm Mills were heretofore standing within the tything, hamlet or liberty of Codsall" together with all ponds was worth 6s. 8d. per annum.

		£	s.	d.	
(Summary)	Out of Lands and Royalties	23	8	7	£38 rent payable to the late dean
	Out of Tithes	14	11	5	
	Quit Rents, Royalties	70	15	5	
	Demesne Lands	72	6	11	
	Tythes in present possession	89	0	0	
	Sum total per annum	£232	2	4	

The second volume of the existing parish registers begins with the notice dated 30 September 1653 that Ambrose Sparry clerk had publicly been elected and chosen to be the parish Register . . . . to Register all marriages solemnized as also births and burials and had taken his oath to do the same according to the late Act . . . . before George Bryndley, a magistrate, who signs this declaration.

This was the work of the "Barebones" Parliament: AN ACT touching MARRIAGES And the Registring thereof and also touching Births and Burials. (24 August 1653). It takes no notice of religious ceremonies and provides for a civil marriage: publication three times in the market place and subsequent marriage before a magistrate. The principal (regularity after much lapse) was good if it could be carried out; but it offended against sentiment, and the machinery to perform it did not exist. Magistrates were few; it was inconvenient and not easy to find them; so the registration was often left incomplete and many were married without registration, and in the end of this period it was left to the clergy to carry out the ceremony as they liked.

The following magistrates sign marriages in the register: Mathew Moreton frequently, sometimes at Engleton (near Brewood); George Bryndley (of Kinver); Henry Stone (of Walsall); Sir John Wyrley (of Hampstead); John Whorwood (at Dunsley, and Compton near Kinver); Thomas Whitgreave (of Burton by Stafford); Lancelot Lee (of Coton, at Claverley); Henry Mott (at Lichfield). There is a marriage at Tamworth 17 June 1656. From 1657, 28 August Ambrose Sparry and John Reynolds perform marriages at Wolverhampton. There is also Mr. Andrew Bailey who became Sacrist in 1661, and Mr. Thomas Badland the minister at Willenhall.

Something should be said of the public generosity of John Gough, father of Sir Henry, who died 30th January 1665. His sword was a thing of the past though it was not a ploughshare. "He set up (says a Latin account) as an everlasting monument of his love of the town, almost at his own cost, a building fit for a council house, market hall and court of law, and would have done more had not death alas, intervened." Otherwise he was a great peace-maker and lived beloved of all. His monument, in Bushbury Church, does not tell us this, and but for the taste Mr. John Coles the Grammar School head-master had for oratory and versification it would have been unknown. The building itself was demolished in 1780 to make more room in the Market Place, but a thumb-nail sketch of it is found on the map of 1751, and it seems to be of the nature of that still standing at Bridgnorth, a large room on arches, which belongs to the same period and may even have inspired Mr. Gough.

"So shall his name oblivion's waves outvie,
Remaining famous to Eternity.
And that which his short life hath left undone,
Shall be completed by his virtuous son."[1]

chanted Mr. Coles.

One other important building had also newly risen. This was the Deanery Hall standing secluded behind a high wall off the Horsefair to the N.E. of the Church. Its builder had a faith in the post-war stability of the times, which was in the end disappointed. One can speculate as to its predecessor, which was likely to have been of timber construction. When the ground was cleared for the Technical College, which stands on its site, earlier foundations of stone were uncovered not quite in line (as it appeared) with the demolished Deanery House. These may very well have supported the usual stone plinth for the wooden superstructure.

Richard Best, the builder, does not seem to have had any previous connection with Wolverhampton. He had been a bookseller or publisher established at Gray's Inn Gateway, Holborn, in 1640, from which address many, usually small, works had been issued (yet he shared in the publication of the large 1652 edition of Raleigh's History of the World). During the Commonwealth he "farmed the Excise" which was, it seems, profitable, as he was able to buy Perry Hall, Handsworth, and "wished to purchase more land in the country". The Royalist holders or "farmers" of the Deanery lease were in difficulties in 1652 and by 1654 had sold their interest in this estate. Richard Best bought the remaining years of the lease in October 1656, and then built the large brick house, whose appearance is well vouched for by photographs and drawings, if not by memory, at a cost he claimed of £3,000.[2]

The style was that of Sir Christopher Wren (son of the late Dean), and it is possible that his master hand directed the plans.[3]

The carved panelling still preserved in the Principal's room in the Technical College which now occupies the site, shows that Richard Best did not skimp matters, and that the demolition of the old building is an irreparable loss. It was that to the builder, for at the Restoration and the re-appearance of the Dean and Chapter, Richard Best "feared he had not a good title to the lease" and tried to have it confirmed. Manorial courts were held in his name up to 14 March 1664—5. He was then a seller and borrower, and had disposed of Perry Hall to Henry Gough. The tide had turned. Mr. Best of Perry Hall and the Deanery, Wolverhampton is in the list composed by Sir Simon Degge (appended to the 1723 edition of Erdeswick's Survey of Staffordshire) of those new-comers to the county who would "take it ill if you write them less than Esquires."[4] He died, it seems, at Shifnal at the end of 1687.[5] His son, Richard Best of Walsall, married Anne the second of seven daughters of Colonel John Lane, which accounts for the following entry in the parish register: "Elizabeth the daughter of Mr. Richard Best borne att Bently and baptized the 17th of January (1664—5)."

At the Restoration the Deanery Hall was occupied by Sir Clement Throckmorton, the young M.P. for Warwick (1660) who died here 10 November 1663, leaving a widow. He was, says Mr. Coles, "truly noble and eminently learned" (and he had much more to say).[6] Sir William Dugdale once asked him to copy Sir Richard Leveson's epitaph for him; but he did so badly (and only half) that it had to be done again.[7] Dugdale spent the

1 School History, 153.
2 Chan. Proc. C.7. 324/88, (1672) and C.7.504/14. Best v. Hy. Gough.
3 See the "Case for the Preservation of the Old Deanery", 1915.
4 Dated 20 Feb. 1669–70.
5 Admon. 18 Jan. 1687–8 at Lichfield.
6 See W.A. 252, 364.
7 W.A. 331. letter Dec. 1665.

night of 10 April 1663 at Seawall, his nephew John Huntbach, the Antiquary's house. He was then making his heraldic Visitation as Norroy King of Arms. He had indeed spent the first year of his married life there. As saviour of St. Peter's Church from complete ruin (the tower but for him might have collapsed) the town should hold him ever high in honour.[1]

Let us not forget young Mr. Thomas Pilkington one of the Queen's Musicians who caught a fever and died at Wolverhampton, and lies there buried (20 November 1654). Sir Aston Cokayn wrote his epitaph and also a funeral elegy in 62 lines of punning verse. These were printed in his extremely scarce book (why does this rarity always attach to Wolverhampton?) "A Chain of Golden Poems" printed in 1658. He was "Musicks prime Master of our Land" for monumental purposes, but in practice invented the Orphion, a word which according to the New English Dictionary (where the date is wrongly given) is only known by this one reference.

Colonel John Lane was captured finally at Ashby-de-la-Zouch in February 1646. His father who lived at Bentley, whereas the son was of "the Hyde" near Brewood, was able to keep out of hostilities and to compound for his estate, and lived just long enough to welcome the King's return. John and his father were imprisoned for the part they took in the King's escape, and again in Booth's rising in September 1659. The standing of Colonel Lane is shown by the fact that he was only released on a bail of £4,000, a higher price than that of any other Staffordshire man.[2] He was one of the intended Knights of the Royal Oak, and Colonel of one of the newly raised regiments of Foot after the Restoration. His monument says he fought against the Dutch (which can only have been in 1665). His membership of the "Pensioner Parliament", sitting for Lichfield, may have accounted for his death in London, 31st August 1667, aged 58.

The church register has: Buried 7th September 1667 "John Lane of Bentley Esquire." He left no will.

His tomb in N. transept has recently been moved for the second time, with the advantage that the sill of the window (east) then behind it has been laid bare, showing the remains of the original mullions of that now very odd-looking piece of architecture, and the manner of placing the panels on the wall, which originally contained an altar.

There has grown up a belief that this tomb was erected at the cost of the nation, "Parliament voting £1,000 for the purpose on the colonel's death in 1667". (Masefield, *Staffordshire*—Little Guides (Methuen, 1910 p. 259.)). On this head Allan Fea, The Flight of the King, 2nd edn. 1908 (first edn. 1897) p. 93 note, writes:—

"In the year 1667 Colonel Lane received a gift from the King of £2,000—Domestic State Papers, February 22, 1667. A thousand pounds was voted by Parliament to erect the monument to his memory. It is engraved in Shaw's "Staffordshire"."

Enquiry shows that in March 1667 a sum of £2,000 was granted to Colonel John Lane from the King's Privy Purse (not Parliament) for services to the late and present King. But there seems to be no record of the £1,000 voted by Parliament for the tomb.[3] (Besides, as money was valued in those days, £1,000 would have far exceeded the cost of the tomb).

That the Colonel was not forgotten at the time of his death appears from the last few lines of the epitaph: (translated)

1 Married 17 Mar. 1622–3, Margery 2nd d. of John Huntbach of Seawall, gent. "After which he tabled with his wife's father, untill his own father dyed, viz. 4 July, 1624" (Diary, p. 8).
2 S.H.C. 1920, 129.
3 Search of Journals made Oct., 1932.

"His remains, moreover, from a sense of pious and grateful affection, The King would have interred with great funeral pomp, Among the Royal Tombs at Westminster, Had not the hero's modesty, in his dying moments, Resisted so great an honour." But there is a clue which might point to a solution of this difficulty, a public collection of a different kind.

In the second volume of the Codsall Registers, under the date 29 January 1681—2, is the entry: "Collected then upon a letter of request from Wolverhampton upon ye account of John Lane the summ of £00 02s. 9d." (This may be compared with a similar entry of 14 December 1684: "for re-edifying St. Paul's London 7s. 9d.").

These entries, which are common in parish registers of the period, are notes of the money collected—usually quite small sums—for "Briefs", *i.e.* appeals widely dispersed for charitable objects, set out in the form of a proclamation, and carried out by certain authorized collectors.

The date is of course nearly 15 years after the event, but repairs and alterations, and presumably additions, to the church at this time were only slowly effected. The ruined chancel was not repaired until 1685. And it is to be noted that the royal augmentation to the Lane coat of arms appearing on the tomb and mentioned in the epitaph, was not granted until July 1677. There had been a lapse of 10 years.

Gregory King, Rouge Dragon, in his *Note Book* (edited S.H.C. 1919, p. 201.) mentions under August 11th 1679—"Mem. the Colours of Capt. Lane's Crest are thus given to the Stone cutter: a demy Horse Strawberry colour bridled gules bitted and bottoned or, supporting an Imperial Crown proper",—which proves the date of the tomb. (It is a pity that the recent painters think a strawberry roan horse is of chocolate colour).

Having got so far let us with the help of Mrs. Arundell Esdaile identify the "stone cutter".

Dr. Plot shows by the attention he gave Lane's tomb in his "Natural History" 1687, that he was particularly interested in it. He copies the grant of arms and also the epitaph, and mentions with approval the skill of Mrs. Rebeccah Normansell (the mother of one of his subscribers) who had "so excellent a hand in the management of her *Cisers*" that she cut out a representation of the Tomb in paper, to which the Doctor had never seen anything equal "outside the Musaeum at Oxford".[1]

Sometime after 1671 Doctor Plot had put up a tomb in memory of his father, Robert Plot, esquire, of Borden, captain of the local troop of militia near Gravesend. The design bristles with spears, cannon and warlike material. The same may be said of John Lane's tomb, and also the tomb put up to Sir Richard Astley (now a baronet) and his two wives to be seen in Patshull church (Sir Richard died in 1687) and likewise engraved for "Shaw" vol. II. It has a low relief picture of Sir Richard mounted at the head of his troops. (In his quieter days he invented, with the approval of Dr. Plot, a *collistrigium* or pillory for measuring game cock to $\frac{1}{8}$ part of an inch.)

Finally there is the tomb in Christ Church, Oxford (with which Plot must have been familiar) which is the only monument in Oxford to bristle with arms and banners arranged in a manner startlingly like those on the Plot monument (says Mrs. Esdaile).[2] It is to the young Viscount Grandison slain at the siege of Bristol in 1643, erected by Barbara Duchess of Cleveland to her father's memory, and signed by Jasper Latham.

1 Plot: NAT. HIST. STAFFS., IX, 100.
2 Acct. in "The Times", 10 Aug., 1938. See illus. of Plot monument in Engl. Church Monuments, 1510–1840, K. A. Esdaile, London, 1946, pl. 109.

Wolverhampton did not take amiss the Restoration or the Monarchy. Some old faces reappeared while others went into quiet retirement. In the church Andrew Bailey returned and John Reynolds wrote in the register "here endeth ye exercise of Mr. Reynolds".[1] But he remained in the district and practised medicine.

King Charles II was acclaimed at Wolverhampton with some ceremony. On 19th May 1660 there were present at the proclamation Lord Ward, Sir Brian Broughton (the high sheriff) with divers gentlemen of quality including the chief officials, Lord Aston, Sir Hervy Bagot, Thomas Wilbraham and Robert Leveson esquire (son of Colonel Leveson), and at least 200 horse and 100 musketiers. We are told no more.

It was this, or like, occasion that John Coles, the schoolmaster, siezed for his Loyal oration in Latin which he afterwards printed for a wider audience.[2]

1 Pr. Reg., p. 254.
2 School History, 145.

CHAPTER VIII

UNQUIET YEARS: 1660 to 1713

WHEN John Reynolds the Minister wrote in the Parish Register, November 1660: "Here endeth ye Exercise of Mr. Reynolds", he still had twenty years of active life before him. His more famous son, John Reynolds, non-conformist minister of Shrewsbury, was born here, 19th February 1667, and there is other evidence that he did not immediately leave the neighbourhood. He won the praises of Dr. Edmund Calamy (one of the leaders in non-conformity), and at the time of the Savoy Conference in 1661 his judgment was sought not only by Baxter but by several members of Parliament. The differences between the various dissenting bodies were slight, and the King desired a wide toleration, but so certain were the sects that each was right, a scheme of Comprehension was impossible. The interference of Parliament, easily swayed by enthusiasm or fears, brought persecution upon both extremes.

So Dissent, no longer within the Church, now had a legal status and rights, and was recognised as a permanent fact.

Richard Baxter knew his Wolverhampton. In his opinion it abounded with "Papists and Violent Formalists".[1] Known personally to every household between Kidderminster and Bridgnorth, his "Saints Everlasting Rest" (1650)[2] brought him an audience far and wide.

Baxter said he thought of Heaven with the more pleasure, because he should meet there with Peter, Paul . . . . . Brook, Pym, Hampden and others of his way of thinking.[3] His readers were often of other opinions and critical of his list. So eventually Baxter, lest they should "stumble" (take offence), caused these names to be blotted out in the later editions, telling the Reader that by so doing he did not change his judgment of the matter. In any case the list contained no Wolverhampton name.

The clash did not come till June 1669, when Baxter was inconvienced but not silenced by the Five Mile and Conventicle Acts, and living at Acton, Middlesex, of which the Dean of Wolverhampton was Rector. John Reynolds, now practising as a doctor (his "Discourse upon . . . . . the famed Derbyshire Damosell" belongs to 1669) had a somewhat heated argument with Richard Bracegirdle, the doctor, and pillar of Wolverhampton church, during which he flung at him words to this effect: "the Non-conformists were not so contemptible for Number and Quality as he made them, that most of the people were of their mind, that Cromwell though a Usurper had kept up England against the Dutch . . . . . and that he marvelled that he would be so hot against private meetings, when at Acton the Dean suffered them at the next door".[4] Surely an indiscretion on Reynolds' part, for Bracegirdle wrote to the Dean, the Dean hurries to the King "as if it were the discovery of a Treason"; the King takes umbrage at the name of Cromwell; and Baxter undergoes a short restraint in Clerkenwell new Gaol.

1 W.A. i. 395.
2 Do.
3 A. G. Matthews, Annotated List of the Works of Ric. Baxter, pp. 2–3.
4 W.A. i., 395 — Bracegirdle v. Baxter.

The old Race-course

South side of High Green shewing High Hall *By R. Noyes.*

This incident may have suggested that obscure allusion to Gaius on Bracegirdle's monument now in the North aisle of the church. He is there declared "a steadfast son of the Church of England hostile to each extreme, so much so that Dean Bruno Ryves deservedly called him Gaius in accordance with holy writ".[1] (As to whom see the Third Epistle of John).

Tradition gives John Reynolds (who died December 1683) the credit of being the founder of Non-conformity in Wolverhampton. His name is jotted down in the Register Book of the Old Meeting House (No. 72, Stafford, in Somerset House) as the congregation's first pastor, and in the controversy of 1818 he is again referred to as "the father of this congregation of Dissenters".[2]

Difficult as was the religious position, the civil side was complicated too. There was a minority who did not approve of the new government; Cromwell's old adherents were unemployed.

At Beaudesert, near Cannock, was established Sir Brian Broughton, a magistrate and Deputy Lieutenant, who took upon himself the duty of secret service agent. His reports to the principal secretary of state, dating from 1663 are to be found among the State Papers (Domestic), but they are so illiterate that it is difficult to follow them. Besides he was jumpy and saw plots everywhere.

"Pardon the trouble of this ill pen that dare trust noe other. Immediately after my last I went to Colonel Lane to see what hee had done" . . . . . he sends the information "for feare the other miscarried" . . . . . he awaits "a more perfect discovery". The conspirators' watchword is "the sword hewes before the sythe mowes". "It is very strange there should bee so much smoke in these parts and none in others" . . . . . Three weeks since "one Renalds preached at a conventicle, a thing hee ever did when plots weere in agitation, many of the oulde souldiers and officers at it. On wenseday the 20 of this instant (May 1663, (Major Edmund) Waring, formerly governor of Shrousebery, (Henry) Stone . . . . . governor of Stafford, Backehouse Oliver's governor of Stafford . . . &c. . . . . . met at Wolverhampton market. What was their business wee know not". Their designs were chiefly carried on by drovers, and markets were their meeting places. The constables' presentments gave a list of 1128 old soldiers who had borne arms against the King; but of these only 20 were from Wolverhampton.

Again, writing on 7th November 1663, he says:—

"Sir, I sende this paper to tell (what) to my apprehention is improbable, but my informer tells me its confidently beleeved . . . . . that they have intelligence to Wolverhampton once every fortnight out of the North . . . . . (he speaks of landings in Scotland from Ireland) . . . . .

My scout hath bin in the darke by rason of a sore foote, but now hee promiseth I shall heare more which shall bee faithfully communicated by Sir

your most humble servant

B. Broughton".

In a letter of 24th June 1663, he tells of the meetings (as a justice of the peace informed him) of Backehouse, Waring, Daniell and several other officers . . . . . "at Wheelers house" in Wolverhampton every market day for six or seven weeks. "Its said that greate sommes of moneys have bin observed to bee counted there . . . . . this looks like a grande Committee of several counties", (says Broughton).

1 W.A. i., 396.
2 Congregational Magazine, i., 275.

On 8 July, he tells of more meetings in the town including Colonel Crompton (the last governor of Stafford) Captain Gent, and more strangers, at Captain Backehouse's house. "It is difficult to dive into their councills, they manage them with so great caution", he writes. An old soldier of Oliver's "is full of moneys and why a person that is so (should live in a cottage) makes mee wonder!"

The fact remains there was no rising, probably because it was never intended there should be, save by a few hotheads.[1]

The Restoration reopened the old Chancery suits conducted by the Prebendaries. Much groping in the dark produced much argument. It was the taking over of the ashes of history long extinct. Their cause was hopelessly lost in the past when the College was suppressed in the time of Edward VI. Ownership of the church lands, except for small rent-charges, then passed elsewhere. The defendant, now Robert Leveson, was a grudging and unwilling party to the proceedings, but the law was ready. In one case the Lord Chancellor said he would hear the plea at 8 o'clock in the morning (June 1663). The plaintiffs were Thomas Wren and Cesar Callandine (3 February 1663-4), prebendaries of Willenhall and Hatherton. The bill is again and again dismissed and renewed. Once (24 June 1666) the instrument of proxy by which Dr. Wren was installed prebendary of Willenhall was not forthcoming and caused him to be non-suited at the Stafford Summer Assizes, without even coming to the merits of the cause; but again he is given another chance. On another occasion they decide to try a test action of Trespass and Ejection to a piece of land called Pepper Croft, but nothing comes of it and on 22 May 1667 the Lord Chancellor ordered that the plaintiff's bill "be from henceforth clearly and absolutely dismissed out of this Court".

It had long been the custom at Wolverhampton to distribute the prebends in the proportion of 50-50 between residing and absent prebendaries. The latter were sometimes foreigners, who knew well the nature of sinecures. Here then comes Mons. Samuel de l'Angle as prebendary of Kinvaston to be installed (with the customary fee of one guinea) on 21 November 1684. He succeeded Mr. Andrew Durell of the Channel Islands, a nephew of the Dean, who had died suddenly of an apoplexy. De l'Angle had lately fled from the persecution of Protestants in France,[2] where he was famous as minister of Charenton, near Paris. Settling in England he was created D.D. at Oxford, 12 February 1682-3, and was a prebendary of Westminster until his death in 1693.

It fell to the Rev. Thomas Allestree to attend him at Wolverhampton, and he put him down for a subscription of £12 10s. 0d.—one of the highest—to the rebuilding of the Chancel. Writing the new Dean, Dr. Hascard, in November 1685, he says: "I desire you when you see Dr. de l'Angle to present my most humble service to him. I assisted him, when he was here, the best I could according to your order, and he was very kind to me". And further: "Mr. Humphrey Wyrley, who is a very worthy person, came not long since to Wolverhampton, and invited me to dine with him and some other Justices of Peace at the signe of the Cock where wee drank your worships health. I shall be very glad to see you at Wolverhampton, and the sooner you come the better, I have severall things to impart to you . . . . . " He was accustomed to preach the Dean's "Courses" at £4 per annum, which he deducted from the Dean's rents.

It is likely that the new prebendary was told on one of his visits (he was here on 10th October 1685) what a gold mine his stall could be if only the Court of Chancery would take a rosier view of his claims. For sure enough, Samuel de l'Angle, D.D., prebendary

1 A. G. Matthews.
2 S.H.C., 1915.

of Kinvaston in the Collegiate Church of Wolverhampton, filed his Bill, as plaintiff, on 25 November 1689, against Robert Leveson, esquire.

The case is peculiar.

It appears that Robert Leveson had paid him for two years but not for the last three, and owed £67 10s. 0d., and now pretended he did not hold the tithes or any part of the estate belonging to the prebend, and that he had paid the rents by mistake. The Plaintiff was in an unhappy position, having no deeds or evidence to support his case. "And the truth is", he pleaded, "that divers papers and counterparts and other writings . . . . . were in the custody . . . . . of Dr. Durell, who was uncle to the plaintiff's predecessor Dr. Durell, who managed the revenue of the prebend for his nephew, he living very remote from the same". The papers were lost and with them the plaintiff's case, unless the defendant supplied the information, and this was desired in full detail.

Just within a year, 10 November 1690, Robert Leveson filed his Answer, which starts with the year 1550. It appears that the Sequestrators during the Commonwealth had charged his father's estate with the payment of £22 per annum to the person who then enjoyed the prebend, and the defendant "being a stranger to his estate" continued the payment, not knowing but that the same might be due. Now, "having lately recovered some of his writings" he believes that he made all those payments in his own wrong. He believes the plaintiff holds the prebendal lands of Kinvaston free of any lease. But if the defendant is allowed to enjoy the tithes, he will continue with the payment of £22 per annum willingly. Samuel de l'Angle died before the case was concluded and was buried in St. Margaret's, Westminster. The son and executor, John Maximilian de l'Angle arranged for the dispute to be settled by arbitration. (Chancery Decrees and Orders, 2 May 1694). But this one prebend henceforth remained the prebendary's own estate.

Soon after the accession of James II in 1685, the town became the headquarters of the College of St. Chad. The atmosphere favoured the old religion, and quarters were available of the best. The Fathers had in fact taken over the large house known as the Deanery Hall, owned then by Thomas, Lord Windsor as tenant of the Dean of Wolverhampton. It was, says a contemporary account,[1] "one of the most pleasant and convenient in the whole town", its extensive gardens, surrounded by a high wall, opened out upon the fields and a "delightful country'.' In the house was a spacious chapel, which was well attended and a large school, where the Fathers taught nearly 50 children out of the town (of which 12 were convictors, or boarders). The scholars were soon able to compete with the students of the older protestant schools and to carry off the palm in "disputations".

It will be remembered that the intended President of Magdalen College, Oxford, was a Wolverhampton man, Bonaventure Giffard.[2]

But all this prosperity was short-lived, as it was bound to be for an unpopular minority. Soon after the landing of the Prince of Orange in November 1688, all was upset. A "riotous mob" . . . . . "destroyed everything with fire and sword". The Constables' accounts significantly touch upon this:—[3]

		s.	d.
1688—9, 23 December	Paid a Messenger to High Constable Hall's "to warn in the Militia Horse"	1	0
7 January	Paid a Messenger to fetch the Coroner from Kidderminster to sit upon the men killed at the Chappel	1	4
	Paid for summoning the Jurymen from Willenhall and Wednesfield		8
	Paid for Ale for the Coroner and the Jewry (sic)	3	0
	Paid William Persehouse (mercer) "for pouther & torches at the Rising"	9	2

1 The "Annual Letters" for the years 1685–90, cited Foley, V.450 & 420.
2 For an account of whom, *vide* Oxford Hist. Soc. trans.
3 See for this valuable source W.A. ii.

The Roman Catholic account mentioned continues:

"We have made a calculation of the damage done to us, enumerating singly our special losses; the altar, altar rails, pulpit (which was quite a work of art) have been either destroyed or applied to profane uses. The greater portion of our library which was well stocked, was burnt in the market place. The schools were demolished (the houses we rented of the Earl of Plymouth were through fear left untouched), the benches, reading desk, chairs, the ornamental woodwork, framed after the model of our continental schools, also the entire household furniture—all was either plundered by the mob, or appropriated by the Commissioners who were sent. These, however, we do not despair of recovering in due time. But the sacred furniture, including chalices, vestments, ornaments of the altar, &c. were saved. The Superior, with another of the Fathers, was compelled to fly into Lancashire in order to avoid the fury of the populace and the iniquity of the times, to which both, had they remained, would certainly have fallen victims. After their flight the rage of the mob increased, and they threatened extreme measures. Another of the Fathers, in his attempt to escape, was less fortunate, being seized on the road and at once thrown into Stafford Gaol, where he remained for a year. He was then removed by writ of Habeas Corpus to London, and discharged by order of the judges. The Superior, after a six months' retirement in Lancashire, has returned to his College and set about collecting the scattered fragments of the wreck, to prevent their utter loss".

There was hope of some restoration; but the mission and schools came to an end. The wreck caused by the Revolution on Roman Catholic hopes was extensive, and in 1701 only four Fathers worked this Midland district.

The reign of James II ended in a period of alarms and excursions.

William III landed at Brixham in November 1688, while James took boat below London Bridge, and Lord Chancellor Jeffreys was taken in disguise at Wapping.

In London there was Interregnum and uncertainty, from 12 December 1688 to 12 February 1689; at Wolverhampton, the local magistrates were stirred into uncertain activity. Of these there was only Robert Leveson, father of the Colonel of Dragoons, on the spot; but Sir Henry Gough was at hand and very old Sir John Wyrley at no great distance. There was Squire (John) Chetwynd at Stafford and Squire Gray at Enville. Foremost was Edward, Lord Ward, at Himley.

But a "glorious Revolution" even of the mildest and launched among the warlike must cause anxiety.

The accounts of the two Constables, Thomas Loxdale and Michael Brown, as we have seen, drop significant hints.

On 30 December and later, a number of soldiers are found quarters on their way South "to the Prince of Orange", while on 19 January a guide is provided for a body of Lord Delamer's troops proceeding to Stafford.[1]

At home remained Robert Leveson after the Order summoning the Convention Parliament was "published" at Wolverhampton on 18 January—two days later than in London. Justices Gough, Chetwynd, Grey and Ward were members of this Parliament, all Tories, and the first three distinguished themselves by voting that the throne was NOT vacant.[2]

Leveson was a protestant and content to become a whig, having seen his family's wealth dispersed on lost causes and every evidence (as in his ruinous Old Hall) that it

1 See D.N.B. He was son of 1st Lord D. who, as Geo. Booth, was one of Cromwell's presbyterians who went to welcome Chas. II. The son, who became E. of Warrington, was a Whig, but a relation by marriage with the families of Grey and Ward, who were Tories.
2 S.H.C. 1922.

did not pay. He was the last of his line. He ordered the proclamation of the King with such military display as the Trained Bands afforded.

The new High Sheriff was proclaimed on 3 May; the Coronation was celebrated not without evidence of good cheer on 26 May. That is as much as we are allowed to see of Wolverhampton's part in the Revolution.

The Constables so touch upon this in their Accounts:—

		£	s.	d.
1689 April 11	Paid William Allison (of the Swan) for 12 bottles of wine and two of sack (at the Coronation)		16	0
1689 May 26	Paid my mother-in-law (Mrs. Pountney of the George) for a half hogshead of Ale which was dranke at the Coronation of King William		10	0
1689 May 3	Paid William Hollier (of the Cock) for wine at Proclaiming of King William	1	14	0
	Paid for Ale at the proclaiming the High Sheriff (William Cotton in place of Francis Eld)		2	0

One of the most frequent entries at this time is in connection with soldiers whether disbanded (with passes) or deserters (which meant "hues and cryes" at 3d. each), or "poor soldiers", or quarters for the sick. (A sick officer is carried to Stafford by means of two horses—20 April 1689—a soldier's cost is 4d. a night, or with small pox, 7d.). In short, there is an endless ragged stream of broken men, heroes perhaps, passing through the town, and paid to do so, to their homes and kindred, and the Irishman, who is "distressed", is also found (3 October 1689).

It is very noticeable what a great horror each parish or community had of paying money to those of other parishes, the unthrifty traveller, the migrant, the woman with child: all regarded as a waste of hard earned income and no concern of theirs. This is abundantly clear from a slight acquaintance with any parish or constable's accounts before modern times. Pauperism must be discouraged or at least marked where it existed. The days of branding were lessening but paupers wore a badge, and in the Bilston Constable & Chapelwarden accounts for 1704 there is the entry:

"for setting ye Badges upon 8 persons 1.4"[1]

It is not a distinction that appeals to us now; we have advanced in some ways since Queen Anne.

On the other hand the practice of the leading townsmen of drinking and entertaining with drink at the public charge was of frequent occurrence, especially at times of rejoicing. An entry which we find at regular intervals is that of "wine, sack and bisket to treate the Judge and his retinue" (17 July 1689). It only too frequently happened that the town was not disinterested, having made an unhappy contribution to the same assizes which had been sent ahead for its better custody.

The Oxford circuit then worked in a different direction, and the judges arrived from Worcester, to be met here by one of the bailiffs (if a later practice was followed) who guided them to Stafford where the Sheriff met them at Moss Pits. It is a question whether the road was generally fitted for a coach in the time of Queen Anne, or until the Turnpike Trusts improved it. So the "judges" then meant a cavalcade on horse-back (like Queen Elizabeth in her day and Celia Fiennes on her side saddle at this very time—about 1690).

1 Register, Vol. III.

DR. ROBERT PLOT'S IMPRESSION OF WOLVERHAMPTON AT THIS PERIOD.

Dr. Robert Plot, Keeper of the Ashmolean Museum and Professor of Chymistry in the University of Oxford, dedicates his "Natural History of Staffordshire" to King James II in 1686. It is a work of "great Industry and Charge", finished by 1680; not a guide-book, but an account of such things, and they were many, as struck him as wonderful. He would have stayed at Wolverhampton, that is likely enough, and it is likely too that he stayed with the Normansells of the High Hall on High Green (the Tudor house whose removal in 1841 was regarded as a great and good clearance) for not only did he admire Mrs. Rebecca Normansell's scissor work,[1] but he obtained her son, Richard Normansell, as a subscriber. There is entered on the Map, as some return, the family coat-of-arms (properly those of Normanville) as one of the six who being natives were "gentry with no seat in Staffordshire".

Dr. Plot found the town's origin "very uncertain", yet made some serious attempt to unveil the past by using the chronicles of the realm which were to some extent in print. So he had read of the Battle of Tettenhall, of Wulfrun the Saxon (the wrong one), and of Peter of Blois' troubles here in the time of King John.

He noticed the shortage of water, which was fetched from the springs "in great leather Budgets" on horses in the mediaeval manner. He found the town's high position made it healthy in spite of "fumes" from the coal mines. This healthiness was proved, he suggests, by the fact that they suffered the plague seldom, but the small-pox frequently "both signs of salubrity" in his opinion.[2]

Certainly iron-working had made some strides in this century. He found the art of Lock making to be far advanced towards perfection; and yet until this time it had met with little or no notice. How the trade started in Wolverhampton and at what date, are matters which sadly await evidence. The method of hardening iron to suit it for polishing (by covering it with a nitrogenous mixture) tickled his chemical fancy.[3] The pranks of Thomas Wall entertained him, for he could bend large nails or tenterhooks between his teeth, being blessed with "incisores" of unusual thickness.

A lunar Iris (rainbow) seen at Tunstall in October 1678 by Mr. Francis and Mr. John Wightwick was reported to him. Sulphur waters found at Monmore Green near the town were duly noted. He tells us indeed that among the springs that would not answer to his experiments, "but nevertheless had some virtue whereby they perform unaccountable cures", was that "in a narrow lane about midway betwixt Wolverhampton and a house call Sea-wall, which was anciently of such repute that it still retains the name of the Spaw". This was the house of that "ingenious and most oblieging Gent., Mr. John Huntbach" (of Fetherstone) another of the local subscribers.

Dr. Plot disliked the peal of bells, then numbering seven, and points out however they were rung the sound could "never be gratefull". He was not impressed with the Deanery, saying merely "there yet remains some umbrage of a Dean and Prebends here to this very day".

It hardly does the position justice, for at this time, 1680, there emerges a new feature in the three "Readers". These were in fact a kind of curate, to be abolished by the Act of 1811 (which appointed a Perpetual Curate). Whether they grew out of the Lecturers

1 Plot, Nat. Hist. Staffs., IX, 100.
2 Do. II, 12.
3 Plot, Nat. Hist. IX, 73.

(those paid to preach and do nothing more, popular to the "low" churchmen) there is not the evidence to show. The tithes of Wolverhampton were subject by prescription, and probably by express grant, to the payment of £12 annually to the Choir of the Church.[1] They appear in the parish register as "singing men".

THE FIRE OF 1696.

But 10 years after Plot published his "Natural History", rural Wolverhampton was wiped out by a fire which began in Barn Street (Salop Street). This was on 10th September 1696, and the testimony of the Rev. Mr. Ames of Bilston is of interest:[2]

Thus, 1696 September 10. "On which same day about 4 of the Clock, afternoon, there happen'd a Sad and Lamentable Fire in Barn-Street . . . . by which the general part of Barn-Street, and almost all Boblake was laid in Ashes, the wind being at that time very high. It was said to be occasioned by some Harvest-Hay in the Barn of (one) Stych, which took fire it being ill gotten in."

Within 5 hours over 60 dwelling houses, 60 bays of barns full of corn, stables and other buildings, the possessions of over 80 inhabitants were consumed by the flames. It was estimated that the loss amounted to £8,680 in value, and the blow was heavy as modern insurance was unknown.

The magistrates at Quarter Sessions petitioned His Majesty for a licence under the Great Seal to ask for contributions and benevolence from all well wishers. Such documents are rarely preserved, as they were intended to be returned, with the money collected. Notes of small sums of money from far distant churches can doubtless be found when occasion allows. The contribution of Bilston on this occasion was a record, £10, their usual collections being often under 2/-.[3]

The Constables accounts notice the Fire mainly by payments for Ale drunk but a move to buy a Fire-Engine with 24 buckets was set on foot and brought to a conclusion by September 1703.

CHURCH AND CHAPEL AGAIN: THE 1696 ASSOCIATION ROLL. MR. AMES & CHURCHGOING. THE CHAPEL IN JOHN STREET.

Thomas Allestree, M.A., who appears as "Minister" in 1676, has left several reminders of his existence and activities. His claim at his death at Hamstall Ridware (vide his monument) on 30th June 1715, aged 77, to have composed 500 sermons and to have preached 5,000 times is not without printed testimony. He published "A Funeral Handkerchief" while Rector of Ashow, Warwickshire, in 1670, and dedicated it "To the Right Honourable Thomas Lord Leigh, Baron of Stoneleigh, his singular good Lord and Patron", who had, we learn, a "smiling countenance" for his new domestic chaplain.

"When a Friend", he begins, "is going a long Journey, it is a commendable piece of civility to go with him some part of the way, and to weep at parting . . . So when our Friends depart and go to their long home, from whence they shall never return till time shall be no more, is it not good manners to accompany them to the Grave, and shed some tears for them, whom we shall see no more with mortal eyes?"

It is a pleasant introduction to the 300 pages which follow, and as "A Posy is not cast away because made up of several Flowers", Mr. Allestree adds "Three Sermons Preached at Coventry". The book was re-issued with a new title-page in 1692, which in the prevailing taste of the time is adorned with skulls and other emblems to encourage a hesitant buyer.

1 G.R. tithe map.
2 Lawley, Hist. of Bilston, p. 59. Printed Register of Bilston, p. 15.
3 S.H.C. 1938, 224.

When he signs the Association Oath Roll in 1696, Mr. Allestree starts a new membrane or sheet, calling himself "preaching minister at the Collegiat Church of Wolverhampton". Henry Bracegirdle comes next as "Sacrist", followed by J. Bailye, the curate. Then comes John Hillman, "usher of the school of W'Hampton", and Nath. Mansfield "Preacher", who was non-conformist minister at Walsall. Afterwards came Nath(aniel) Lawrence who was Presbyterian minister here from 1692. Conspicuous in his absence is the head-master. The town paid Mr. Unett, the book-seller, 2/- for "Parchment for the Association", in June 1696, and 6d. "for a List of the Papists and those that would not signe the Association". It may be that the Rev. John Plymley, the headmaster, preferred this list, but this point has not been pursued. Mr. Plymley was one of our unsuccessful headmasters, and had to be dismissed in 1710, being old beyond his years and doing so little work that "many of the schollars have themselves complained that they had more hours of play than of learning", though "tender of doing the Master any Injury".[1] He continued as one of the prebendaries of the Church till his death in 1734.

The Association Oath Roll itself as it concerns the town[2] is a useful check upon the inhabitants and lends itself to study. There are about 1026 names. They cannot all be signatures, for many could not write. It is clear that father and son (or sons) in numerous cases signed together.

It should be mentioned that the Oaths originated in plots in favour of the exiled monarch brewed in Lancashire in 1694. The Queen died at the end of that year, and the King's life was threatened in 1695. A revolt of feeling in favour of the King followed, and he made the most of the situation and carried the country with him. The voting for Association in the "House" was 400 against 113. They realised that[3] "the welfare and safety of this Kingdom and the Reformed Religion do next under God intirely depend upon the Preservation of Your Majesties Royal Person and Government . . . . . ". The exiled James was, in fact, at Calais waiting to take charge of the French Fleet.

Attendance at church in the time of Queen Anne was a duty which was very generally practised. The law was on its side, and one kept on the side of authority by going to church. If a person was not considered worthy there were ways towards forgiveness. The official process of the church did much to direct the proper use of men's lives. For instance, in 1694, the Bilston Chapel accounts preserve the entry "To Mr. Allestree for ye Fast Booke and Proclamation . . . . . 1 3d. "which evidently refers to the power entrusted to Mr. Allestree as "Official acting for the Dean[4] of granting licences to the needy for eating flesh during Lent, a custom with many centuries of use behind it, and still, it seems, being regulated.

That morals were not neglected some entries by Mr. Ames in his parish register amply show. It followed a similar process of legal authorization.

8 Feb. 1718-9 (penitance of a Wednesfield woman in Bilston) "by vertue of a schedule of pennance from Mr. John Hillman Official".

The victim stood before the congregation holding a white wand and wearing a white sheet (provided by the parish).

1 Hist. of W'ton. School, by the author, 1913, p. 175.
2 P.R.O. Petty Bag. C213/258.
3 Preamble.
4 S.H.C. 1915, p. 333.

8 March 1719-20 (Another case). "She appear'd by her much weeping to be truly penitent".

5 May 1723 (A woman) "did publick pennance" at Bilston; it "being injoyn'd her by Rev. John Hilton LLB. Official of Wolverhampton".

Sunday Feb. 7 1724-5, a woman did penance "enjoined by Mr. Craddock ye Official".

12 June 1726 (A youth) "apprentice to Amos Parkes of Bilston did publick pennance . . . . . enjoyned by ye Rev. William Cradock A.M. principal Official, dated 9 June. Note I have certify'd it", wrote Mr. Ames.[1]

And finally, 3 Dec. 1727 (A woman) "of this town Spinster (by vertue of a processe out of Wolverhampton Court from Mr. Cradock Official and E. Short, Registrar) was Denounc'd Excommunicate for Contumacy in not appearing. I doubt (adds Mr. Ames) she is a vitious woman, She haveing had Two Bastards".[2]

CONFIRMATIONS.

Difficulty of transport was the main hindrance to a regular course of Confirmation, and this led to lapses of many years and huge accumulations of candidates. When the bishops did appear they took it in their stride.

In 1722 Bishop Chandler of Lichfield came to Wolverhampton with that object—the town, as he reported to Archbishop Wake, "being very populous and without confirmation these twenty-seven years, will afford business for two or three days".[3]

Let Mr. Ames also take up his pen.

"July 8, 1722. Dr. Edward Chandler Lord Bishop of Coventry and Lichfield preach'd at Wolverhampton in ye morning and his chaplain (Mr. Millward) in ye afternoon. The Bp. confirm'd in ye afternoon & likewise on Monday, on which day he was treated att the Cock att the Publick Charge. The Prebendaries then Attending were Rich'd Ames (myself) Prebendary of Monmore. Mr. Tho: Hall Prebendary of Hilton & Mr. Craddock prebendary of Hatherton. Mr. John Hilton, Prebendary of Willenhall was then Ill of ye gout and could not Attend".[4]

But it seems that the Bishop was wrong in his calculation for (as Mr. Ames reports) "Dr. John Hough . . . . . did preache and Confirme att Wolverhampton, being Requested so to do by Mr. Henry Wood in the name of the Deane & prebendaries of ye Collegiate Church . . . . . " on 6 August 1706.

On 13 August 1727, being the 11th Sunday after Trinity, Dr. Edward Chandler returned and, in the afternoon, preached the Charity Sermon and Confirmed. "He also Confirm'd (says Mr. Ames) after Sermon in ye Morning. It happened to be my course then and I preached upon Psal. 76, 11, and dined with his Lordship att Mr. John Hayes's".[5]

It was when the Bishop was at Walsall confirming in June 1726, that John Lane, senior, Esquire of Bentley, "moved his Lordship to Consecrate Willenhall and Bilston Chapel-yards for Burial places, which (writes Ames) his Lordship seemed inclinable to do.[6] The Mayor of Walsall treated his Lordship and the Company then present".

The need for this was a grievance of long standing, and was a matter of fees. When burials took place at Wolverhampton, the mother church, fees were forthcoming; but when the chapelries could bury their own dead, what happened? Wolverhampton was clear there must be double fees. On that rock the question stuck.

1 Reg'r., p. 93.
2 Ib., p. 104.
3 Sykes, Church & State in England in 18th c. Vide also: Ames' Register, p. 119–20.
4 Bilston P.R. (printed), p. 77.
5 Steward of the Manor.
6 Ibid., p. 93.

The Wolverhampton Chapter debated this at Oxford on 17 August 1709. There was a full attendance under the dean, Dr. Thomas Manningham, except that Mr. Allestree was represented by Proxy. Certain orders were made which controlled their own actions.

(1). That the Prebendaries shall preach their courses as often as conveniently they may, and such persons only shall preach for them as shall be approved by the residing Prebendaries: That a Table of their Preaching courses shall be made and hung up in the Chapter house of the Collegiate Church of Wolverhampton. That the course shall begin on the first Sunday after Michaelmas next, the Dean to begin the course and the several Prebendaries to follow according to the priority of their Stalls.

(2). It is resolved by the said Dean and Chapter that the Cure of Souls and visiting the sick doth under them appertain to the Sacrist, and that all future Sacrists shall at their admission into the said office undertake the same and shall be obliged to perpetual residence, unless dispensed with the Dean. But in regard the present sacrist Mr. Henry Wood (also Rector of Aldridge, d. 1718) was not apprized of this duty at the time of his admission into the said Office, the said Chapter do content themselves with his solemn promise made to the Dean, that upon application made to him for any persons that is sick, he will look upon himself obliged to visit such sick person, during the time of his residence at Wolverhampton.

(3). Resolved that in case the Inhabitants of Wolverhampton shall desire to Erect a Gallery in the Parish Church of Wolverhampton the Licence of the Dean and Chapter shall be sufficient for their so doing, the occupiers of the seats therein keeping the Gallery in repair.

(4). Ordered that the three Curates of the said Church upon application made to them shall be obliged to visit any sick person in the said parish.

(5). Whereas it has been represented to us by the Inhabitants of the Chapelries of Bilston and Willenhall that several Inconveniences frequently happen on the account of Carrying the Dead within the said Chapelries to be interred at Wolverhampton, and are desirous to have the Chapels and Chapel yards. . . . to be consecrated in order to the burial of their Dead therein: the Dean and Chapter have here unto given their consent provided the Inhabitants of the Chapelries aforesaid shall at all times hereafter pay the Customary Levies to the Mother Church and likewise pay the burial Fees to the curates of the said Chapels as well as to the curates of the Mother Church and also shall defray the charge of the Consecration.

It is the resolution of the said Chapter that for the future no double fees shall be demanded for Marriages and that the curates shall pay a constant attendance on Divine Service unless sufficient reason be given for their absence and that if any one offend in any of the aforesaid particulars he shall be subject to such censure as the ordinary (that is, the Dean or his "Official" or Chancellor for him) shall think fit.

(*Signed by*) Tho: Maningham Dean of Windsor and Wolverhampton.
Richd. Redding Preb: of Kinvaston.
John Plymley Preb: of Fetherstone.
Richd. Ames Preb: of Monmore.
Henry Wood, Sacrist.

In passing, it should perhaps be mentioned that Ames' own great day came on 14 August 1727, when the consecration at Bilston was carried out. He describes this at some length in his Register (at p. 229). The "Act of Consecration" was read, in Latin, by Mr. Edward Short, the Wolverhampton Registrar. As well as Ames, Mr. Cradock and Mr. Jesson, prebendaries of Wolverhampton, were present. We also read the names of Mr. Daubrie (headmaster of the Grammar School); Mr. Downes (his Usher); and Mr. Possu, a Swiss, (his "Assister").

On the same day the consecration at Willenhall took place.[1]

THE CHAPEL IN JOHN STREET, WOLVERHAMPTON.

The epoch of chapel-building followed the Toleration Act of 1689. Then meetings of Protestant bodies (not Unitarians) for worship, were legalised and the building of

1 This account is to be found in Bilston Parish Register printed by Staffs Par Register Soc. and "History of Willenhall" by N. W. Tildesley.

meeting-houses allowed. Within the next 30 years over 4,000 of these were in use. Wolverhampton lagged somewhat in this enterprise, but before the close of the century, two ministers, Daniel Greenwood and Nathaniel Lawrence, had contrived to eke out a rather lean existence here. There was room for more strenuous endeavour, and on 18 September 1701, John Russell conveyed the land on which the Meeting House in John's Lane was built, for £10 to Joseph Turton, senior, Thomas Sutton, John Scott and Abraham Pearson —good Presbyterians all! The chapel dates from that time.

It did not stand unscarred and in peace and quiet, but became rather a centre of storm and resistance.

The death of Queen Anne brought politics again to the front. The powder was there for an explosion if a suitable spark was found to set it off. Mr. Thomas Story, Quaker from America, had on 20 May 1715 a successful meeting at Wolverhampton, and departed well pleased towards stormy scenes at Oxford.[1]

The annual Fair altered this. Squire Archibald Grosvenor was, as his epitaph remarks, when a military officer, active, brave and honourable, and when a civil magistrate, just, ready and impartial.[2]

On Wednesday evening, 29 June, the day of the Fair, he and his friends while in a public house, heard in another room "some old seditious song", and the singer who refused to be quiet and shouted "Down with the Roundheads" was put in "the crib or stone house".

Mr. Grosvenor tried to stop a rescue by "drawing his sword and with it hurting one or two that were about the crib: the Mob was enraged and in all likelihood had killed Mr. Grosvenor had he not made his escape".

Immediately the rabble ran down into John's Lane "and very much defaced the Presbyterian meeting-house there". The proceedings were opened by an address from the roof, where the ring-leader called for cheers for King James III. To the mob, "a gang of ragamuffins, pick-pockets and Gaol birds", he cried "Fall on, boys", and they fell on with a will. Seats and moveables were carried off to burn in the market place, thus endangering the town; but the destruction at the chapel must have been more than this, as the later depositions show.

Mr. Stubbs, the minister, for his safety was hurried out of the town, and a guard of 20 to 30 men set that night before his house.

Mr. John Scott's house, higher up the street, was also threatened: "he is very rich and a non-conformist",[3] says the newspaper account. Samuel Clemson's house, next door, must have been badly wrecked; it was the only house singled out for special compensation.

The number of persons punished for this rioting was not very large. The heaviest sentence was passed on John Wild—two years' imprisonment and "to be whipped twice round the Town Hall at Stafford for rioting at Wolverhampton and West Bromwich". Lives of his more famous brother, Jonathan, say he was a "public officer" or "Cryer" in Wolverhampton—otherwise a "catchpoll" (bum-bailiff), and we meet with his name so employed in the Constables accounts.

1 W.A. i., 165.
2 Plant, 83.
3 W.A. i., 29.

Authority was slow in taking action, and it was towards the end of July before Dragoons appeared and quiet was restored.

The Nonconformists were identified with the Whig ministry which bringing the accession of George I was unpopular with the Tories. A contemporary view of the situation is given in a letter of Richard Ames, curate of Bilston, to William Ward, one of the County members (and Ames' old pupil), which was read before the House of Commons on 16 July, 1715.[1]

The performance of the Wolverhampton Mob, he points out, was followed by the demolishing of the Presbyterian Meeting-houses at Stafford and Walsall "and ('tis said) at Stone and Longdon: yesterday a Parcel of the Wolverhampton Folks set forth in order to attack (West) Bromwich Meeting-house: These People took Bilston, Darlaston and Wednesbury, in the Way; so that there were a great number: But the Dissenters having Notice of what was intended, came together in great Numbers, Horse and Foot, furnished with Guns, Swords, &c. and attacked the Rioters, and drove 'um off; several of whom they have wounded . . . . . The Truth of it is, there is no such thing as appeasing 'um with good words; and, I think, to cure it by Force will be but an uncomfortable Matter. As far as I can learn, these poor Fellows have got a Notion, that the Ministry and Dissenters have ruined Trade, on purpose to make the Nation out of Love with the late Peace (of Utrecht in 1713) and Peacemakers . . . . . Hunger, and Want of Sleep, perhaps, may tame 'um in a little while; but, if Things don't mend in a little time, Parishes may be burthened with their Families . . . . . "

After order was restored, in response to a petition from the House of Commons, the King, on 20 September, 1716, appointed Commissioners (including Archibald Grosvenor) to inquire into the damages which any of His Majesty's Protestant Subjects in the County had sustained between his accession and 1 August, 1715, in buildings and goods by reason of the riots. The depositions still exist.[2]

John Wylde, of Wolverhampton, Carpenter, aged 44, deposed that on 29 June, 1715, and some days following rioters had pulled down the chapel and burnt the premises, and that it would cost £254 : 16 : 2d. to rebuild and refurnish. Edward Pagett, of the same, mason, aged 31, deposed to the same effect.

Samuel Clemson, of the same, currier, aged 33, deposed that on 11 July, 1715, a great number of rioters attacked his house, being his inheritance, broke the windows, flung great stones and pieces of timber into the house. threw down the pewter from the shelves, wounded and bruised the deponent and his wife, and threatened his life so that he was forced to keep a number of armed men in the house for a fortnight. Damages were estimated at £20.[3]

The damages for the County were £1,722 : 17 : 8d. (the highest). The total for the whole country was £5,580 : 4 : 7½d.[4]

Old Sir Henry Gough wrote to his son from Perry Hall where he was snowed up:—

"This weather almost kills me, and impoverishes the country to that degree, that, if it continue, it will ruin many families, and destroy abundance of creatures. It seems a just judgment on the mob, for their wantonness and wickedness in raising such tumults amongst us. I cannot but pity many of the poor and

1 A discovery of A.G. Matthews, who prints it, as from Commons' Journals, XVIII, 227 in Trans. of Congreg. Hist. Soc. Vol. XII, no. 1, p.6 (April 1933).
2 PR.O. – copied by Matthews, ibid., 7–9.
3 Cong. Hist. Soc. XII. 1, 9.
4 Matthews, op. cit., p. 128.

ignorant, but wish the first promoters were well known and punished. Many (women especially) continue insolent and foolish in their talk, but a little time perhaps may calm them. We are much easier than we have been hereabouts. We must be content to pay for our disorders. God grant the Rebels may be everywhere suppressed, and the King and Government no more forced to extremity, which must be when no other method will do."

EDWARD ELWALL.

The town had its full share of eccentrics and of these Edward Elwall was conspicuous. He was born, it appears, at Ettingshall. His baptism, Edward son of Thomas and Elizabeth Elwall of Ettingshall, nailor, took place at Sedgley on 9 November, 1676. He himself claimed that his ancestors had lived at Wolverhampton "above eleven hundred years, ever since the Saxons conquered the Britons", and he certainly lived here for many years, serving the office of Constable in 1709-10 (the accounts show his signature), and being a grocer and mercer, and successful in trade. He built with his savings seven brick houses off the Dudley Road, on the boundary of St. John's parish, which were known as "Elwall's Buildings" while they stood. They are now forgotten or demolished.

Dr. Johnson said that Mr. Elwall failed in his scheme of making himself a man of great consequence; but the fact that the Doctor had once dined with him and twice was drawn to refer to him in Boswell's presence, had added to his glory.

It was when he turned to religion that he lost his mental balance and showed that marked eccentricity which made him famous. Once a member of Mr. Stubb's flock in the John's Street Chapel, when he ceased to be a Trinitarian, he drew the minister's preaching against him. After an argument with the Archbishop of Canterbury (Wake), he became a convinced Unitarian and Sabbatarian with a leaning towards the Quakers—in fact, an "Elwallian", and acted the part by growing a long beard and assuming the flowing garments of the East. Undiscerning people thought him a Jew.

From 1724 he issued several tracts of an impudent and abusive nature, defending the first and fourth commandments. These are interesting as the first fruits of the Wolverhampton press, and they quickly ran into other editions printed in London. They caused considerable annoyance to the clergy and those not of his mind.

It was thus on the subject of toleration that Boswell was able to twit Dr. Johnson with "his countryman Elwall". Johnson replied: "My countryman, Elwall, sir, should have been put in the stocks—a proper pulpit for him: and he'd have had a numerous audience. A man who preaches in the stocks will always have hearers enough".

Elwall was often threatened and sometimes attacked by ruffians of the neighbourhood; others wished to send him to prison. But the magistrates were not unfriendly to him. At length the clergy, especially those of Wolverhampton, procurred an indictment against him for heresy and blasphemy at the Stafford Assizes before Mr. Justice Denton in 1726. The Judge allowed him to address the Court for about three-quarters of an hour, feeling perhaps helpless where the Archbishop of Canterbury had failed, and on evidence of good character quashed the case. Thus Elwall was able to print "The Triumph of Truth", being an account of the trial, which subsequently, 1772 and 1783, was reissued by Joseph Priestly as a Unitarian text book. Another edition appeared so late as 1817.

THE BACHE PEDIGREE

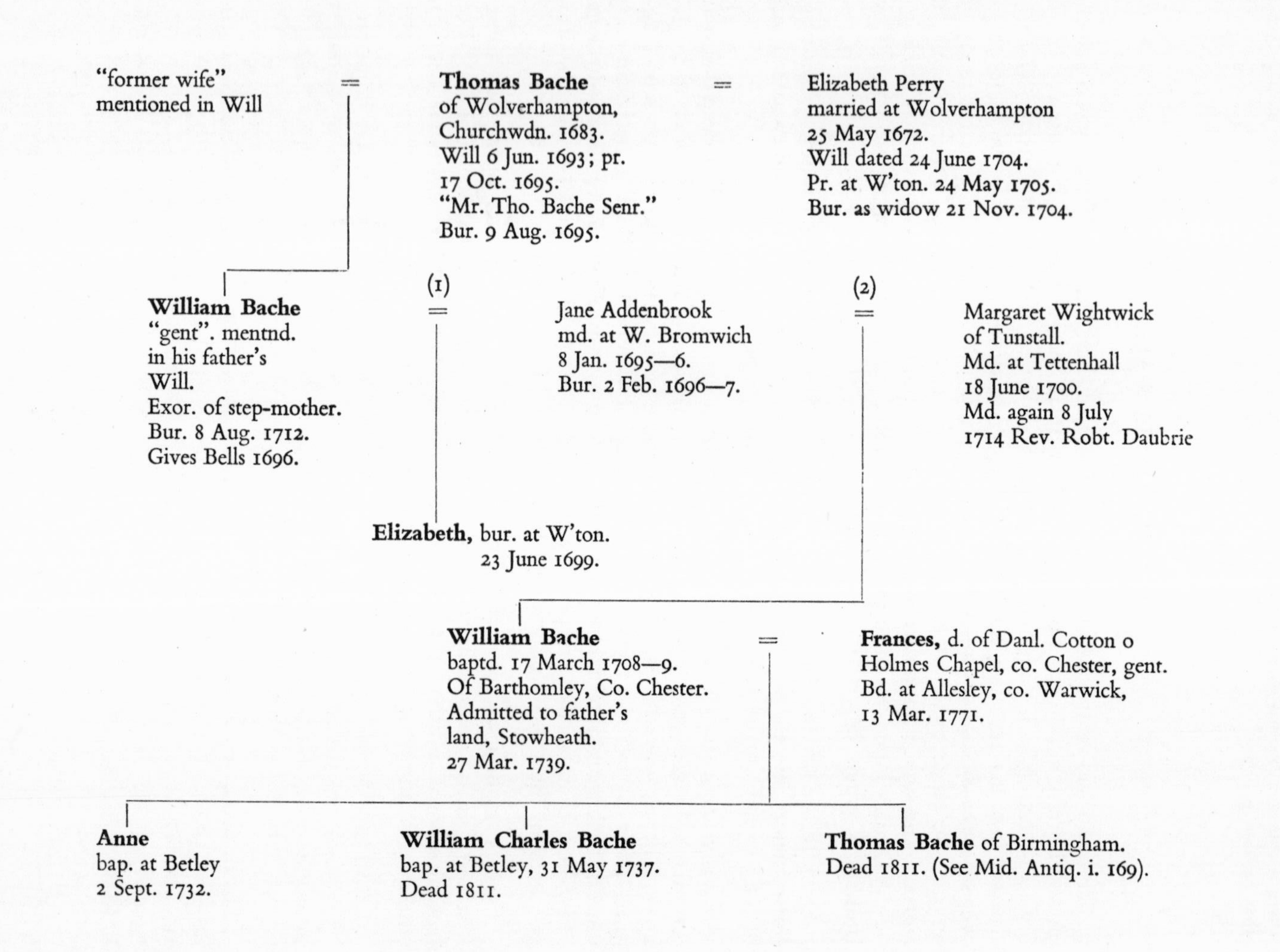

SOME OTHER WOLVERHAMPTON MEN OF THE PERIOD:
William Bache and the first Steam Engine in Wolverhampton.
Joseph Turton, Ironmonger.
William Wood, Ironmonger.

WILLIAM BACHE.

It is now generally recognised that William Bache of Wolverhampton fixed the first steam engine to raise any quantity of water at Wolverhampton.

That was in March 1712, a date to put in our diaries for annual celebration. That he died in August of the same year possibly hindered greater contemporary recognition. His father, Thomas Bache, descended from a family of that name at Penn, was churchwarden here in 1683 and died in 1695. The son signs the Association Oath Roll "Will:Bache", in a prominent position, and the statement "Wm. Bache Gent. gave 12 pound towards casting us 1698" appeared on bell number 9 in St. Peter's Church.[1]

His son, William Bache, born in 1709, is styled Ironmaster when he succeeds to land in Stowheath in April 1739. He was living at Doddlespool House in Barthomley parish on the North West county border near the furnaces of Heely Castle in 1733, and his children were born there.

There are about the year 1700 quite a number of prominent names of those called "Ironmongers", an earlier form of "Ironmaster" such as William Bache was. Edward Sheldon, Richard Molineux, William Stokes, William Wood, Joseph Turton (and family), John, father of Edward Pearson, and several others may be included in this category. Joseph Turton and William Wood need some further remarks.

JOSEPH TURTON.

Joseph Turton, ironmonger, was drawn to Wolverhampton from Rowley Regis, where he was a member of a family of "ironmongers", and was baptised in 1641.

He had certainly settled in Wolverhampton by 1666, where he followed the family trade, and issued his brass ½d. token in 1670. For this he can never be forgotten. His trade was continued by his sons, Joseph, Benjamin and (probably) Thomas. He was churchwarden in 1681, and his children were baptised at the Collegiate Church up to 1685. He was High Constable for the Hundred in 1690. As Joseph Turton, senior, he was one of the first trustees of the Presbyterian Chapel or Meeting House, and his son followed him in this belief. He died in November 1709.

The second Joseph Turton (1671-1729) who prospered in trade is styled in the Parish Register "Iron Factor". It is not quite clear whether he or his father purchased (about the end of the 17th century) the Old Hall on Snow Hill, then ruinous, and restored it in the fashion of the day, by inserting sash windows and removing the upper storey. He may have taken up residence on his marriage (January 17th, 1694-5) with Ann Clemson, a sister of Samuel Clemson, the ardent non-conformist of John's Street; in which event Dr. John Turton, his son (1700-1764) was born here, as was his grandson, John Turton (1735-1806), Physician in Ordinary to the King and Prince of Wales.

The Hall was licensed in 1715 as a place of worship under the Toleration Act,[2] doubtless as a temporary refuge for the congregation ousted from their place of worship during the Riots. Under this family the house became known as Turton's Hall ("Mr. Turton's",

1 W.A. ii, 46.
2 Matthews, p. 126.

it is called in the Constables' Accounts for 1718), and continued to be so described long after it had again changed hands—in fact, to the end of its days, 1883. A photograph of it in its last state is preserved in Wolverhampton Public Library.

WILLIAM WOOD.

William Wood was born on 31st July, 1671, and baptized at Wolverhampton on 10th August of that year. His father, Francis Wood (d. 1721) was a silkweaver; his mother was Mary Granger, daughter of Hugh and Isabel Granger, a notable family of Bellows-makers.

Hitherto, William Wood's wife, whom he married on 22nd February 1690, when under-age, has been described as "Mary Molyneux of Witton Hall".(D.N.B.). Actually, this is a mistake, due to a mis-reading of the family handwriting, for *Margaret* Molineux of *Willenhall*. It is a matter of some importance, as her brother John, and half-brother Daniel Molyneux, ironmongers, set up in business in Meath Street and Essex Street, Dublin, and were involved in the troubles there. They were children of Richard Molineux of Willenhall, who died in 1724.[1]

Twelve of William Wood's 15 children, appearing from 1692 to 1714, lived to grow up and become a proud, if crowded, exhibit in the family pew in church. In the register the father is described as "Chapman", "Iron-monger", "Iron Factor". He is said to have owned large copper and iron works in the west of England, and to have had a lease of mines upon Crown properties in thirty-nine counties of England and Wales. Undoubtedly at times he was prosperous. At Wolverhampton he lived at the Deanery, and when he left it for Hampstead he still rented it, and laid out a walled fruit garden.[2]

But it is Dean Swift, of St. Patrick's, who in the shape of a "Drapier" wrote the Drapier's Letters, 1724, against him, that makes him a character whom the town must always regard with interest and subdued admiration.[3]

Among his many enterprises, Wood found a way of issuing coins of good quality to governments needing currency. He had already obtained a patent for issuing coins for the North American colonies for 14 years (on 12 July 1722)—300 tons in all. "The Plantations" accepted them without eagerness. This should have been a warning. After the South Sea Bubble, (and even now), people find currencies uncertain blessings. It was agreed that Ireland wanted a coinage; but they claimed they did not want so much as was being forced upon them. Sir Isaac Newton at the Mint showed that their claim that the quality was bad was untrue. To William Wood it was all a matter of business between him and the Government. If they backed out of their bargain, as they did in the end, he expected to receive compensation. Meanwhile, the Irish found that any piece of Wood would serve to beat the Government. On September 7 1724, the people of Dublin hung him in effigy. They had been unable to find him himself; it is likely that he was no nearer than Bristol, for William Wood knew his Irishmen. He is reported to have declared himself "surprised at their Impudence and Insolence", and considered it was the Papists who were against him; that Ireland was ripe for rebellion and ready to shake off its dependence upon the Crown of England. How awkward was all this for his brothers-in-law in Meath Street, who had been, to some extent, his agents. An Advertisement might help them. "Whereas", they write on 22 August 1724, "several Persons in this

1 W.A. ii, 29.
2 Lease: Feb. 1726-7, for 21 years.
3 Swift stopped writing Gulliver's Travels in order to proceed with his attack.

The Deanery

Photograph by Bennett Clark

The Old House, Victoria Street

Kingdom suspect that John Molyneux of Meath-Street, Iron-Monger, and his Brother Daniel Molyneux of Essex Street, Ironmonger, are Interested in the Patent obtain'd by William Wood for Coyning of Halfpence and Farthings for this Kingdom. Now We the said John Molyneux and Daniel Molyneux, in Order to satisfy the Publick, Do hereby Declare, that we are in no Way concern'd with the said WOOD in relation to his said Patent; And that we never were possess'd of any of the said Halfpence or Farthings, except one Halfpenny and one Farthing, which I the said John Molyneux receiv'd in a Post-Letter, and which I immediately afterwards deliver'd to one of the Lords Justices of Ireland.

And We do further Declare, that We will not, directly or indirectly, be any Ways concerned with the said Wood's Half-pence or Farthings; but on the contrary, act to the great Advantage and Satisfaction of this Kingdom, as good loving and faithful Subjects ought to do. And We do further declare, that to the best of our Knowledge, the said WILLIAM WOOD is not in this Kingdom".[1]

We do not know the effect, but in the "Full and True account of the solemn procession to the Gallows, at the execution of William Wood, Esquire, and Hard-ware-man", his brother-in-law and "a certain sadler, his intimate Friend" find place. "Each had a small Kettle in his Hands, wherein was a reasonable Quantity of the new Half-pence".

William Wood died in London but was buried at Wolverhampton, on 6th August, 1730. The entry in the Register is: "William Wood Esqr.".

His eldest son, William, cast the Iron railings at St. Paul's. They were of Sussex Iron. It was probably this person (and not his father) who was the writer of the impassioned letter to his lady-love (dated 1714) found at the Deanery House during its demolition.[2] He was born in 1694, and so was 20 years old.

THE TOWN AND ITS NEW BUILDINGS DURING THIS PERIOD.

The end of the 17th century marked a general change in the appearance of the town. Hitherto the prevailing type of house was one of half-timber, with a roof often of thatch. Fires made this type of roof unpopular, and thatching was finally forbidden in the Town Act of 1814.[3]

In 1675, we get the name of the Brick House given to a house in Cock Street, evidently that of an unusual and distinctive building. It marked the turn of the tide in fashion towards that very pleasant work in brick of William and Mary and Queen Anne. How little of this has lasted in the town! Some of it is known from old views, and a few early Georgian buildings remain: Giffard's House, 1726; "Cope's", 1736; but the most charming of all, number 19, Bilston Street (built by Thomas Turton who died in 1733), was ruthlessly demolished in 1954. The Red Lion Hotel, built on the site of the present Town Hall about 1697 was the first inn of red brick, and gained by this newness, and the large assembly room it provided.

Another enterprise was the New Town Hall, a building with a turret, which seems to have been finished, after a slow start, by 1703. There is a large payment, £16, for glazing the New Town Hall in 1712, while Mr. Atherly is paid £6 10s. 0d. for a Town Hall clock, a competitor of the one in the Church Tower and the sundial over the church porch.

1 Herbert Davis, Drapier's Letters, p. xxxvii.
2 W.A. i., 231.
3 There is a photograph of what was probably the last thatched house in Wolverhampton in the Public Library. (J.S.R. 1955).

There was probably much need for a building which could serve as a parish hall. It is difficult to say much about its appearance, but its site is shown on the map of 1750 (by Isaac Taylor), opposite the Angel, and forming part of High Street which extended to the Church gates. Near it was the new Crib (1707), the pillory and the stocks.

A general meeting of the townsmen, "Gentlemen and Inhabitants", called to make regulations for its future on 25 February 1702-3, decided that Timothy Lilly, junior, should have free use of it "to teach writing and accounts at 20sh. for one year provided he take care to use his diligence to teach ye Towns children as they ought to be". This ordinance was the germ of the subsequent Charity School, which established itself here for the best part of the century.[1]

It was also provided that the Constables should have the "privilidge", to which they were accustomed, of letting the hall for the benefit of the town. There are 32 interesting signatures appended to this document of the townsmen who were present.

The income derived from this source was inconsiderable.[2] Apart from the regular 20/- received, the Constables' accounts tell of a "waxman" and an "auction man" in 1699, actors and rope dancers in 1700, and actors again in 1701; but the details are not always given. In 1718-19, there was a puppet show,[3] an exhibition of fencing, and (once a month till June) 2/- was paid by Madam Fowler "for the Assembly in ye Town Hall". One may be quite wrong in suggesting that this was a card party; perhaps they only drank the new infusion called tea!

And who was madam Fowler? William Fowler, a younger son of the Pendeford family, was a leading townsman at this time. She is therefore likely to be the mother of Samuel, Richard, Elizabeth, Mary, Honor, Anna Catherina, Diana and Thomas Fowler, baptized at the church between the years 1700 and 1713.

We have seen that Robert Leveson, esquire, (d. 1709) was the last of his line at Wolverhampton. He had sold his lands at the turn of the century, and outlived his entire family, who were in no case blessed by a long life. His daughter Sarah (1658-1701) married at Lichfield Cathedral, on 19 April 1687, Charles Fowler of Pendeford, (d. 1731), who seems to have succeeded his father-in-law as the magistrate on the spot. (He signs in the Constables' Accounts in 1710).

Richard Leveson the eldest son had a career of some distinction. Born on 12 July, and baptized on 28th, 1659, at Wolverhampton, he became a Colonel of Dragoons, and Major General in 1696. He was M.P. for Lichfield 1685-7, and 1692-5, and Governor of Berwick from 1691 until his death in March 1698-9. Of his wife, we only know her name was Penelope and that she was buried at Wolverhampton on 14 December 1697, having died in London.

The eldest child, Catherine, is more of a mystery. She was born on 18 August and was baptized on 6 September 1655, at Kinver. She seems to be the only candidate for the position of "the honoured and worthily esteem'd". Katherine Leveson, to whom William Congreve, the poet and playwright, dedicated in 1691 his first work, Incognita, "a novel". He remarks upon her "clear wit, sound Judgment and Merciful disposition". He was then 20, she 36.

His family had returned from Ireland at the time of the Revolution. He had had a serious illness and a long convalescence, spent, it is supposed, in Staffordshire.

She died unmarried in October 1692.

1 Mr. Matlock had paid £1 "for ye use of ye New Hall" from 1695.
2 In 1693 £1–8–0d. was paid "for ye use of the ha'll".
3 The large sum of £1–10–0d. was received from a "poppet-showman for the Town Hall", in 1721–2. 7s. 6d. "Cash from the Actors" in 1728–9 seems rather small.

CHAPTER IX

THE CHANGING TOWN

THE 18th century was a period of material progress, and it witnessed a tremendous growth in the population of Wolverhampton and the surrounding area. Coal and ironstone had been found in great quantities in the district and mining and iron making attracted many workers. In 1750 the number of inhabitants in the town had risen to 7,454[1] and the growth of some of the adjoining parishes had been even more spectacular. It was this increase in the population of the outhamlets of Willenhall and Bilston which was the primary cause of their agitation for greater independence which culminated in 1727 in the consecration of their burial grounds. But they were still chapelries with no cure of souls and marriages could only take place there with the express licence of the Dean of Wolverhampton. These restrictions irked them, particularly when they found they had to pay double fees for the meagre privileges they possessed.

It had been customary from very remote times for the chapelries to pay lewns or rates to the mother church and this usually amounted to about £4 per annum but about 1714 the churchwardens began to infringe the old custom of confining themselves to a single levy and sent several of these demands out each year. The churchwardens of the Collegiate Church were faced with increasing bills, for the fabric of the church was old and greatly decayed, and although Dean Turner had, after much agitation, restored the chancel the rest of the building was in sore need of attention. The organ, restored by Thomas Bracegirdle after its destruction during the Civil Wars,[2] again needed some repair and the clock in the tower had to be replaced. All these things required a great deal of money and extra rates levied by the wardens on the townspeople were very unpopular. It was fatally easy to unload some of these liabilities on the chapelries and the lewns for those areas rose steeply. The amount of the lewns remained the same but the number levied each year increased until the annual demand from Willenhall and Bilston rose to £56 each.

Bilston was the first to object to the imposts and in 1740 the chapelwardens William Walker and Joseph Parkes refused to pay any more and the churchwardens at Wolverhampton proceeded to sue them in the spiritual courts. The people of Bilston duly responded by passing a resolution, recorded in the Bilston register, that their church officers should "be borne harmless from all costs and necessary expenses that shall be incurred in defending the said suit". The defending chapelwardens carefully prepared their case[3] and went, at some length, into the past history of the parish and chapelries.

"Formerly Bilston and Willenhall usually paid each the sum of four pounds per annum to the Mother Church, and that (as they apprehend) towards the repairs of the fabric of the Mother Church only, at which time three treble lewns for the (whole) parish were £29 1s. 4½d. and the chapelries never paid above £16 in any one year, until the year of Our Lord 1716; since which time the Churchwardens of Wolverhampton have called upon

1 See Taylor's Map in Shaws "History of Staffs". Vol. II.
2 This is recorded on his tablet in the nave of St. Peter's Church.
3 Lawley's "History of Bilston" p. 96. See also "History of Willenhall" by N. W. Tildesley p. 73 et. seq.

them for £28, £32, £40, and £56, in short, what sum they pleased without the consent of the inhabitants, and have made them pay it, but have never called for less than £16 since the year 1724. All that these chapelries receive from the Mother Church is only bread and wine for the Sacrament, four times a year, for which they paid £4 per annum, saving that the Chapelwardens of each place have for collecting it—at Bilston of threepence in the pound, and at Willenhall fourpence in the pound. All the rest of the villages have been forced to pay in proportion with these two towns. Between thirty and forty years ago, an organ was by voluntary contribution bought and set up in the Church of Wolverhampton. For about twenty years the salary of the organist, viz., ten pounds per annum, has been paid out of the churchwardens levies; many ornaments also, within this time, have been placed in the (Mother) church, viz., a large branched brass candlestick, a large picture for an altar piece, etc., and also on the outside of the church, that is, gravel walks have been made, trees planted in the churchyard, two old stone windows have been altered to modern fashion, and the Church itself has been chipt, the expense of all of which have been very great, and, as we apprehend, have all been paid out of the Church levies, of which the outhamlets pay such a proportionable part as above".

Bilston tried to get support from the people of Willenhall in this important matter but Dr. Richard Wilkes the Willenhall chapelwarden and spokesman did not approve of Bilston's tactics and would not join with them. But Willenhall was not to be out of the picture for long and in 1750 they too refused to pay the increased demands of the Wolverhampton officials. The chapelwardens of Willenhall at that time were Dr. Richard Wilkes and Samuel Hawksford, both men of wealth and influence, and they were determined to fight the churchwardens of the mother church, cost what it may. In January 1750 Dr. Wilkes received a demand from John Snow the Wolverhampton churchwarden for £32 as a proportion of a levy granted to the collegiate church for repairs, made up of eight levies instead of one, for which the Willenhall people could get no satisfactory explanation. Willenhall were further hampered at that time by the cost of rebuilding their own church, so, in February 1750, they paid £8 to Wolverhampton in the fond hope that this figure would satisfy the officials there. When no more money was forthcoming legal pressure was applied and eventually a suit was filed in the Wolverhampton Peculiar Court where churchwardens and other officials were both judge and jury.

Dr. Richard Wilkes and his fellow warden retaliated by filing a suit in the Court of Chancery[1] in which they set out their case at great length. In the schedule they gave details of the money they had paid and the way it had been spent and stressed their great objection to the growing demands of the Mother Church. The case was heard on 14th March 1753, but on the advice of Counsel, the plaintiffs agreed to withdraw their Bill on the understanding that the churchwardens would stay their case in the spiritual courts.

Attempts were made to bring the parties together and in 1754 the Earl of Stamford, a generous benefactor of St. John's, Wolverhampton, endeavoured to persuade the two sides to agree to arbitration but whilst the Willenhall people expressed their willingness to do this the officials at Wolverhampton remained adamant in their determination to follow the case through in the spiritual court. Later on in the year however, John Brevitt one of the Wolverhampton churchwardens died and this meant a fresh start to the proceedings. Later on in 1755 wiser counsels seem to have prevailed and the cases in both

1 Chancery Proceedings C.12/2329/67.

courts were withdrawn. It was agreed that whilst double fees should no longer be demanded of the chapelries they would in future refrain from conducting marriages in the chapels, this being the sole privilege of the Collegiate Church. Other demands were also dropped.

Although the storm had abated the people of Bilston and Willenhall had an uncomfortable feeling that at any time the case might be reopened so to protect themselves and their successors they drew up an agreement in the form of a joint memorandum, written in the Bilston parish register and signed by all parties, in which they agreed to stand together against any further encroachments by Wolverhampton. This was the end of the difficulties between the Collegiate Church and the chapelries but it was another hundred years before the latter obtained their parochial freedom.

About 1750 it was obvious that the provision of another church in Wolverhampton was a priority and to this end a voluntary subscription list was started and a favourable site on the western side of the town offered to the authorities.[1] Contributions arrived slowly, however, and little progress seems to have been made with the proposed scheme until about 1754, when the Earl of Stamford offered to give the sum of £1,000 to the building fund, on condition that he and his successors might have the perpetual right of presentation to the living of the new church. There were, however, several practical difficulties to be overcome before his offer could be accepted. One of these arose from the necessity of obtaining a private Act of Parliament, because of the condition imposed by Lord Stamford on his gift, and a certain amount of delay unavoidably occurred before this received the Royal Assent in 1755 and a start could be made.

The numerous provisions of the Act were to be carried out by trustees or "commissioners", 34 of whom are named, and, in addition, any person who contributed £20 or more to the building fund automatically qualified as a trustee and his name was added to the list. At their head was the Dean of Windsor and Wolverhampton, Dr. Penyston Booth, one of the few deans ever to reside in the town, through whose enthusiasm Wednesfield Chapel had been erected in 1746. Amongst the other names on the list we find those of William Archer—who was later to provide £200 towards the purchase of the famous Renatus Harris organ; a factor, Rowland Carr of Queen Street; an upholsterer, James Eykyn; four "ironmongers"—including the celebrated Benjamin Molineux, of Molineux House; and one of the early Wolverhampton japanners, Thomas Wightwick of King Street.

Five of the trustees[2] who were owners of an extensive area of land known as the "Cock Crofts"—stretching from Snow Hill across to Worcester Street—had made a free gift of some two acres of this as a site for the new church and burial ground, and once the Act for the building of the church had become law, a start was possible.

The choice of an architect and builder was the first problem, but in this instance it seems to have occasioned little difficulty. It is now virtually certain that for their builder the trustees selected a Wolverhampton man, Roger Eykyn, who was responsible for much good class work in the district including the alterations to Oakeley Park for Lord Powis 1748-58, Bellaport Hall for William Cotton in 1755, and Hankelow Hall and Brand Hall in 1756.

Eykyn's father—the James Eykyn already mentioned as a trustee—was well known in the town. His premises were in High Green (now Queen Square), where he carried on a flourishing trade as an upholsterer. His son Roger, appears to have taken an interest in

1 I am indebted to Mr. J. S. Roper M.A. for the whole of the article on St. John's.
2 John Jesson, George Saunders, Thos. Wightwick, John Pershouse, James Raby.

building quite early in life, and soon became an "amateur" architect of the type so frequently found in England at this time. The experience he was to gain in the building of St. John's probably enabled him to design his own church, St. Paul's, in Birmingham in the 1770's. This bears a striking similarity to St. John's in many of its details, and was almost certainly modelled on it.

Closely associated with Eykyn at this time was the architect, William Baker[1] of Audlem in Cheshire whose name first becomes known to us in 1743, in which year he designed the Butter Cross in Ludlow. From then onwards he was engaged on a number of Midland buildings and in 1749 he went to Patshull Hall to work under the instructions of its owner, Sir John Astley, Bt., who was then in the course of reconstructing the house. At this time Baker was engaged on a number of projects in South Staffordshire including alterations and erections at Penn Hall for Thomas Bradney 1748-54, the building of Pattingham House in 1753 and alterations to outhouses and stabling at Enville for Lord Stamford 1748-51. It was probably his business association with Eykyn and Lord Stamford that recommended him for the post of Architect of St. John's. Sir John Astley had, about 1742, engaged James Gibbs—Sir Christopher Wren's successor—and architect of St. Martin-in-the-Fields, London (1722-6)—to redesign his house and church at Patshull, but it appears that Gibbs was unable to complete the work there, probably on account of ill-health, and Baker took over from him. According to Baker's own account book, he was at Patshull fairly regularly from 1749 until about 1759, so it does not altogether come as a surprise to find the following entry in August 1755:—

July 28-Aug. 5. Paid Expens to Patshull & Surveying of (?) Plans for W'ton Chapel: 9/-.

Several entries similar to this follow; Baker was at the stonelaying ceremony in April of the following year and charged a further guinea for his trouble. Between that date and the end of 1759 his accounts show that he received about £190 as fees from one or other of the "commissioners" of St. John's. There seems little doubt on this evidence that Baker did in fact design the church though we should not dismiss entirely the possibility that Eykyn himself drew up the plans, and that Baker acted as overseer of the work, as he most certainly did at Penn Church in 1765.[2]

Whatever the answer, building went on apace. The new church was of brick encased in Perton stone which was brought from Lord Wrottesley's estate—an "excellent stone", as Dr. Richard Wilkes, the famous Willenhall antiquary described it when he saw the building in the course of construction.[3] By 1758 the nave, chancel and tower had been erected and the interior of the church was being plastered and fitted out. As the present spire was not at the time intended—probably because of expense—the building must have been almost ready for use. And then disaster occurred.

Wilkes tells us all about it in an account which Stebbing Shaw the famous historian of Staffordshire thought fit to include in his description of Wolverhampton later in the century: Speaking of St. John's he says:—

. . . . . after it was covered and plastered in 1758, when the wainscoat for the pews or seats was all finished, and ready to be fixed, a fire broke out in the night (the workmen having left some in the steeple, and well-secured it as they imagined), which burnt it all, and did some damage to the roof, the whole loss amounting to 7 or 8,000 £.

His estimate of the damage caused is an exaggeration. Baker himself came over early in November "to survey the Expence done", and his figure is much more conservative,

1 Staffs. Hist. Coll. 1950–1 p. 109 et seq.
2 Ibid p. 133.
3 S. Shaw "History of Staffordshire" Vol. II p. 164.

£350 12s. 6d. But this was serious enough in a church barely completed and still in need of funds. How the difficulty was overcome is not really known. Wilkes goes on to tell us that the inhabitants of Wolverhampton "went to the principal towns, and gentlemen of fortune, to ask their assistance", and says this was so rapidly forthcoming that they were able to clear the debt already outstanding on the building fund and carry on with the work of repair. He may, of course, be right, for there appears to be no record of the more usual remedy of "briefs" being resorted to, although we certainly read of a church rate of 5d. in the £ being levied on the parish for the "repairs and other uses" of the church shortly after its opening in June 1760.

Unfortunately, there is little or no record surviving of the actual opening ceremony. The Chapelwardens' Accounts begin on the 30th June 1760, with the record of a vestry meeting in the new church—called St. John's—and it is made plain that notice of the meeting had been given both at the Collegiate Church and at St. John's itself on the previous Sunday. This may conceivably have been the first occasion on which the building was used for public worship.

The choice of wardens fell to the lot of the first vestry and they chose William Hilliard and Roger Eykyn for this office. Hilliard was well known in Wolverhampton for his efforts to reform the Grammar School, and it is pleasant to think that the builder of the church himself was appointed to play an active part in it during its early years. He remained warden till 1763. Hilliard was succeeded after one year in office by Thomas Wright, an ironmonger, of Snow Hill.[1]

As first minister for his new church, Lord Stamford, as patron, selected the Rev. Benjamin Clements, B.A.—a Dudley man, who had recently come to Wolverhampton on his appointment as headmaster of the Grammar School. His early career at St. John's seems to have been quite uneventful, but after the opening of the Roman Catholic School at Sedgley Park in 1763 we find him engaged in a vigorous campaign against popery. Many of his printed sermons testify to his feelings on this subject. He remained at St. John's until his death in 1768, though he had become a hardy pluralist, holding the living of Braunton, Devonshire at the same time.

It is odd, perhaps, that the only other official of whom anything is known during these first few years is the dogwhipper, that "important subordinate of the wardens", whose duty it was to expell from the church such dogs as did not behave well.[2] This was usually done by gripping them about the neck with wooden tongs, several pairs of which remain still in various parishes about the country. At St. John's the office was filled by William Shaw, who was paid an annual salary of 6s. He was still serving in this capacity in 1778, when the wardens' accounts record the purchase of "a pr. of second-hand Breeches for old Shaw" at the price of 1s.

After the opening of the church, preparations for its final completion went on apace. The chapelwardens were continually finding money for some new addition to the fabric. In August 1760, for example, the bell arrived, having been purchased from George Birch of Birmingham at a cost of £35 1s. 8d. and brought to Wolverhampton for a further 15s. As the work was still continuing on the spire, temporary arrangements had to be made to hang the bell in the lower part of the tower and a special floor was constructed for this purpose. It now transpires that this bell, cast in 1706, belonged at one time to St. Martin's Church, Birmingham and the inscription, of which there is a facsimilie in the west porch of St. John's, bears the names of an early 18th century Rector of Birmingham, William

1 So it appears—Sketchley & Adams Directory 1770.
2 Tate—"The Parish Chest" Cambridge 1951, p. 106.

Daggett, and his two wardens, Robert Hicks and George Hallham. Perhaps this bell was removed from St. Martin's when the "ring of twelve musical bells" mentioned by Hutton in his History of Birmingham was placed there.

The next acquisition of which anything is known was the magnificent set of Communion plate, consisting of a "silver flagon, two chalices and two plates" as the Benefactions board has it. It was given by Samuel Whitehouse one of the original trustees of the church and a man of some fortune who died in 1762. An interesting entry in the warden's accounts on 7th August 1761 relates that John Carter was paid 4s. "for horse hire to carry the Communion Plate to be engraved and to fetch it back", but we are not told where the work was done.

It would appear from the church records that the famous Renatus Harris organ was not installed until some time after the building was opened, and that during the first two years of its history, St. John's had the use of "the little Organ" supplied on loan by a Mr. Abraham Adcock of London. This instrument seems to have caused nothing but trouble, for the wardens had to pay for substantial repairs twice within the course of the next few months, and it cost them nearly £12 to send it back to London after it had fulfilled its purpose. One wonders if this unfortunate experience prompted the opening of a subscription list for the Harris organ. The Benefactions board states very precisely that it was purchased by a subscription of £500, "towards which Mr. William Archer contributed Two Hundred Pounds. Anno Domini, 1762". The story of this superb instrument is an interesting one.

It is now generally accepted that the organ was acquired for the "town of Wolverhampton" from the widow of John Byfield, an 18th century organ builder of considerable repute and skill, and probably son-in-law of John Harris his partner. Harris was himself son of the famous Renatus Harris, one of the two great organ builders in England in the latter part of the 17th century. How Byfield came by the organ is an oft-told story, but it will bear repetition, together with, perhaps, a few suggestions as to its authenticity or otherwise.

In 1682, the ancient Temple Church in London—spiritual home of the two societies of the Inner and Middle Temple—was in need of an organ. There appears to have been some dispute among the Benchers of the respective Inns of Court as to who should build the instrument; it is suggested that the Inner Temple supported Renatus Harris, whilst the Middle Temple favoured his great rival, Bernard Schmidt (Father Smith), who had come to this country from Germany, in 1660, but a few months after the arrival here of Harris and his father from France.[1]

In an attempt to settle the dispute as to who should build the instrument, both Schmidt and Harris were permitted to set up organs in the church, and the famous "Battle of Organs" thus began. By 1684, if we are to believe the rather scanty records which exist, the instruments had been completed, and the trial began. This was to last for four years, during which period many eminent musicians are believed to have been engaged by the rival contestants to play their organs. It is said that Henry Purcell, John Blow and Giovanni Draghi (organist to the Queen) were all involved in this long drawn-out struggle. New stops were added from time to time by each builder in an attempt to outdo his rival—but with little or no success.

Finally, in 1688, a decision was made and it was in favour of Smith. Harris' organ was rejected and he was asked to remove it from the church, though "without loss of prestige"

1 The "Universal Magazine" for Dec. 1778 seems to be the chief source of the story of the "Battle of Organs".

and, moreover, he received £200 for his pains. Part of the Harris organ was eventually conveyed to Dublin and installed in Christ Church Cathedral. It is possible that the superbly carved case—with its Crown and Mitres—dates from this time. The organ remained in Dublin for just over 60 years. In 1750 John Byfield was asked by the Dean and Chapter to repair it, but it seems that he managed to pursuade them that a new instrument would be a better proposition and he took the Harris organ in part exchange for it. It seems that Byfield had some difficulty in disposing of the organ and it was not until after his death that his widow in 1762 sold to to St. John's for £500.

Building operations continued at St. John's for some 14 or 15 years after the opening of the church for the erection of the spire,[1] commenced after the fire of 1758, was a lengthy task. It seems, therefore, all the more commendable that during this period the wardens put in hand, and indeed completed, the laying out of the churchyard, with its walks and avenues, in preparation for the planting of the lime trees a few years later. The brick wall surrounding this two acre site was also finished, and an order placed with "Mr. Hilliard and Co." (probably the Mr. Hilliard who was elected warden with Roger Eykyn in 1760) for "the Iron Gates at the East End of the Chapel Yard Wall". The pair of wrought iron gates now displayed in the Art Gallery are probably the ones Hilliard supplied. If so, it is of interest to read that his account for them came to £10 1s. 9½d. Gates of a similar design were placed at the opposite end of the churchyard in 1775.

We are fortunate in knowing pretty well what the interior of the church looked like during this first phase of its history, and the opportunity will be taken at this stage to say a few words about this. The body of the church was occupied by large box pews quite common at this period, each with its door on which was displayed very prominently on the outside the number. Along the tops of the pews, at intervals, were wooden candlestick holders—for there was no gas lighting in the church until well into the 19th century and the wardens' accounts contain reference to the purchase of "dozen-pounds" of candles at 5¼d. per pound, and of candlesticks at 3d. each. Lighting was not a particularly serious problem at first for the services were usually held during the hours of daylight. Evening Prayer was usually held at 3.30 p.m., after which the church was closed for the rest of the day.[2]

The pulpit was similar to many of the three deckers still to be seen up and down the country. The minister's entry and exit were controlled by a door, and above him was the sounding board—a device which enabled his voice to carry to the more distant parts of the building. This was later ornamented by a carved dove—probably in the manner of the pulpit in St. Swithin's Worcester—and must have been one of the most delightful features of the church.

There was, of course, no stained glass in any of the windows, so that the interior was much lighter than at present, especially as the walls were as yet unpainted. The first attempt at decoration, in fact, appears to have been left until 1787, when the wardens were authorized to have the inside walls painted "with oil colours of a light colour, and also the pillars". They had previously been whitewashed.

Several additions to the church had, however, been made before the date of this improvement, and among them were some of the more familiar features of the present interior, including the magnificent Coat of Royal Arms, now hung on the front of the west gallery. These were set up in 1778 or 1779, at a cost of £9 9s. 0d.—no small sum of money at

1 Shaw "History of Staffs." Vol. II p. 164. It has always been assumed that the money collected as a result of the fire allowed the spire to be added.
2 As late as 1833 there were no evening services—Bridgen's Directory.

that period. Their authorship is uncertain, though it is high'y probable that William Ellam, who executed the table of Commandments at the same time, had a hand in them. The hanging of the Royal Arms in churches had become compulsory in 1660, and sometimes it was the custom to set them up over the Commandments, at the east end of the church.

During the course of the following year, 1780, the wardens were given authority "to article with Mr. Josh. Barney Jun'r" to paint and complete "a new altar piece for the east end of the church." The result of this commission was the splendid copy of Ruben's "Descent from the Cross", which today forms part of the Altar reredos. Barney came of a Wolverhampton family, and was born in the town in 1751. When he was 16 he was sent to study under Zucchi and Angelica Kaufman, but he eventually returned to England and took up an appointment as drawing master at the Royal Military Academy, Woolwich. This post he held for 27 years, and he must have gained considerable distinction in it, for we find him as painter of fruit and flowers to King George III, and an exhibitor at the Royal Academy from 1786 onwards. Ultimately he settled in Wolverhampton again and became a decorator of japanned trays for which the town became famous towards the end of the 18th century. According to Pearson & Rollason's Trade Directory of 1781 he had a house in the Horse Fair, now Wulfruna Street.

His fee to St. John's for painting the altar piece was £50. This was paid in April 1782, so it is probable that the work took about 18 months to complete. As a proof of the esteem in which the painting was held, the following memorandum was inserted in the church-wardens' account book in 1806:—

> " . . . . . a Curtain shall be put up to the window on the South side of the communion place to prevent the sun damaging the altar piece".

It is unfortunate that we have no view of the interior of the church as it was after these many additions had been made, for it must have appeared very different from the rather bleak interior seen by Dr. Richard Wilkes before the fire. Few chapels-of-ease, for that was the status St. John's enjoyed, a propos of the Collegiate Church, could have claimed to be more handsomely appointed.

This fact does indeed prompt us to consider the people the new church had come to serve during the first 40 years or so of its history, for many of them played an important part in beautifying and adorning the fabric, and in serving one or other of the church's offices, such as wardens, beadle or clerk.

When St. John's was opened for worship in 1760 it stood in comparative isolation. The square which now surrounds it was not yet begun, nor had George Street or Church Street been built up. Temple Street (Grey Pea Walk) was, as its old name implies, a mere footpath from one side of the town to the other; whilst the west side of Snow Hill had but a few houses on the edge of the great fields which stretched from Worcester Street to the main Dudley Road, and were known as the "Cock Closes". And yet, during the 20 years or so which saw the completion of the church, changes of unparalleled consequence for the town took place. The Industrial Revolution had come to Wolverhampton.

The 17th century was a period of repression for all faiths except that of the Established Church and it was not until the passing of the Act of Toleration towards the end of the century that things became easier and all forms of Dissent were able to develop.

The old Catholic faith had never completely died out in Wolverhampton due largely to the fact that many of the large landowners and principal inhabitants remained true to

Street where they were served for the next sixteen years by students of the Countess of Huntingdon's Connexion. The last of these preachers was Mr. Thomas Thorne who was there in 1798 and was probably then the settled pastor of this little church. Members from the Temple Street church moved to Snow Hill to form the Congregational Church there and others, including John Mander and his family, joined the other community when, in 1800, they bought a piece of land in Princess Street and built a new chapel there to which they moved in due course from Pountney's Fold. This chapel served its purpose for 12 years when a new chapel, on the site of the present one in Queen Street, was built.

The irreligion and general apathy towards spiritual matters of the 18th century was one of the factors which encouraged the rise of the various dissenting bodies, but this in its turn produced the religious revival of this and of the following century. In this the Wesleys and their friends have for ever left their mark. The early story of Methodism in Wolverhampton is principally concerned with the many visits of John Wesley to the town. Although the Methodist movement started at Oxford in 1729 we find no evidence of its spread to the town until the middle of the century, when George Whitfield, a friend, and, in the early days, a colleague of John Wesley wrote from Wolverhampton on 27th October 1753 that on the previous evening he had preached there.[1]

It was not however until 8th March 1760 that Wesley himself records in his journal his first visit to the town. This is strange when we recall that he was at Bilston as early as 1743 and he must have passed through the district on many occasions when he visited his old friend John Fletcher at Madeley, Salop. Of his first visit he writes:—"I was surprised at coming into Wolverhampton, which is what Dudley was, to find the people so still; many gaping and staring, but non-speaking an uncivil word. 'Aye', said a well-meaning man, 'we shall not find them so civil by-and-by'. I wish these croakers would learn to hold their peace. I desire to hear no prophets of evil. What do they do, but weaken the hands both of preachers and people, and transfuse their own cowardice into others.

But this prophet of evil was a false prophet too. For neither while I was preaching, nor after I had done, did anyone offer the least rudeness whatever; and we rode quietly out of the town as we could have done out of London or Bristol". The magic and power of Wesley's preaching drew large congregations and gave great strength to the little community during its early struggles. With apostolic zeal he continued to visit them throughout the next thirty years of his long life.

About the time of Wesley's first visit or shortly afterwards the Methodists had erected a preaching house which, although small, met their needs and they prospered. But this state of affairs was not allowed to continue for long. In 1763 a Mr. Hayes an attorney (who should have known better) led a mob which destroyed the small chapel. Alexander Mather, one of Wesley's veterans, thereupon sought the help of Lord Dartmouth whose intervention at the County Sessions compelled Hayes, under threat of legal action to promise a complete restoration of the premises and in due course this promise was implemented. Those were the days of mob violence, as we have seen in the case of the chapel in John's Lane. On Wesley's second recorded visit in 1761 he tells us "I came to Wolverhampton. None had yet preached abroad in this furious town; but I was resolved, with God's help, to make a trial, and ordered a table to be set up in the inn yard (i.e. the Angel in High Green). Such a number of wildmen I have seldom seen; but they gave me no disturbance, either while I preached or when I afterwards walked through the midst of them".

1 Much of the history of Methodism in Wolverhampton is taken from John Wesley's "Journal".

Of his next visit on 23 March 1768 he writes:—"After preaching at several other places I rode on to Wolverhampton. Here, too, all was quiet: only those who could get into the house made a little noise for a time. Some hundreds attended me to my lodging but it was with no other intent than to stare". Wesley loved to preach to the crowds in the open air, a practice much frowned upon by his brother clergy of the Established Church, and on his next visit on 21 March 1770 he preached to a large gathering in the High Green from the doorway of the house of one Denman[1] the printer. Amongst his hearers was a locksmith named Moseley, a notorious drunkard, pugilist and gambler. On one occasion, we are told, Moseley flung a stone at the great evangelist which struck him on the head causing blood to stream down his face. The memory of this vicious act haunted Moseley through the years and later on, in the Noah's Ark Chapel he was converted and became a preacher, remaining a staunch Methodist until his death at the great age of 90.

As the years went by the Methodist cause continued to flourish and in 1786 Wolverhampton was formed into a separate circuit. In a letter to his brother Charles in the early part of 1786 John Wesley tells him that his friend Melville Horne was to be ordained on the following Trinity Sunday to a curacy under his old friend Thomas Fletcher at Madeley, and in due course the ordination took place, but Melville Horne was irresistibly drawn to Wesley and his cause and shortly afterwards he joined him. In 1787 we find his name, as supernumary, included, together with those of John Leach and John Brettell, as a minister of the Wolverhampton Circuit.

With the spread of Methodism the preaching house at Wolverhampton became hopelessly inadequate for the needs of the growing church. A new chapel was built in Wheelers Fold at the rear of the Noah's Ark Inn in old Lichfield Street. Although larger than the original chapel it was comparatively speaking, a small building being 38 feet long and 32 feet wide. It was pewed in the centre of the floor and contained a gallery for the choir at the end opposite to the pulpit. From its situation it took the name of the Noah's Ark Chapel and was famous in South Staffordshire Methodism until 1825 when the chapel in Darlington Street was built. The registers of baptism for this chapel commence in 1795.

John Wesley came to Wolverhampton for the opening of the new chapel and records in his Journal "1787. Wednesday, 28 March: In the evening I opened the newhouse at Wolverhampton, nearly as large as that at Newcastle-on-Tyne. It would not near contain the people though they were wedged together as close as possible. I believe such a congregation was never seen in Wolverhampton before; not only so serious, but so well behaved. I hope this is a token for good".

Twelve months later Wesley was again in the town, coming here from Dudley where he had preached "with much liberty of spirit; but with far more at Wolverhampton in the evening, the new house being sufficiently crowded. What a den of lions was this town for many years! but now it seems: the last will be first". On Tuesday 23 March 1790 John Wesley made his last visit to Wolverhampton being then an old man of 87 but still a vigorous preacher. He writes "We had a pleasant ride (from Dudley) to Wolverhampton. This evening the rain began, and continued about 24 hours, after more than 24 weeks of fair weather; such a winter I never before saw. A melancholy event fell out the day before. The mistress of the house (adjoining the one where Wesley lodged) was boiling some varnish, it boiled over, and took fire, which seized on her,

1 The Hippodrome now occupies the site of these premises, No. 44; he was still in business here in 1844.

Old Lichfield Street

St. John's Church

St. George's Church

Photographs by Margaret Roper

and burnt her so that her life is despaired of. The rain lessened a little the congregation so that the house contained us tolerably well; and many, even of the genteel hearers, seemed almost persuaded not to halt between two opinions". The opening years of the 19th century saw Methodism well-established in Wolverhampton and well on the way to becoming an important force in the spiritual life of the community.

The centre of Wolverhampton, that is to say the area around Queen's Square and the Collegiate Church, was entirely built up by the middle of the 18th century as Isaac Taylor's map of 1750 well shows but the buildings were old and in many cases dilapidated, and no powers existed in those days to clear them away. Many of the streets were narrow and winding and much of the property abutting on them dated from the Tudor period or earlier. Lichfield Street, then about 15 feet wide and lying much on the same course as the present street, ran only as far as the passage-way at the side of the Midland Bank and through this the traveller passed into the Horsefair and Canal and Berry Street.

As the town grew any new buildings had to be erected farther afield and so we find such areas as Queen Street and Snowhill and the new square around St. John's Church being developed. King Street was constructed about the middle of the century and access was gained to it through an archway in Dudley Street, the clearing away of which was one of the special provisions of the Wolverhampton Improvement Act of 1777. This street still retains a number of nice Georgian houses built about 1750 by the more substantial tradesmen of the town. Towards the end of the century St. John's Square became the fashionable residential area of the well-to-do and is indeed the first example of town planning in Wolverhampton.

A photographic survey made in 1871[1] gives a good idea of the number of Georgian houses built during this period. There were some fine examples to be found in Dudley Street, Great Berry Street, Victoria Street and Bilston Street, but with the march of progress these have nearly all disappeared. As industry increased and the town grew the more prosperous tradesmen built substantial houses near to their places of business and we find these larger dwellings dotted about the town. The largest, although perhaps not the most striking of these houses, is Molineux House, now known as Molineux Hotel. Here in the middle of the century lived in some state Benjamin Molineux, "ironmonger" or, as we should describe him today, ironmaster. He was one of the sons of John Molineux[2] who probably founded the family fortune and built the house, sometime between 1740 and 1750. Another son, Thomas, built a house, not quite so imposing, in Dudley Street and on the rainwater spout caused his initials, with those of his wife and the date 1751 to be recorded. This house had a garden stretching back to Pipers Row with imposing entrance gates, on the posts of which were elaborate urns bearing his coat of arms. Molineux House remained the home of the family until the 1860's when it was sold to a Mr. McGregor and then converted into licensed premises. The central part of the house is probably all that John Molineux first built but later on Benjamin added north and south wings and altered considerably the general arrangement of the house. The interior still contains some very fine panelling and a staircase with spiral fluted balusters very similar to that in Giffard House nearby and probably the work of the same craftsman. The magnificent gardens of this house, which swept down the hill to what is now Waterloo Road, are today the headquarters of the Wolverhampton Wanderers Football Club. The Molineux's continued to flourish throughout the 18th century and ranked amongst the gentry. George Molineux became High Sheriff of Staffordshire.

1 Copies of these photographs are in the Reference Library.
2 The family came to Wolverhampton from Willenhall.

Of Giffard House we have already spoken. Another nice Georgian house stood in North Street on the site of the Civic Hall and yet another, probably belonging to the Giffards and later on to the Jesson family stood at the west side of Victoria Street and which, towards the end of its career became a cinema. On the north side of Queen's Square a member of the Persehouse family built a very fine house which afterwards became known as Cope's Wine Lodge. It bears its own date, 1726 and represents a high standard of craftsmanship and design such as are to be found in buildings of that period. An extension of the premises was carried out in 1755 and this date was also recorded on the spouting.

The initials on the lead rainwater spout are seen to be W.P. reversed and conjoined which we may be fairly sure represent William Pershouse. Who he was is not so certain. By chance one of the very few Wolverhampton deeds preserved at the British Museum (Add. Charters 41,831) illustrates without settling the point. It is an indenture dated 28th February 1727 (a significant date) between John Fowler, mercer, and Sampson Nocke, vintner, both of Wolverhampton, whereby Nocke receives a lease for 21 years from the 29 February last at £18 per annum of all that messuage in "the High Green having a dwellinghouse of William Pershouse in the holding of Henry Wood, the New Town Hall and a backside on or near all or most parts thereof", and all lately held by Joseph Perkes, and a cellar under the shop of John Fowler, all now held by Sampson Nocke. It is a legal statement of the clumsier kind which embodies the truth in some confusion. We can however reform the plan of this corner site by its means.

The style of "Copes" can be traced to the arrival here of George Cope in 1818, as successor to John Lilkey (or Likly) who had been established for 30 years. That takes us back to 1788. Previously this house was in the hands of John Crutchley, described in 1781 as "upholsterer and auctioneer", so the wine was kept underground; but it is not easy, without seeing the title deeds (which seem to have been dispersed), to distinguish the houses which make up this block of buildings. A Mrs. Pershouse, widow, was still occupier of one of the houses in the Rate Book of 1777. High Green as it was known in those days (it was renamed Queen's Square after Queen Victoria's visit in 1866) was very different from the square we know today. At the entrance to old Lichfield Street stood Davenhills, an inn dating back to pre-Reformation days. It was half-timbered with gables and a jettied upper storey. The east side of High Green was almost completely rebuilt in the 18th century and part of these Georgian houses survived until about 1912, when they were demolished to make way for a cinema. The Swan Inn which stood here was cleared away when Lloyd's Bank was built.

On the south side of the square near Dudley Street stood an old half-timbered gabled building faced over with plaster which for many years was the headquarters of George Smart, bookseller, stationer and printer of the Wolverhampton Chronicle. A little to the west, projecting out into the square, stood the High Hall which in Tudor times was the home of wealthy James Leveson. When the Levesons migrated to their country estates the Hall passed to the Normansells who lived there throughout the 17th century and probably later. It eventually passed to James Hordern who in the late 18th century founded his bank there and it survived until 1841 at which time it was occupied by William Warner, chemist.

A shadow of its former self, but still picturesque, it began to be something of a problem to its owners. There was for instance difficulty about its drains, the water from which, if allowed to wander, would have taken a course towards the Town Hall, the pump at the top of Cock Street, which had to be avoided. In the end Mr. Warner cut the Gordian Knot by demolishing the building, intending to rebuild but this happily was not proceeded with.

The 18th century High Green was not the open area we know today, as Taylor's map and Rowlandson's drawing[1] eloquently testify. The entrance to Cock Street was narrow and restricted and Darlington Street had not then been constructed. The markets and the fairs were held here, the latter being a common feature of Georgian England. At its eastern end the square was cluttered up with buildings, the principal being the Town Hall and the Charity School, both of which Taylor depicts on his map. The Town Improvement Act of 1777 gave the Commissioners powers to clear this area. The Town Hall, which had been rebuilt about 1687, was the scene of most important events in the town. It was also used as a theatre and here such famous personalities as Sarah Siddons and her brother, John Philip Kemble entertained our forebears. The Town Hall had been used for this purpose as early as 1754 when the local verse maker, William Vernon, wrote two epilogues[2] for the use of " a company of players, who met with little encouragement on their first appearance at Wolverhampton".

"The gentry yet, have hardly shewn their faces.
They take our bills; but never send for places".

He tells us that they prefer to gather at two of the respectable local inns for their entertainment rather than patronize the playhouse. One hears similar remarks these days. A theatre bill of about 1770 has survived which announces the appearance of the Kemble family in a comic opera called "Love in a Village". Roger Kemble, the father, was an actor-manager and a number of his children became famous in their profession. Sarah, who married William Siddons, appeared on several occasions at Wolverhampton and eventually became famous as a tragic actress on the London stage, appearing for many years at Drury Lane. Her brother, John Philip Kemble, made his debut as an adult actor at Wolverhampton on the 8th January 1776 in Lee's "Theodosius". He too went on to become a great actor, appearing at Drury Lane and Covent Garden. It is of interest to recall that he received his early education at the Roman Catholic Seminary at Sedgley Park.

As the Town Hall had become out of repair and was unsatisfactory in other ways for theatrical purposes a new theatre was erected about 1779 at the rear of the Swan Inn and this served the town until another building was erected at Snowhill which survived until the close of the 19th century. In its early years the Town Hall was also used by the Charity School. This school, for the education of poor children, probably owed its existence to a bequest by the Rev. Charles Winn, vicar of Penn, 8th May 1669, of £6 per year to trustees to help pay for the schooling of poor children of Wolverhampton and to buy them Bibles.

About 1695 the inhabitants of Wolverhampton made an agreement with Mr. John Matlock, a writing school master, that he should have the New Town Hall for life for the rent of £1 per annum. The terms seem easy ones and the payment is entered among the receipts until 1702.[4] Possibly Mr. Matlock died or retired; but there was a new and more careful agreement on 25th February 1702/3:—

1 Now in the Art Gallery.
2 "Early Wolverhampton Books & Printers" by G. P. Mander, 1922, p. 35.
3 Ibid. p. 37.
4 Account Book of Charity School—Wolverhampton Public Library. This account of the Charity School is compiled from notes prepared by Mr. Mander.

"At a general meeting of the Townsmen concerning the disposal of the New Town hall it was agreed & ordered by the Gentlemen & Inhabitants whose names are hereunto subscribed that Timo(thy) Lilly, junr. shall have the free use of the New Town hall to teach writing & acc(oun)ts at 20s. for one year provided he take care & use his diligence to teach ye Towns Children as they ought to be (. . . . deletion). The Constables shall also have the same privilege (sic) they use (sic) to have in making what they can of the hall for ye benefit of ye Towne". (34 people sign).

This agreement is evidently an advance on the previous one with the writing master. It seems also to have been generally agreed that the education of the town's children was a matter of public concern. They consented for instance to set apart a public building for the purpose, and it is clear from the Contables' Accounts that the payments for mending the windows and repairs swallowed the bulk of the rent. The old Minute Book of the trustees which starts in 1716 has survived.[1] The first two pages is occupied with the "Rules for the Charity School for Boys in the parish of Wolverhampton". The staff of the school consisted of a master, a mistress, and a "dame" (in the early 1800s called a governess) and later on a matron. They were paid, in 1718, £26, £12 and £7 16s. od. per annum.

It is clear from the original Rules that the master's equipment for teaching need only be slight; and there is no reason to suppose it to have been anything more. A large class of scholars was the normal thing in those days, and we can imagine his attention being fully occupied by the presence of 50 more or less unruly boys. He had his remedy, the time honoured one of the birch rod, and he also had assistance. We find in August 1725 that eight senior boys were chosen to keep order and report those who cursed or swore or told lies or "spoke unmannerly one to another or to anybody else". In 1757 they are mentioned again. If late, or at fault, boys were to have six blows with the birch and the girls were to be whipped.

The chief trouble the trustees had to contend with was truancy. At harvest time it was particularly prevalent, and an uphill fight was conducted between the trustees who insisted that the children should work at their books and the parents who were determined they should work in the fields. In July 1719 an order was made "That no body have leave to go a leasing & if any do they are to be immediately crost off the book and dismist & that the subscribers be acquainted therewith".

Nevertheless when September came some of the parents took their children away. There was also the complication of clothing, for the trustees, at considerable expense, made themselves responsible for dressing the children in a school uniform. In August 1722 some girls were removed after they had been newly equipped. The remedy was to insist that the clothing must be handed over when the scholars left; but it was sometimes necessary to bring the parents before a magistrate before this could be effected. On one occasion the master and mistress took with them the Beadle and seized the clothes of those who neglected to come to school. There is at least one case of a parent returning in person his children's clothes "with a deal of ill language".

On the north wall of the south transept of the Collegiate Church high above the arch is a large painting on canvas recording the various benefactions to the Charity School. It was erected in 1719 or 1720 and bears the names of the two churchwardens for that time, Henry Price and Thomas Brett and on either side of the picture is portrayed a boy and a girl dressed in the rather quaint costume of the period.

The school was supported mainly by subscriptions. One of the sources of income came from the collections taken at the time of the Charity Sermons. This was one of the

1 The original is now in America but a photographic facsimile is at St. Peter's Church.

chief events of the town and took place during the summer. There was considerable ceremony. The name of the preacher and the time of the sermon was advertised and those members of the community who enjoyed the title of "gentlemen" were reminded of the occasion. The trustees met at the school and followed the procession, composed of school children and apprentices, to the church, at the doors of which stood the churchwardens to receive them. The Grammar School gallery was used for this event, the usual seats being (at a later date at least) under the organ loft.

On one occasion it was directed that "an Anthem be sung". Considerable trouble was taken to find a suitable preacher and the clergy from various parishes round about were invited to give the address,[1] but often one of the prebendaries, who was usually a trustee, delivered the sermon. Apart from some endowments the rest of the income of the school came from the pockets of subscribers and as, doubtless, they were all considered trustees and the more interested attended the periodic meetings of the board, we find their names duly recorded in the Minute Book of the Charity.

One of the most interesting and colourful of these supporters was Button Gwinnett who in later life attained to fame in the American colonies. Gwinnett, the son of a clergyman, was born in Gloucester in 1735 and came to Wolverhampton as a young man probably in the course of business. On 19th April 1757 he was married at St. Peter's Church to Ann, the daughter of Aaron Bourn, a prosperous grocer of the town and after the marriage joined his father-in-law in the business. They lived in a house "in the churchyard". Gwinnett took an interest in the Charity School and attended three meetings of the subscribers in 1761 when he duly wrote his name in the Minute Book. But he was of a roving nature and in about 1762, after the birth of his third child he departed for the Plantations of Georgia[2] where he had received a grant of land. In due course his wife and their only surviving child followed him to America there to share with him the ups and downs of a planter's life.

He took an interest in the political activities of the colony and as one of its representatives signed the Declaration of Independence in July 1776. Shortly afterwards he had a violent quarrel with another prominent colonist, Lachlan Mc'Intosh, and died of wounds which he received as a result of the duel which followed. Owing partly to his early death his signature is scarce and as a result has become of great value to those Americans whose hobby it is to collect the signatures of the Signers of the Declaration. He had the distinction of being the first Governor of Georgia.[3]

At the other end of Cock Street in John's Lane stood that other centre of learning, the Grammar School,[4] which had catered for the children of the better class parents of the town since its foundation by Sir Stephen Jenyns in 1515. In 1714 the school was completely rebuilt by the famous Warwick architect, William Smith, who was also responsible for a number of other buildings in the district.

The rapid growth of the town in the 18th century created its problems. In spite of its ecclesiastical importance and the eminent position of its deans, Wolverhampton had never been favoured with a charter of incorporation and as a result local government was confined to the activities of the manorial courts and the Vestry, both of whose powers were extremely limited. In 1777 the town's first Improvement Act became law, and the Commissioners, who derived their powers under it began a programme of clearance and destruction hitherto quite unheard of.

1 A list can be compiled from the Minute Book.
2 For an account of his life see "History of Button Gwinnett" by Chas. F. Jenkins, 1926, Doubleday, Page & Co. New York.
3 Ibid.
4 For the complete history of this school see Mr. G. P. Mander's "History of Wolverhampton School".

The preamble to the Act of 1777[1] makes it clear that the measure was one of urgent necessity, stating that Wolverhampton "is a large, populous, and trading town"; that many of its streets "are narrow and incommodious for Passengers and Carriages";[2] and that with the recent opening of the canal,[3] the number of carts used for the conveyance of merchandise has greatly increased, and should therefore be placed under proper regulation.

125 Commissioners to administer the terms of the Act are named, in addition to the Stewards of the respective Manors of the Deanery, the Prebends and Stowheath. Many of those named have connections with Wolverhampton's industries, but there is also a fair sprinkling of professional men, clergy, tradesmen and innkeepers. The powers given to the Commissioners differ little from those contained in many "Town Acts" of the period, but particular emphasis is laid upon the purchase and demolition of buildings which have become obstructions; and on the levy of and collection of a town rate, a necessary evil if the Act was to work at all.

A Schedule of buildings to be demolished is appended and included among them are the Market House in High Green, the Shambles and Water Cistern adjacent to it; a "Gateway", leading out of Dudley Street into King Street; the Roundabout houses at the bottom of High Green; a number of houses, barns and stables in the Tup Street and Dunstall Lane area. The work of destruction was, in fact, carried out with expedition. Fortunately, the Minute Books kept by the Commissioners have survived,[4] and they provide us with an insight into the day-to-day workings of this new-fangled authority.

At the third meeting, held on the 20th June 1777, the order was made for the serving of notices to quit on the occupiers of some of the scheduled properties. At the next meeting, held 4th July, it was ordered that "a certain ancient building" in the Market Place, called the Slaughter Houses and Butchers' Shambles be taken down immediately. The demolition of the Market House, "being 60½ feet by 31½ feet" was to follow, but no action was, in fact, taken until the following February, when a poll was held. 25 of the Commissioners were found to be in favour of its removal as against 23 who wished it to remain, and its fate was, therefore, sealed. Wolverhampton was thus less fortunate than Bridgnorth and Tamworth, or even than Dudley, which was allowed to keep its Town Hall until 1860. The removal was, however, appreciated in at least one quarter, as an introductory note to "Wolverhampton" in Pearson & Rollason's Trade Directory of 1781 proves:—

"... . the butchers' shambles, market cross, or town hall, have been taken down, which is a vast improvement to the town, which now is a handsome well built place, most of the streets being new built and new paved".

In other matters, too, the Commissioners seem to have worked with some speed. As early as the 20th June 1777, their Minute Book records that they "are open to receive tenders for Glass Lamps for lighting the Town, also Lamp Irons and Oil and Lighting". On the same occasion, an order was made for the numbering of the houses and the naming of the streets. For this latter purpose, "Mr. John Smith" was engaged and we read that he was "to paint up the names . . . . . (in white on a black ground) at 2/6 each name".

Many entries relating to the appointment of scavengers appear during the early years of the Commissioners' rule. John Newbold "of Ettensall (Ettingshall) Park", and Thomas Miller of Dunstall, both described as yeomen, were appointed early in October 1777, "for cleansing, sweeping and carrying away the ashes, dust, rubbish, dirt, dung or other

1 We are indebted to Mr. J. S. Roper M.A. for this article on the Improvement Act 1777.
2 Printed copy of the Act—Wolverhampton Library.
3 Canal at Newbridge constructed by Brindley in 1772.
4 In the custody of Town Clerk. See also Wolverhampton Antiquary Vol. I p. 18.

filth or annoyance whatsoever". Their appointment was for one year only. In March 1779 a committee, consisting of four Commissioners, was given the task of supervising this department, and early in the next year, it was ordered that they obtain the best price for the "Muck, Dung or Manure" collected by the Scavengers in the course of their duties". Thus did Wolverhampton's first public health officers go about their problems.

The collection of the Town Rate, levied under the terms of the Act, appears to have constituted a major difficulty for the early Commissioners. At their meeting on 29th August 1777, it was ordered that a rate of 4d. in the pound be levied on buildings of a yearly value of £4—£7. This was to be increased by 6d. for buildings assessed at £7—£14, and by 1/- for those assessed at £14 and upwards. There were many objections to the actual values placed on some of the properties; the first Rate Book, a copy of which has been kept, is full of notes to this effect, and the word "Appealed" frequently appears. The Commissioners, however, seem to have pursued their course determinedly. Notices were served on those refusing payment of the Rate, and proceedings ordered. Entries relating to "Arrears" soon became common.

A salary, on the basis of 6d. in the pound collected, was paid to those responsible for this task, which was a half-yearly one. On one occasion (6 February 1782), it is recorded that Joseph Jobbern was "granted 2 gns. for his trouble in collecting overdue rates". On the whole the Commissioners seem to have achieved a remarkable improvement within a short time, and there is little evidence during the earlier years, at any rate, of abuse and apathy so commonly associated with these statutory authorities. It was not until the Cholera epidemic of 1832 had devastated the town that government by Commissioners was proved to be inadequate for a place of Wolverhampton's size and importance. Even then another 16 years were allowed to pass before the town received its Charter of Incorporation, and the Commissioners were finally deprived of office.

So much then, for some of the more important outward changes which occurred in Wolverhampton during this period. The building of fashionable town houses; the development of new streets; the opening of another church and burial ground; and the attempts to clear away much of the old town that was both undesirable and a practical obstacle to further expansion; meant that Wolverhampton had kept as well abreast of the time as the majority of her neighbours, and had, indeed, outstripped many.

Shaw, writing in his "History of Staffordshire" at the very end of the century, praises the town and its amenities. By reason of the improvements made in it, he says, and the fact that "excellent accommodation is to be found at the principal inns", it was much frequented by travellers going from London to the North-West, " . . . . . who have the further advantage of good roads and a picturesque country from thence to Shrewsbury". He tells us encouragingly that Wolverhampton "is nearly surrounded by gardens, which add much to the health and pleasure of the inhabitants". Blind as he so obviously was to many of the town's shortcomings, his assessment of it is one with which a large number of his contemporaries would have agreed. Few places in the West Midlands had as yet taken such steps as Wolverhampton to set their houses in order, and by comparntive standards its record during the 18th century was a good one.

Besides being a market town, Wolverhampton was also situated on the branch of the Holyhead Road which passed through Birmingham and the Black Country and was thus a halting place for traffic passing from London to North Wales and Ireland. Inns where travellers could obtain rest and refreshment and, when required, a night's lodging, were very necessary and the "Swan" and the "Angel" largely filled this need with a success to which, as we have seen, Shaw bears eloquent testimony. There were, of course, other hostelries—of lesser fame—such as the "Bell" the "George" the "Red Lion" and the "Cock", which did a thriving trade, particularly on market days. We should not lose sight of the distinction between these places of rest and refreshment, so vital to the comfort of the travelling public in those days before the railways, and the taverns or alehouses whose primary function seems to have been to quench the abiding thirst of the more humble townsfolk of Wolverhampton.

The "Swan Inn" was the most important of these hostelries and seems to have occupied this position from quite early times. It stood on the east side of Queen's Square, on the site of Lloyd's Bank. Over the main entrance was fixed a large model[1] of a swan. The inn yard at the rear was approached from the square beneath an archway; it also communicated with Berry Street and the road to the east, so that coaches coming from Willenhall and Bilston could draw into the yard without the trouble of negotiating the windings of Lichfield Street and Berry Street. The coaches were thus able to stand off the highway whilst horses were changed and passengers refreshed. The "Swan" was also one of the centres of social and business life in the town. At least one of the Freemasons' lodges met here as an advertisement in the Wolverhampton Chronicle of 12 June 1792 bears testimony. The Town Commissioners occasionally did their business here, as did also the manorial courts, and it was customary for the Consistory Court of Wolverhampton to adjourn here from the cold and draughty atmosphere of the church. Later on, in the following century the Pitt Club held their dinners at the "Swan" and convivial gatherings they must have been to judge from the minute books that have survived.[2]

In the early part of the 18th century the proprietor was William Newcombe; he was followed some time later by Joshua Latham. Latham, who was born in Chester in 1733,[3] was mine host until his death in 1771 when he was followed by Richard Green. Later on in the beginning of the new century Mrs. Ann Gale kept the inn.

A few doors from the "Swan" and nearer Dudley Street stood the "Angel", which rivalled its neighbour for first place in popularity. James Walker was the proprietor in the middle of the 18th century and is so described on the tombstone of his wife Eleanor, placed over her grave in the cross aisle of the nave of the Collegiate Church. He married twice more, and had a son, grandson and great grandson,[4] who were all clergymen—the two former being officials of Wolverhampton church. James Walker died in 1783, and his will was proved in the Wolverhampton Peculiar Court, 28 April 1783.

The "Red Lion" in Tup Street (now North Street) was the more usual rendezvous of the Town Commissioners, and was eventually purchased by their successors as a site for the new Town Hall. In Victoria Street (formerly Cock or Tunwall Street) stood the "Cock" Inn, on a site near the present mock Tudor public house known as "Giffards Arms". Its history can be traced to the early part of the 16th century when it was sold by James Byng to James Leveson. After the Restoration the proprietor issued a copper token with the quaint inscription "Kitt oth' Cock".[5] In the early years of the 18th century it was kept by the family of Hollier and in 1770 the proprietor was William Bamford. It was then known as the "Cock and Bell".

1 This can still be seen over the entrance to the "Swan & Peacock" on Snow Hill.
2 Wolverhampton Antiquary Vol. II p. 10 et seq.
3 His baptism appears in Holy Trinity Register, Chester.
4 See his Memorial in St. Peter's Church.
5 A specimen in possession of N. W. Tildesley.

The "George Inn" formerly stood in Queen's Square on the site of premises now occupied by Messrs. J. Lyons & Co. Ltd., but it was moved about 1735-40 to its present position in Stafford Street. Before its removal Edward Henney kept it and afterwards Christopher Pountney was proprietor. The new inn was much in favour at this time when the "Swan" was in the process of being rebuilt. Dean Lyttelton notified Dr. Richard Wilkes from Hagley, 3rd October 1753 . . . . . "I have wrote to Mr. Buckeridge at Lichfield (to whom I sent my folio, Staffordshire manuscript), and desired him to send it to the "George", at Wolverhampton direct to you . . . . . " on the 5 November 1734. The Town Constables paid Christopher Pountney 8s. od. for 4 bottles of wine; and 18s. 6d. for "wine at ye George" in 1749.[1] This inn was used for post office purposes and so to a less extent were the "Red Lion" and the "Swan".

In old Lichfield Street stood the "Noah's Ark Inn" whose chief claim to fame lay in the fact that in a room at the rear the early Methodists held their meetings and here was built the Noah's Ark Chapel which survived (although not used for its original purpose) until the clearance of the area in 1877. It was in this chapel, as we have before mentioned, that the Rev. John Wesley preached, the last occasion being on 23 March 1790, when he addressed "a numerous and respectable audience". The proprietor at that time was William Horton who had taken over the premises a few months earlier. In 1791 he advertises as a rum and spirit dealer. He was very active in the affairs of the town and his florid signature is to be found at this time in both the Vestry Minute Book and the Charity School Minute Book. After a successful business life he retired to Tettenhall where he died in 1825. Other members of his family were also engaged in the business of victualling. His niece was married to John Hargrove who kept the "White Rose" in old Lichfield Street and later the "Black Boy" in the Horse Fair and his sister-in-law was proprietor of the "Golden Fleece" in Dudley Street. This latter place, which stood at the corner of John's Lane, was more of a tavern than an inn, but it was very popular and at least one fortune was made there. The early title deeds of these premises have survived and from them we learn much of its history.[2]

In 1698 it was known by the sign of the "Welsh Harp" but later on, in the early part of the 18th century the name was changed to the "Fleece" and later on to the "Golden Fleece". About 1794 it was purchased by Thomas and Mary Faulkner. They had both been in the service of the Molineux family, he as footman and she as sewing maid, and it is possible that they were able to start in business as a result of a legacy which one of the Molineux's left to each of his servants. Mary Faulkner remained as proprietor of the "Golden Fleece" until about 1816[3] when she retired and left the town for the more salubrious climate of Tettenhall. Although she had little schooling, she was a shrewd business woman, of strong physique and masterful mind, who managed her husband, the inn, and her customers with equal ability. If any man became drunk and troublesome she was in the forefront in superintending his ejectment and her sharp tongue soon subdued any who became argumentative. She had three husbands and all submitted to her will. She married her last husband when she was 43, and they lived long enough to celebrate together their golden wedding. She died in 1859 at the great age of 94.[4]

For the greater part of the 18th century Wolverhampton was without any local newspaper of its own and had to depend for what news it received on Aris's "Birmingham Gazette" which started in the middle of the century, and what London papers filtered

1 Wolverhampton Antiquary Vol. II p. 115.
2 They may be seen at Public Library Ref. Dept.
3 In 1818 Benjamin Butler was proprietor—Wolverhampton Directory.
4 From the family records of the editor.

through to the Midlands. In 1789 the "Wolverhampton Chronicle" came into being but the men of enterprise who, under the name of Proprietors founded it, have hitherto preserved their identity in dignified silence. That they ultimately lost their money was of no particular matter, with the exception of the printer, for they were all men who could well afford it. The Continental Revolution which burst upon them before their child had found its legs upset the conditions under which prosperity could be found—a public eager to search for news among the advertisements and advertisers ready to rush into print, and both ready to pay. A leaf from the Stock Book of the Company[1] has survived and this tells us something of their financial vicissitudes. They went off to a shaky start, but before they ruled off their venture as hopeless they ploughed some more money into the business.

"August 18 1789. At a meeting of the Proprietors of the *Wolverhampton Chronicle*, and *Staffordshire Advertiser*, held this day, ordered that a call of Ten Pounds p. share be made and paid into the hands of Mr. Hordern".

Other meetings were held on 26 October 1789 when there was a further call of £5, on 6 February 1790 when £10 was called and on 31 May 1790 when £15 was called. Mr. Smart the printer who was also a bookseller and stationer in the High Street, and to eke out a precarious existence sold pills, potions and patent medicines, was Secretary of the Company. The proprietors, who sign the stock book, but never all together, numbered ten and the value of a share was apparently about £50. The following sign the book:—George Molineux, P. Hinckes, Richard Tooth, Robert Morrison, William Tindall, James Hordern, Joseph Smart, William Beto Taylor, Isaac Scott, and Joseph Lane.

The first number of the "Wolverhampton Chronicle" came out on Wednesday, 2nd of September 1789 and was priced 3½d. (stamp duty 2d.). The proprietors assure the public that they had not "been induced by lucrative motives", they would "find this paper open to every party, biassed by none; free from a wanton Detraction of Private Characters, yet ready to attack the Vices of the Day, though supported by Wealth, or patronized by Power". The inhabitants had "long submitted' to receive their intelligence from the neighbouring counties—a Staffordshire PAPER is now presented to them".

By 30 September 1789 (no. 5) the paper claims to have had "a rapid and extensive Sale" and was beginning to feel its consequence as a County Paper. But this was not to be. The county had to be shared and before the paper recommenced in 1810 under Gower and Smart, a rival (but Saturday) paper had started in Stafford in 1795. The proprietors struggled on manfully until 1793 when the newspaper ceased publication and for the next seventeen years the town was without its local Journal.

The provisions set out in Wolverhampton's first Improvement Act to deal with the cleansing and scavenging of the streets leaves us in no doubt that by 1777 the town's industries were often a major source of nuisance and obstruction. Anyone found "washing any Brass Dirt or Ashes, or any kind of Metal" outside their shops or yards was liable to a penalty of 10/-; the common practice of using the street itself for these purposes was now forbidden.

The inconvenience of carts "used in carrying and conveying Goods and Merchandize" from the newly opened canal to the town centre and back was also to be checked by the terms of the new Act, and the detailed regulations imposed on these vehicles and their drivers points directly to the great increase in their use by those engaged in industry. Other credible sources of our industrial history at this period confirm the general im-

1 At the Public Library—Mander Collection.

CHAPTER X

THE REGENCY

To BEGIN this chapter at the beginning of a century gives us the advantage of a round figure only, for the year 1800 was in the middle of a European war with no decisive victory to point to a conclusion, nor had there been any special landmarks or change in the conduct of the Town. A break in the issue of the local Newspaper in 1793, though it had never been very remarkable as a local chronicle, helps to widen the gap in our knowledge of the period.

There was, however, one notable event which had just occurred and was made manifest by a publication of this year (Remarks on A Tour to North and South Wales in August of the year 1797, by Henry Wigstead, with plates by Rowlandson, Pugh, Howitt and etc. (Aquatinted by I. Hill) London. Published by W. Wigstead, No. 40 Charing Cross, 1800), namely the journey of Thomas Rowlandson, the artist, and Henry Wigstead in search (like Dr. Syntax before them) of the picturesque. They approached Wolverhampton from Dudley finding the road "but indifferent", being kept in repair mostly with clinkers and cinders from the adjacent forges, but were relieved in finding "a neat market town" and the road to Shifnal "very pleasant".[1]

The visit gained for posterity a lively sketch of the Market Place, looking up the "High Street" towards the church. It is in Rowlandson's inimitable style and forms, apart from the church, the earliest view of the town. (The original water-colour drawing is preserved at the Art Gallery). Conspicuous on one side is the old gabled half-timbered corner house at the turning into Lichfield Street, (it stood over the modern road). Above, it contained the town clock, below was T. Bevan's brandy shop. Matching it on the other side is John Likley's wine and spirit store (to become in December 1818 the long established business of George Cope) a stately Georgian brick building dated 1732. The foreground shows the meat market or shambles, with butchers working at their stalls. The scene has much that is charming of the past, a setting which J. M. W. Turner later in more elaborate fashion also depicted from the same point of view a position opposite the Swan Hotel.

The recommencement of the Wolverhampton Chronicle as a weekly newspaper on Wednesday, January 9th, 1811 at a price of 6d. (of which 3½d. was tax[2]) added to the amenities and excitement of the town. It is true that the local news is rather sparse, partly because there was no great demand for publishing information that was already stale, and for the reason that two of the four pages were filled with advertisements, principally of sales by auction and those always attractive patent medicines, and there was abundant European news. Of local events one cannot help being struck by the prevalence of professional pedestrianism and shocked by the constant inquests on victims claimed by the unguarded coal pits and unprotected machinery. State Lotteries still guided the money of the speculator into the public funds, and the possibility of repressive Parliamentary action stimulated the ticket distributors to more urgent appeals.

1 "Remarks on a Tour to North and South Wales in August of the Year 1797" by Henry Wigstead. Published by W. Wigstead, London, 1800-p. 8.
2 Afterwards 7d.: 1816.

It was a time when the protracted European warfare was beginning seriously to curtail the local export trade, but news from Lord Wellington in the Peninsula was regularly cheerful and overshadowed any cloud looming over America; yet increasing poverty and high prices made grievances enough.

We have to look to this time for the vocal evidence of the Radical party who with the Whigs voiced the need for Free Trade and supported the manufacturing interest. Principal among these were Richard Fryer, a banker, and Joseph Pearson, a merchant. The former took the chair at a Town's Meeting to protest against the East Indian Co.'s monopoly, asserting that British subjects had the right of Free Trade with every part of the British Empire. His speech, we learn, was "short but animated", and, it may be judged, flowery. "Open those ports—those seas (he said), then again would the loom and the anvil sound responsive to the song of cheerful industry; then would the ships which now crowd our harbours . . . with swelling sails plough the trackless ocean to the most distant climes . . ." It was the speech of an Imperialist and "completely successful. Not a dissenting voice was heard." It was, besides, the earliest reported effort of our first M.P., who then lived in Lichfield Street (probably over his Bank, a dignified Georgian edifice which survived into the 20th century).

The compulsory General Fast and day of humiliation held in February or March at this period was not the only sign of Christian endeavour. As early as 26 January 1810, Mr. John Freer Proud M.R.C.S.[1] had pointed out the expediency of establishing a Dispensary in the town; but with no practical result.[2] Attention also had been turned, with the support also of the Non Conformists, to the "London Society for promoting Christianity among the Jews"; the County was also being canvassed for the formation of Auxiliary Bible Societies;[3] while the Vestry held a meeting to consider the pressing necessity of providing an additional Burial ground.[4] But perhaps no more striking example could be given of the tender conscience of the inhabitants than the remarkable order promulgated by the constables which to be appreciated must be set out in full. One cannot help thinking that a game of marbles had its less innocent side.

SABBATH BREAKING

Whereas, the Practice of Sabbath Breaking, by Boys playing Marbles and other unlawful Games, has arisen to a shameful Height in this Town; NOTICE IS HEREBY GIVEN, that a strict Watch will be kept in future, and whoever is found offending will be apprehended and punished with the utmost Rigour of the Law; and all Parents, Guardians, and Masters, are hereby required to prevent, as far as lies in their Power, the Commission of such Crimes.

W. READY } Constables, Wolverhampton
J. BROWN } March 17, 1812

It could probably be shown that the move towards Sunday Schools started with the Protestant Dissenters in their chapel school-house in St. John's Street in 1785, for at the 28th anniversary in July 1813, it was claimed that upwards of 1,200 children had been educated at that school.[5] Nevertheless the Established Church was alive to such benefits, and £110 was collected for the purpose of Sunday Schools in May 1813.

1 Wolverhampton Chronicle 27 Feb. 1811.
2 Wolverhampton having to share with what success they may with the local branch of the Seisdon Hundred in the County of Stafford General Infirmary of which, in 1812, James Hordern and John Mander "esquires" held office as stewards. Wolverhampton Chronicle, 29 Jan. 1812.
3 Do. Apr. 1812.
4 Do. 9 Dec. 1812.
5 The Rev. J. Steward had also a private "Seminary" for the education of 20 pupils at his Manse (43 St. John's Street).

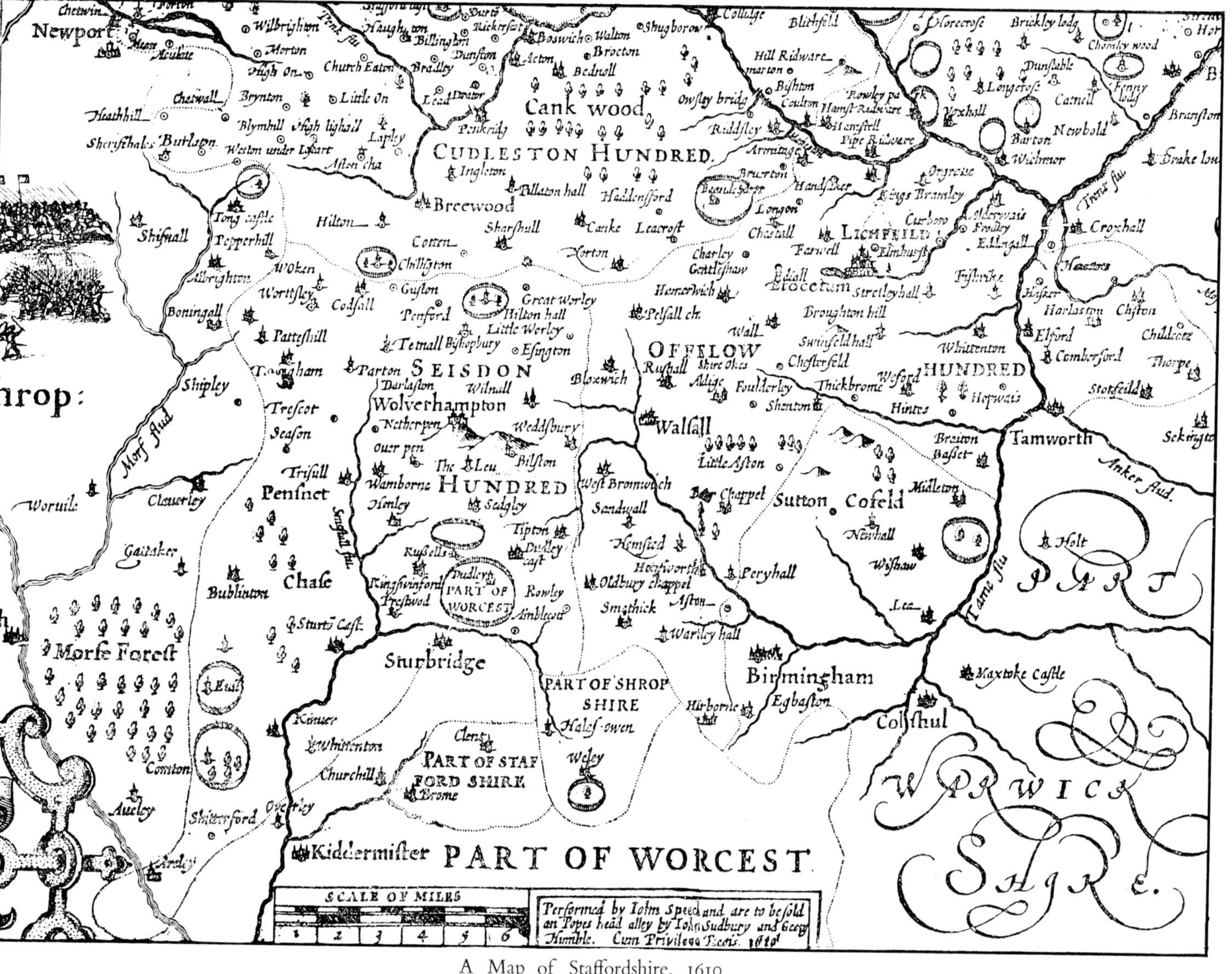

A Map of Staffordshire, 1610

Lichfield Street and High Green, 1870

The 2nd September 1813 saw the opening of the newly built Queen Street Chapel with sermons both morning and evening (the latter by J. A. James of Birmingham who was one of the celebrated preachers of his day[1]). It was a brick edifice of the usual architecture of that period with the round-headed windows and low pitched roof, on the same corner site as that of the present distressingly ugly building of stone. The ground, as was that of its predecessor in Princess Street, was owned by one of its members, John Mander, whose memorial slab within describes him as "the unwearied and munificent friend of religion and education." He had conceived[2] of the business-like idea of letting the cellars to Joseph Barber, "a Wine and Brandy Merchant", which inspired some ribald lines about the different spirits "above and below", and must have led to some head shakings in that strict and grave society.[3] With what satisfaction must the Landlord, a regular attender in the chapel portion, have lent himself to his devotions secure in the knowledge that the basement also was paying its way!

Activity at the Old Church was signalised by a visit from the bishop of the diocese on a rare and long overdue business of a Confirmation. The ceremony was promised well in advance, and came to be of portentous proportions when it took place on Sunday 28th August 1814. It involved a week-end stay for the bishop at the Lion Inn where he arrived on Saturday evening, presumably from Eccleshall; but he cannot have grumbled at the result. The amazing number of 2,919 persons were in fact then confirmed, being a record for his episcopate hitherto and probably for the town.[4]

The newspaper tells us that "thanks to the arrangements the ceremony was gone through with the utmost decorum, without any accident, and in much shorter time than could be expected."

It has already been hinted that the inhabitants, loyal, long suffering, martial (in that they readily provided their quota for the militia by volunteers rather than by ballot) and if necessary bellicose, were also war weary. They looked eagerly for peace beyond the haze of decisive victories. But the battles near Leipzic brought general rejoicings, and this, followed by news of the Marquess of Wellington's successes in France and the surrender of Dresden in Saxony, whether the figures given of the French losses were true or not, "occasioned the highest exultation." The concerted action taken to show these manifestations took the form of general illuminations, bell ringing, the playing of patriotic airs by bands, and frequently by banquets for the aged poor. It was estimated that on Monday 29th November 25 sheep and 2 cows were roasted at the different public houses and that at 2 o'clock nearly 2,000 persons "were regaled with excellent dinners and quart of ale each". Statisticians conjured with figures and stated that at the Peacock Inn alone 150 diners had the united ages of 10,433 (being an average of 69¼) and other inns were not dissimilar. Owing to the exceptional inclemency of the weather two large fires were lighted in the Market place, besides others in various parts of the town. A chastening incident was caused by the cannon fired by Mr. W. Tortoiseshell to give expression to his feelings, which burst into a number of pieces, so that "part of the cannon or its contents" pierced his fragile exterior, with damaging yet not with fatal results. But all this was somewhat premature it was not until March 1814 that the probabliity of a settled peace was discussed. becoming a matter of daily import when Napoleon had retired an exile to Elba. While the negotiations proceeded, the town witnessed the daily passage of French prisoners of

1 Wolverhampton Chronicle, 1 Sep. 1813.
2 Ibid. 20 Oct.
3 Matthews "Congregational Churches," p. 205.
4 At the confirmation on Sat. 2 Oct. 1789 by the Bp. of Oxford, (late Dean). 1,785 persons "redeemed the pledges of their sponsors"—Wolverhampton Chronicle, 6 Oct.

war who had been quartered at Bridgnorth and beyond on parole, and the converse flow of war-worn soldiery, both returning home. The winter of 1813—14 was exceptionally cold with prolonged frost and snow, which interrupted communications with the outside world.[1] Memories had to go back to 1795 for such another; and considerable distress was caused to the "Lower Orders". The people were however cheered by the "probability of peace", while sympathy was sought for the "suffering Germans" and a considerable sum of money was raised for their alleviation.[2]

The tidings of Peace following Napoleon's exile in Elba reached Wolverhampton early on Friday morning 3 June 1814 and a special leaflet describing the Definitive Treaty was printed off to meet the occasion. The church bells awoke the inhabitants and the joy soon became general. The various coaches that passed through the town bore a festive appearance, and the eight horses which drew the mail coach from Birmingham were particularly observed. The feeling of the townsmen favoured illuminations for expressing their sentiments and it was decided to hold these, which would take some preparation, a fortnight later.

By 8-30 in the morning of the day selected the Change Ringers in the Church tower had completed their 3 hour peal of 5,040 grandsire triples in six courses of 840. Shops were closed at 12 and business ended, and the town was given over to good cheer and feasting in which 4,000 of the poor, distributed among the numerous public houses, were willing to share. The newspaper gives a full description of the many Transparencies "large and elegant" which were illuminated at 9 p.m. These in their simpler form showed the word "Peace" and a Lion or a Britannia or some other loyal emblem, and were evidence that the artists in the many japanners' work had been actively employed. It is difficult to appreciate how much interest and pleasure could come from the contemplation of these Transparencies which glowed faintly and feebly in front of a colza oil lamp or a row of tallow candles; but the town tried nobly to make darkness visible at least on this occasion. It is mentioned especially that Messrs. Ryton, C. Mander and Illidge gave dinners to their workmen.[3] But the greatest enterprise in this direction occurred on Thanksgiving day (Thursday 7 July) when Samuel Fereday (Ironmaster) and his partners marched 5,000 of their workpeople to church and then dined them in the field in front of his house at Ettingshall Park. An attraction was 100 barrels of "Stout Staffordshire ale" and 100 tables set out in two rows. At a bugle note a solemn benediction was pronounced in the most impressive manner by the ubiquitous Rev. J. Clare. It is stated that nearly the whole of the population of Wolverhampton poured out of the town to witness so novel an event. But such feasting was merely transitory, and the country had they known it, was rushing towards a collapse. The peace signed with America (24 December) left the town unimpressed; but the Profanation of the Sabbath called forth protest as "a very notorious and growing evil." The clergy, church and chapel-wardens and the two Constables gave notice that the laws enacted for the proper observation of the Lord's Day, would forthwith be put into execution. Tippling in Public houses; exposing meat and goods for sale; the use of carts and waggons in their ordinary occupations; the idling of profane persons in the streets during Divine Service, and the marble-playing boy: would all be matters for the attention of the justices. And it was no idle warning, for with the exception of Sir John Wrottesley and Joseph Lane (Wombourne), the local magistracy were all Reverend sirs, A. B. Haden, John Clare, Charles Wrottesley, G. W. Kempson, P. H. Petit (Hilton) and Nathaniel Hinde (Kingswinford).

1 Wolverhampton Chronicle 26 Jan. 1814. 2 Ib. 6, 13, 20 April. 3 Ib. 22 June 1814.

The corn laws too met with stormy protestation. A meeting of the inhabitants with Mr. Joseph Pearson in the chair, in March 1815, called attention to the fact that rents were high and should be reduced: the population, during a war of unprecedented length and expense had endured privations and was chiefly composed of small manufacturers whose earnings were barely sufficient for their support. Cheapness of labour on the continent (still is the story told) gave their manufacturers a decisive advantage, and the price of food must not be advanced merely because the Farming Interest were temporarily depressed. Mr. Pearson and his friends were not adverse to cheap labour.

The Wolverhampton petition against the Bill was signed by 6—7,000,[1] and was presented by the Rt. Hon. Lord G. Leveson-Gower on Friday 10 March 1815 (though he could not bring himself to vote against the third reading!). The other County Member (Mr. Littleton) was friendly to the principle of the Bill. In Mr. C. P. Villiers Wolverhampton eventually found a man who could voice insistently the other opinion. But the immediate news was not reassuring, for Napoleon was abroad again and heading for Waterloo (18 June). Moreover financial trouble was beginning to make itself felt. A run on banking houses in the north presaged no good, for the disease, and with it alarm, spread. Locally the Bilston Banks, supporters of iron-works now stagnating, were the first to stop payment. Rushbury's stopped; Fereday, Smith and Fisher, and Wooley's, were in difficulties, and a movement among local tradesmen to support them by taking their notes could only for a time restore confidence. The ironmasters of the district claimed to have been losing thousands a week. They pointed out that provisions were cheap and a cut in wages was necessary. The miners and ironworkers may be reckoned as simple, honest, ignorant but seldom truculent and although the greater part of them were in work they struck against this inroad on their standard of living, and on Monday 13 November 1815 some 3 or 400 marched to the town with bludgeons and sticks apparently bent upon riot and depredation. Mr. Fereday whom they had followed from Bilston, addressed them from the window of the Swan Hotel and at the Angel Inn (Dudley Street) and was able to pacify them, though the danger of riot still remained. Special constables were sworn-in that night and two troops of the Staffordshire Yeomanry arrived next morning. In the afternoon their services were called for near Coseley where a great number of miners had collected and were thought a menace. The gallant Yeomanry manoeuvered with difficulty over the broken ground and although they captured two prisoners, the honours may be said to have been with their adversaries. But the magistrates looked seriously upon the matter, which called forth the Lord Lieutenant (Earl Talbot), the Hon. Edward Monckton, and his son Edward Monckton, Esq., Sir John Wrottesley, Bart., and the Revs. J. Clare and C. Wrottesley. Although no harm had been done anxiety continued, especially on Wednesday, market day. A third troop of yeomanry had arrived and also a detachment of 2nd Dragoon Guards and of the Middlesex Militia with some recruiting parties from Birmingham. On Friday a detachment of the 9th Dragoons from Manchester relieved the yeomanry and the rest, and remained quartered in the town.[2] Some of the Berkshire Militia, which had been at Lichfield, were quartered here from 5 to 20 February 1816, and were succeeded by the 73rd Foot.

But although Wolverhampton was not the storm centre, it shared in the depression. In February 1816 Messrs. George Rushbury, senior and junior, coal dealers of Bilston, are bankrupts, and in March Messrs. Gibbons and Co., of the Wolverhampton "Old Bank" owing to the "great and increasing pressure of the extensive Ironworks" with which they

1 9,000 signed at Dudley & 3 000 at Bilston—Wolverhampton Chronicle 15 March.
2 They were called out again to keep the peace under Rev. A. B. Haden at Tipton on 22 Jan. 1816, but there was no violence

were connected, were forced to suspend payment, Messrs. Thomas, John and Benjamin Gibbons, junior, were made bankrupt in March. There was a run upon the bank of Messrs. Hordern, Molineux & Co. but it withstood the shock.

This misfortune is probably the reason for the frequent appearance of bank notes, of £1 and 10s. nominal value, dated September and October 1815, of the firm of Rushbury of Cocksheet's Colliery, Bilston, and also of Messrs. Gibbons of the Old Bank. They were unredeemed and became curiosities and a record of a distant crisis and misfortune. Old Mr. Thomas Gibbons did not live to see this catastrophe. He died 7 June 1813 at Teignmouth aged 83 of society "a useful and exemplary member" and to his numerous family "a most tender and affectionate parent."[1] It is probably to him that the surprising collection of Old Masters, not excluding Titian, N. Poussin, Guido, Cuyp, Opie, Stubbs and Morland, and chef d'oeuvres of Bird "of unquestionable originality", is due. In particular are mentioned "the St. Cecilia and Master Bunbury of Sir Joshua Reynolds; two noble Landscapes by Wilson: the Gipsies and Windmill of Gainsborough". But all fell by the hammer of Mr. Moreton the auctioneer, as well as a library of 3,000 volumes, a pipe of excellent port and 170 dozen of the same in Bottle, in August 1816. Was "the Oaks" on the Merridale Lane to see its equal again? It is doubtful whether Mr. Corser who succeeded to this roomy mansion could match in magnificence these Georgian glories; or, later, alderman John Marston, a water drinker.

The economic distress continued, and in October 1816 it was estimated that upwards of 4,500 individuals, being more than one quarter of the population of the town and mostly unemployed, were in very distressed circumstances. The enterprise of the miners in the heat of the summer of dragging waggons loaded with coal by three different routes towards the metropolis and others towards Liverpool and Uppingham, although they were stopped with great tact just short of their destinations, served to make their distresses known to a wider public. Subscription lists to ameliorate the hardships were being formed both in town and country and were prosecuted with much energy: but it was found that the trading part of the district had its own difficulties and could help but little, while poor rates increased, the power to pay diminished.

Another matter in which Birmingham set an example was in the establishment of a Flour and Bread Company, based on the principle that savings in price could be made if the miller and baker were the same person and the factory was run on a large scale, and if the buyer was secured by being a share-holder in the concern.

The affair was given a semi-public blessing by being launched at a meeting at the Public Office on Friday 28 August 1812,[2] when it was resolved that an Association should be formed "for the purpose of supplying the Inhabitants of the Town with good and wholesome Wheaton Flour and Bread at the lowest Price." The capital was 10,000 £1 shares—of which no person should hold more than 20 (afterwards raised to 40, and capital to 15,000).[3] Richard Fryer marked his approval by becoming treasurer and banker, and a committee of 21 was formed of an equally Radical complexion, whose names, as the names of enterprising men, heading for trouble, may be repeated.

R. Fryer	Jos. Pearson	Robt. Jones	T. Savage	Jos. Underhill
W. Wenman	Wm. Ready	R. Farmer	J. Aston	
J. Felton	George Scott	J. Cornforth	Jos. Baker	
R. Gough	Wm. Clark	B. Mander	Jos. Wright	
T. Timmins	J. Moreton	Wm. Perry	Saml. Wood	

1 Obituary—Wolverhampton Chronicle 16 June 1813.
2 Notice—Wolverhampton Chronicle 26 Aug. 1812.
3 Report at Annual Meeting, 22 Sep. 1813.

The public welcomed the project; the bakers were hostile. It came at a time too when steps were taken to enforce the Statute concerning the size and quality of bread in the county—perhaps reminded the authorities of their duties in this regard.

It was perhaps fortunate that the baking of bread was such an every day domestic affair, because the committee, strong in sentiment, was undoubtedly weak on the technical side. The notice: "WANTED, SEVERAL JOURNEYMEN BAKERS, who perfectly understand their Business" was not without meaning; for Benjamin Mander who, as managing-director, sought their services and was to study their characters for Integrity, Sobriety and Industry, was himself a Japanner. A Bill of Indictment had been found against him and his committee at the Lent Assizes for conspiracy under the Act of 6 Geo. I c. 18 sec. 18 which the booksellers of the town and district were selling, price 2d. The bakers were retaliating. The case was brought to trial at the Summer Assizes at Stafford (The King versus B. Mander and eight others) and proved a fiasco from the bakers' point of view, judge, jury and audience being for the defendants. It is possible that the prosecution was only half-hearted, counsel had only been briefed at the last moment, and vainly did his witnesses show that the Union Mill was "unfair trading", "a monopoly", and would drive the bakers to extinction. The Judge rather pertinently asked how the case differed from the decision given by Lord Ellenborough in 1811, in favour of the Birmingham Flour and Bread Company (The King *v.* Webb) and to that there was no answer. The verdict of not guilty, that the company was not illegally associated, was a popular one; and though the news reached Wolverhampton at day break the bells almost immediately commenced to ring and continued at intervals during the day. The coach bringing the witnesses was met at Gosbrook and drawn through the town in triumph. The crowds assembled were immense, shouting "Justice and Union for ever", "The Big Loaf has won". And yet the wildest rumours had been afloat; that B. Mander as ringleader was to be hanged and the rest transported for seven years; but "it was a long and fair fought Battle and the Victory quite compleat! . . . . if we had not taken a single witness, we should have won . . ."[1]

There followed the inevitable "dinner" at the Swan Hotel, with the usual long list of toasts, including, on this occasion "Sir John Chetwode and a Staffordshire Jury", and "The Union Mill, and may it always be found a public good." It still grinds and a street has long borne its name.

The Town was dimly lit at infrequent intervals by oil lamps during the darker months, to pass from these to gas illumination was progress glorified. The display of this illuminant by Matthew Boulton at Soho in 1802,[2] turned the attention of those who were scientifically minded towards gas lighting, and it was a firm of manufacturing chemists, Mander, Weaver & Co. who first introduced gas into the town, at some unascertained date, to light presumably their own works and for such processes in the manufacture of chemicals as required heat. Two of the partners were among the 57 subscribers who were formed into "The Wolverhampton Gas Light Company" by Act of Parliament on 22 June 1820.[3] Their capital was £10,000 and their ambition "the better lighting of the Town". The enterprise was actively pursued during the summer and autumn; two gasometers were ordered and the prospect of being able to offer gas in January 1821 "of the purest quality without smell or stain"[4] was no small attraction.

1 Family letter, 4 Aug. 1814.
2 "Old & New Birmingham", p. 269.
3 I Geo. IV cap. viii.
4 Wolverhampton Chronicle, 22 Nov. 1820.

The most conspicuous result of their enterprise was the erection of a monstrous pillar surmounted by a lantern on the site of the market cross on the High Green in 1821. The names of the committee of optimistic gentlemen who were responsible for its cost were inscribed on its base, and may be repeated here:—R. Fryer, T. Savage, T. Timmins, T. H. Ward, J. Heape, P. Deakin and W. Parkes. It seems likely that this landmark, which was intended to be ornamental was inspired by the writings of Frederick Accum, who advocated standards of pagoda-like and other strange devices to support the gas jet.[1] But the experiment at Wolverhampton failed, both in its purpose, for the light was too high to be an assistance, and as an ornament, for it was laughed at as a mighty "candlestick", which it closely resembled. It was moreover a nuisance, or the cause of such. By 1826 it had become a scandal, and "disgraced the public situation in which it was placed," being, on account of its want of palisading around it, "a lounging place for the most notoriously vicious, and dissolute characters of both sexes." But some expense would attach to its removal. Was it proper to invite those who had contributed to its erection (including the Lord of the Manor, on whose land it stood) to subscribe again for its demolition? Uncertainty meant respite for many years.[2]

But gases could be put to other uses. In the past 40 years aeronautics had passed through their experimental stage, and a flight in a ballon could be accomplished with fair safety. "Mr. Green the celebrated aeronaut" had made several ascents in the Midlands, but not at Wolverhampton; there was expense in such an undertaking and the risk, so the aeronaut considered, deserved some reward. But public curiosity was not to be denied and a guaranteed subscription encouraged Mr. Green "respectfully to announce" that he would make an Aerial Voyage from the town in his magnificent Coronation Balloon on the 17 September 1824. The payment of 2s. admitted one to the Union Mill Yard, near the Gas works to watch the inflation; the firing of guns marked various stages of this process. It was stated that the town had never been so full, and every eminence in or near it was occupied by a gaping throng, including the top of the church tower. The question whether Mr. Green would be accompanied was settled at 4-50 p.m. when Mr. Edward Clarke, an iron-founder of the town, "took his seat with the greatest composure". To the strains of the National Anthem the balloon ascended upwards of a mile, and in due course landed safely on Dunston Heath, near Penkridge, twelve miles distant. The day was fine but cloudy, and the town had set itself a precendent for ascents of this kind.

As a mirror of the times lawlessness was much to the fore; the local prison, called the House of Correction, had in July 1812, never been so full. With 47 prisoners it must have been overflowing.[3] (Yet there were to be 65 in 18 June 1817 and 268 in the County gaol) Petty cheating too was rampant. On a single day in August 1813, upwards of 40 shopkeepers were convicted for using short weights, several of which were extremely deficient. Yet over 80 were convicted of a similar offence at another inspection in December 1814; whereas 44 publicans were found giving short measure. In January 1814 at the Staffordshire quarter sessions a man was ordered to be publicly whipped at Wolverhampton for stealing a large cheese. As an additional precaution after a Town's Meeting in November 1811, a nightly patrol was established during the winter for the protection of property. Dudley and Walsall took like measures. The exact benefits produced are uncertain. The following advertisement may not be of a private nature:—

1 Letter in Wolverhampton Chronicle, 2 Aug. 1826.
2 There is a drawing of it on the cover of a pamphlet, dated 1833, called "New Year Election Comicalities". Wrote its waggish author, p. 21, "Ten o'clock. The Gas Lamp has been lighted, and, thank G–d, all is darkness and quiet".
3 Wolverhampton Chronicle, 1 July, 1812.

WANTED,
two Men, of good Character, as
WATCHMEN.
Each Man will be required to watch every other Night.
Apply to Mr. JOB HARDING.

Violent crimes were however of too frequent occurrence to be more than a passing wonder; but even so there were occasions when the public mind was shocked, and prominent notice of these was given in the newspapers.

First, no doubt, came news of the assasination of the Prime Minister, Mr. Perceval, on 11 May 1812, the work of a fanatic who was rewarded with a theatrical trial and much press notice. Eager, as so many others, to show their loyalty, the inhabitants of Wolverhampton of all politics and creeds, met, composed and sent an address to the Prince Regent to express their "abhorence of that most attrocious Act."[1] This was all very proper but rather remote; few of them knew Mr. Perceval. Murder unprovoked was brought more vividly before them, by the pistol shot fired at Mr. Benjamin Robins, a gentleman of position in South Staffordshire, when returning from Stourbridge market on Friday evening 18 December 1812 to his home at Dunsley, near Kinver. The victim was able to stagger home and raise a hue and cry, and the wound was not at first thought mortal. A reward of £100 was offered for information which would lead to the apprehension of the murderer, and after what for those days was a remarkable piece of detection, a Worcester man, called William Howe, was arrested in London, and brought to trial at Stafford. There was in this case some departure from the usual sentence which marked such a solemn part of these ceremonies. Public hangings were then regarded as an important warning to those who pursued a career of vice. It was for those of South Staffordshire to be privileged to mark "the retributive hand of public justice"; and so, at the Lent Assizes 1813 the original sentence that the murderer should be dissected and anatomised, was altered to one of being hung in chains. The body was removed from Stafford on Friday 19 March and in the evening of that day was publicly exposed at the prison in Wolverhampton "enclosed in the iron apparatus",[2] which was to hold it together. Early next morning it was conveyed to Kinver Heath, within a short distance of the spot where Mr. Robins was shot, and suspended on a Gibbet about 20 ft. high, close to the road leading from Dunsley to Stourbridge "but not in view of Mr. Robin's house"—a thoughtful touch.

The interested reader maybe referred to the trial itself which was related at length in the local newspapers at the expense of compressing much "political intelligence"; but the story has a sequel—perhaps two.

In the first place there was offered for sale "A Tyburn Ticket, for the parish of Wolverhampton."[3] And then, after menacing the countryside for some eighteen months, the remains were stolen from the gibbet during the night of 3 September 1814. Gibbet Wood, Kinver, still has its place on the map and is not unknown to hunt and hound. It is stated to have been the last case of hanging in chains in the country.

In 1817 two local criminal cases led to an alteration of the law. The one, Ashford *v.* Thornton, properly belongs to Warwickshire; but the trial was printed and sold by the booksellers (Smart and Simpson) of this town, and aroused general wonder and interest, so may be mentioned here.[4]

1 Wolverhampton Chronicle, 20, 27 May, 1812. 2 Wolverhampton Chronicle, 24 March, 1813. 3 Ib., 24 March.
4 Notice in Wolverhampton Chronicle, 11 Feb., 1818. It is more fully recorded in R. K. Dent's Old & New Birmingham, p. 373 seq.

On the morning of 27th May, Mary Ashford, a pretty girl, was found as it appeared brutally murdered in a field near Erdington, and Abraham Thornton, an admirer, was accused of the crime. A jury however, without difficulty, found him not guilty. Whereupon William Ashford, the victim's brother, taking advantage of an almost forgotten law, 'appealed' Abraham Thornton for murder, and at a dramatic trial before several judges on 17 Nov., the *defendant* pleaded "Not Guilty", and throwing down a glove, claimed *Trial by Battel*, a relic of Norman times, last used in 1638. The girl's brother, the prosecutor, being in comparison of inferior physique, and so at a disadvantage, "prayed the judgement of the Court that the said Abraham Thornton be not permitted to wage on him"; but the judges, not regarding the 'appeal' with favour, decided against him, whereupon the case was dropped. The legislature however took steps to end this odd procedure that had outlived its day.

For the other case Wolverhampton provided a background. Let us glance first at the setting. The amount of local crime in 1817 was becoming unmanageable. In March there were over 100 prisoners at the Assizes; in June 268 prisoners were in the county gaol and 65 in the prison at Wolverhampton. The 60 prisoners for trial at the Summer Assizes were mostly there for capital offences (there were no murders, mostly stealing, (*e.g.* horse stealing) in one form or another) and presented, as the judge share, "a long and melancholy list". In this the town had its share:—

Andrew Powell, 40, for a burglary at Wolverhampton.

John Hall, aged 22, and Patrick Morrison, aged 25, for assaulting J. Read in Wolverhampton.

It is the latter case that concerns us, that of two soldiers of the 95th Foot, a detachment of which was quartered in the town, with John Read a civilian. Soldiers were not popular. Already a number of them had been troublesome, not to say offensive, on the anniversary of St. Patrick's Day. So again, on the night of Tuesday 22—23 July these two soldiers, at a loose end and much intoxicated came to belabour John Read in the church-yard (an area not surrounded by railings until 1824) and in the scuffle 1s. and a bad penny of Read's were lost. His sense of loss became a grievance, and Read accused the soldiers of robbing him. His repeated complaints came to the ears of George Roberts "keeper of the house of correction" who, saying it was a "good job", promptly arrested the two soldiers and charged them before a magistrate, Rev. A. B. Haden, (vicar of Wednesbury and "lecturer" at the Collegiate Church) of highway robbery. They were committed for trial at the Stafford Assizes on the Monday following. Quick work. There the prosecution, with witnesses not unmindful, it is believed, of the reward ("Blood money", 4 & 5 W. and M. c. 8) for a conviction for felony (which robbery on the highway of one shilling and upwards constituted) put forward a clear case. This satisfied all those age-long guardians of the innocent, magistrate (a clergy-man), Grand Jury, petty jury and the judge (Mr. Baron Garrow), who had evidently disbelieved the simple story of the defence (who produced no evidence) to the effect that the prisoners were drunk, and so disorderly, and ignorant of wrong-doing. It is significant that George Roberts and his two witnesses received £20, £40 and £10 for their testimony. The injured Read was a miserable specimen of humanity. The judge noted and remarked upon this and spoke impressively about the even-handed justice administered by the law of the land. He then sentenced the soldiers to death. It appears there were 29 "condemned" on this occasion, sentenced mostly in batches of five, of which our prisoners were the last, a "long and melancholy list" indeed. In the majority of the cases the sentence (the only one prescribed by law) was reprieved, and one of "transportation for life" substituted; but on this day seven were "left for execution on Saturday 16th inst."

Up to this point the inhabitants of Wolverhampton had not been interested in the case. Soldiers were birds of passage at the best: if they chose to become gaol-birds it was their own affair. Disorderly conduct must be punished, property protected. Those who had considered the matter at all expected a conviction for common assault. But the disparity between the offence and the sentence came as a shock to sympathetic readers when they saw it much later (as the paper had to carry the news forward a week) in the Wednesday Wolverhampton Chronicle of August 6th.[1] Public opinion was stirred to protect the soldiers, and it was evident that speedy action also was needed if the death penalty was to be averted, for only nine days remained. Mr. Charles Mander, a varnish manufacturer, heard the news from his father who had heard it in the market place, and knowing that legal process must be met in due form they wisely sought legal advice, and in this case free advice, from their solicitor Mr. George Tompson. There must be a petition to the Prince Regent and a 'memorial' to the Judge. Public support was forthcoming; people stirred their memories; additional affidavits were prepared; and the deputation reached London on Tuesday night 12 August. They contrived to see the Home Secretary, Lord Sidmouth, next morning, and that evening he told them he was impressed with their view of the case and that a respite had already been forwarded by special messenger to Stafford. Mr. Mander asked for a copy lest the original should miscarry and this Lord Sidmouth wrote out in his own fair hand:—

Duplicate

Whitehall, 13 August 1817

Sir,

I am to signify to you His Royal Highness the Prince Regent's Commands in the Name and on Behalf of His Majesty, that the Execution of the Sentence of Death passed upon John Hall and Patrick Morrison, now in the Gaol at Stafford, should be respited until further signification of His Royal Highness's Pleasure.

I am, Sir,
Your most Obedient
Humble Servant
Sidmouth.

To the High Sheriff
of the County of Stafford.

The return journey commenced.

The people of Wolverhampton awaited the result expectantly, and the King's Messenger having passed through the town unnoticed (it is possible he went by the shorter, postal, route) Charles Mander was the first to give tidings of his success to an eager throng. He was spared the melodramatic: a last minute reprieve from the scaffold, which retelling the story is apt to inspire, for the final spectacle was not staged, and his copy of the Reprieve was not used. It is preserved, with the affidavits and papers concerned, by his descendants.

The movement towards a free pardon was slower in taking shape, but it was signed a month later. Then the unexhausted part of Public Opinion turned its attention to an investigation into the conduct of George Roberts by the magistrates who appointed him. This caused some heated letter-writing to the Press. There was the die-hard reactionary, a point of view voiced by a long and violently worded letter by an eccentric lawyer who took upon himself to cast doubt on the new affidavits and to point out that had the victims only been sentenced to transportation no one would have taken any notice.[2] How true! but it was not the humane or considerate view. This was taken by the magistrates who "resolved unanimously that it did not appear to them that Roberts was actuated by any corrupt or improper motives in the prosecution of Hall and Morrison and that in their

1 Wolverhampton Chronicle, 6 Aug., 1817.
2 Wolverhampton Chronicle, 26 Nov., 1817.

opinion his character for humanity had not been in any way impeached." The sense of public guilt remained, and this case, with others that had preceded it, was the cause in the ensuing session of Parliament of the repeal of the "Blood Money Act".[1] (58 Geo. 3. cap. 70, which was passed on 13 June, 1818).

And if they could not remove George Roberts, they could remove his post, for Nemesis overtook it. General William Dyott of Freeford, who in his retirement found interest in the question of prisons, when on his way to a visit at Wrottesley (15 March 1820) "took Wolverhampton in my way, for the purpose of inspecting the house of Correction, which I found in a most filthy, dirty, shameful state." (Diary i. 333). Later at the Sessions, he writes "I had a long debate after dinner to support my motion to discontinue the Wolverhampton House of Correction, but I carried my point without a division." Later, the prison was advertized for sale.

A RESPECTABLE TOWN

AT THE end of the reign of George III the Queen Street, Snowhill area, with George Street, (which was built up in 1791) was among the most respectable for dwelling places. Houses to the West of the town, which ended at the Chapel Ash toll-gate, (though Darlington Street was not yet made, and the cottages in Barn Street (or Salop Street) did not extend so far), can be numbered on one hand until one reached Newbridge and the boundary brook. These were "The Corner House" (next to the Eye Infirmary), the "Chapel House", and "The Oaks"; Merridale and Chapel Ash Farm were places rooted in the past. There was besides what the historian W. Pitt 1817, calls the "Elegant Villa" called "The Elms" (now demolished) on the Worcester Road, a Georgian house not unlike "The Oaks", in size and dignity.

That Queen Street was beyond reproach is shown by the number of "Girls schools which it contained:—

Miss Lewis' at No. 20
Mrs. John Jukes at No. 18
Miss Isaac's at No. 6

A 'watch-house' at the end of the street added to their safety, though perhaps not much.

Miss Woodward too, had a flourishing school for a limited number of young ladies at New Cross House with "attendant masters"

French — Mr. Seise.
Music — Mr. Birch.
Drawing — Mr. Noyes.
Dancing — Mr. Lewis.

Cards of terms could be had of Miss Woodward herself or of Mr. Simpson, Bookseller, Wolverhampton.

Chapel House School, we learn, would re-open 28 July 1819, and that Miss Hughes had engaged a resident lady (who has been a considerable time in Paris) to instruct in the French language and in music.

In addition there were numerous schools in the surrounding country which made a choice difficult; at Brewood, Penkridge and Pepper Hill (Albrighton).

But that is a thing we must leave to the anxious mother of the past.

1 An account of this case, in the main features accurate, is given by Peter Burke, "Romance of the Forum", Series 1, Vol. II, p. 18 seq. It is also described by W. H. Jones: "Con. Churches".

THE DEATH OF PRINCESS CHARLOTTE, 1817

THE death of the Princess Charlotte in November 1817 came as a shock both to the nation and to the Royal House itself.

A solitary child of the Prince Regent, all faces had looked upon her as heir to the Crown (with Prince Leopold of the Belgians as Prince Consort) for the royal brothers were, strictly speaking, unmarried and waxing old and had nothing to offer in this respect. To call the nation's loss "ever to be lamented and irreparable" as did the meeting of the inhabitants summoned to vote an address of condolence to their Royal Highnesses, was to use strong language which in the light of Queen Victoria proved to be inexact.

However, the Revs. John Clare and John Reed (of St. John's) knew how to turn the disaster into excellent rhetoric[1] and the two addresses were prepared, adopted and transmitted by the county members to Lord Sidmouth and they and the replies duly appeared in the paper in time for Christmas.

The tomb of the Princess can still be seen, and by some admired, in all the luxury of its setting of chaste white marble and amber glass in St. George's Chapel, Windsor. It occupies, without improving, the chantry chapel prepared by Christopher Urswick, dean of Wolverhampton 1505—15, a curious coincidence; but the tomb of the dean itself is to be seen with his brass effigy at Hackney, London, where he was rector, so no real harm was done.

The public's taste for a good funeral was fulfilled at this period with many of magnificence; as members of the royal family succeeded each other all too rapidly in this mournful reckoning. Princess Charlotte was soon followed by the old Queen (1818), the Duke of York, the Duke of Kent, and the old King.

For Princess Charlotte and her grandfather the "Soul bell" tolled for three days, and muffled bells for divine service on the funeral day (Church-wardens accounts).

In addition there were shuttered shops, the well-attended services, the public mourning, the trapping of woe.

The Newspapers devote whole pages within blackened borders to describe the scenes (the funeral and lying-in-state) and vulture like spread out the details (almost the entrails) over several days, as gruesome and macabre a performance as could be desired. Often this issue is missing from the bound up files, not perhaps from delicacy of feeling.

The Bilston enamellers produced a memorial snuff-box for the Princess in 1817.

WOLVERHAMPTON MARRIAGES IN 1822

IN August 1822 occurred one of those curious psychological movements which so often possess the uninformed. It was inspired by a misunderstanding of the new Marriage Act which was to come into operation on September 1st, Wolverhampton being concerned because doubts had been expressed about the legality of "Licences to Marry" issued by the official of this "Peculiar" jurisdiction (it would have made the obtaining of a licence slightly less convenient; it had not, of course, any effect on the marriage service itself, nor on the more public process by Banns).

Nevertheless the anxiety that marriage should be of the old well-tried and familiar form of wedlock led to a rush towards entering that honourable estate while the going was good, and on Sunday 25 August the banns of 28 couples were published at the Collegiate Church alone, and 27 were married on the next three days, or 44 during the week.[2]

1 Printed 3 December.

2 The Register gives that number from 25th to 31st inclusive. The Wolverhampton Chronicle notices this in issues of 28 Aug. and 4 Sept., 1822 and 23 Apr., 1823.

Subsequently it was ruled that Wolverhampton was unaffected by the Act. Whether these hasty benedicts felt they had been deceived over this matter, or indeed thought at all, history doesn't relate.

THE ACCESSION OF GEORGE IV

THE accession of H.M. George IV to the throne was publicly proclaimed at Wolverhampton on 9 February 1820, and the ceremony was conducted in a manner befitting the occasion. At 11 o'clock the Magistrates, Clergy and principal inhabitants of the town and neighbourhood began to assemble, and shortly afterwards three troops of Staffordshire Yeomanry (in their new blue uniforms) arrived, commanded by Captains Monckton, Crockett and Bickley, when the procession took shape outside the Public Library and News Room in Queen Street, in the following order:—

Special Constables
Trumpeters of County Yeomanry
Kettle Drums
Officer of Yeomanry
Troop of Yeomanry with the King's Standard
Beadles with Staffs
Constables of the town, on horseback
Church and Chapel Wardens
Sidesmen
Overseers of the Poor
Sheriff's Officer with wand
High Constables of the Hundred
Coroner
Stewards of the Stowheath and Deanery Manors
Catholic Clergy
Clergy of the Established Church in their gowns
Deputy Lieutenants and Magistrates
Officers of Excise
Band of King's Own Staffordshire Militia
Banners with King's Arms
Gentlemen of the Town, four abreast
Drums and Fifes
Officer of the Line
Recruiting parties under his command
Deputy Constables
Assistant Constables
Officer of Yeomanry
Troop of Yeomanry

The procession was flanked by files of Yeomanry and at noon moved forward to the High Street, where the proclamation was read a first time. It then passed round the Market Place (Queen's Square) to the bottom of Dudley Street, thence to George Street, thence to Salop Street and then to North Street opposite the house (Molineux House) of George Molineux Esq. the "father of the town", at each of which places Mr. Heape, constable for Stow Heath Manor (the other constable, William Bickley, apparently, was with his Yeomanry, so did not take his turn as his successor did in 1830) read the proclamation "in a most correct and impressive manner". The national air "God save the King" followed the first and last proclamation and was greeted with loud huzzas. Upon the return it was sung again in Queen Street accompanied by the band. The Yeomanry then filed off to the Swan and Lion Inns (we are not told why), then the bells of St. Peter's struck up and continued till a late hour. The windows on the route had been crowded and the yeomanry added much to the general effect.

The new reign started under the worst possible conditions. At Wolverhampton a town's meeting, with Mr. Joseph Pearson in the chair, voiced the anxiety felt for the lamentable state of trade and distress among the labouring mechanics. In this town and neighbourhood it was common to find those who after working 14 or 16 hours daily could only earn a pittance of 7s. to 8s. per week, "while a full third of the population are nearly dependent on parochial Allowance, and the gratuitous distribution of soup". Memory could not tell of so great and general distress as in 1819. New markets must be found and Parliament must do something. They must Petition both Houses, the Marquess of Stafford presenting it to the House of Lords and the Rt. Hon. Earl Gower and E. J. Littleton Esq. to the Commons.

The dissolution of Parliament which came at the end of the month delayed this until 30 May and held up the Wolverhampton Gas Bill (which was one of the first Acts of the new reign) and swept up the Wolverhampton Improvement Bill, which had been ordered to be "laid on the table".[1]

There was no contest for the Members of Parliament for South Staffordshire in the new elections. The Coal and Iron masters met to support Mr. Littleton at the Lion Hotel on Tuesday, 7 March, while the Tories supported Earl Gower at the Swan Hotel. The Seats were divided, a convenient and cheap method of election which had been maintained since 1747.

By the beginning of the year the authorities, the trustees of Wolverhampton Old District of Roads, had decided after long delay how best to tackle the heights of Tettenhall Hill in their progress west. Telford had offered two solutions, (1) diagonally across the Green and ascending the bank by the church, or (2) from the Lion Inn across the valley joining the old road at the Wergs (W. Chron. 14 October 1818).

It was now proposed to excavate the Hill and remove the soil, as an embankment, towards Newbridge, thus spoiling the lower Green. But it was an opportune move and provided much employment for those who did not mind hard work. Darlington Street was formed at this time to introduce the new road into the centre of the town, but it was not finished until 1824, though allowed for in the Town Act of 1814.

Meanwhile the Queen who had been travelling abroad in congenial company returned to England to assert her rights. She was met by a Bill to dissolve her marriage. (I will merely take the words of the chief witness for the defence and say "Non mi riccordo").

The Bill was withdrawn after the voting of the third reading, a very popular proceeding. Many columns of closely typed pages in the press, buttressed by the unanimous vote of the bench of bishops against her, had left the public in no doubt of the Queen's private life. But the populace were not critical of morals, but of the way she had been treated, and the opposition (including the non-conformists) found in it an excuse to belabour the Government. Their demonstration was more successful at Wolverhampton than elsewhere in that the public meeting of householders, called (through the Constables) with Mr. Joseph Pearson in the chair, was successfully 'packed' and voted that the Town should be illuminated to show its rejoicing (having a care for the ordinances about bonfires and firearms). We are told that some houses were illuminated with brilliancy and taste, others seemed to show lights for the sake of preserving their windows; a few remained in darkness

1 Wolverhampton Chronicle, 15 Dec., 1819.

(including those of Mr. Tindall secretary of the Pitt Club). But the Peace was maintained. They were more lively at Bilston, the town's vote being against illuminations, the trouble being started at "a Queen's Dinner" at the Talbot Inn, where ten sheep were roasted and there was an effigy of the Queen. Dudley and Birmingham were quiet; Bridgnorth had rejoicings "for several days"; at Lichfield bells ring: the riot act was read at Oxford: Town and Gown rows occupied Cambridge.

The vote of confidence put forward by Wolverhampton's Tory party was slower in accomplishment, and being "Church and King" had much of the appearance of an announcement of the Pitt Club. It was signed by some 350 memorialists headed by the seven ministers and curates of the two churches:—

"we the undersigned Clergymen, Gentlemen, Merchants, Manufacturers and other inhabitants of the Town of Wolverhampton, viewing with deep regret and abhorrent indignation, the Throne, the Altar, and all constitutional Authorities, assailed by the turbulent and factious, and insulted by the most seditious and blasphemous Publications ever issued from a profligate and licentious press", etc. etc. They put on record their affection to His Majesty's most sacred person, and that they would oppose the seditious and disaffected, and unite to secure peace and security.

JAMES HORDERN — HIGH SHERIFF

In 1823 there came to Wolverhampton a rare honour: the election of its townsman, Mr. James Hordern, to the position of High Sheriff for the county of Stafford. A generation had passed since Mr. George Molineux had held this office (1793) and the actual glory of the proceedings had become a dim memory. With little education but with nascent ability, James Hordern had come from a farm at Saredon, near Shareshill, to William Warner's draper's shop at the old "High Hall" in the Market Place. Hordern's Bank grew up from the financial side of that business (the millinery was downstairs, the Bank above); became independent and prospered; nay, stood firm in times of crisis. And so the owner joined with others—Hordern, Molineux & Co.—bought the Deanery House and gardens; was appointed Deputy Lieutenant for the County in 1814. (Note: With John Pearson of Tettenhall and W. B. Pershouse of Penn, both of Wolverhampton origin).

In appearance he was a small, sandy, rat-faced man;[1] but though spare in body, he was stout in Toryism, as befits a vice-president of the local Pitt Club, though willing to bank for Whigs.

The County Court was then a very real part of the Sheriff's business, but this could be performed by a deputy learned in the law, then Mr. William Keen; in matters of entertainment and display the High Sheriff was left to his own resources and could play his part with startling effect. On Thursday, 13 March, then, the day appointed for opening the Commission of Assize for the County, nearly the whole of the gentry and principal population of the town and neighbourhood assembled at the Deanery to accompany him to Stafford.

There was hospitality on an abundant scale; refreshments—cold meats, fruits and the most choice wines—were set before his guests, some 800 to 1,000 in relays. In the garden a band played "military airs", to cheer the festive board.

"A little before two o'clock the High Sheriff entered his carriage, preceded by his men in costly liveries, and attended by a more splended and numerous retinue of carriages and horsemen that was ever witnessed in this or perhaps any other county[2] on a similar occasion. The streets, and even the road to a very consider-

1 Portrait in possession of Judge Staveley-Hill.
2 Henry Clay, Japanner, of Birmingham—High Sheriff for Warwicks., 1793—must have run him very close. See R. K. Dent, "Old & New Birmingham".

able distance, were crowded with spectators, and the cavalcade which extended more than a mile, formed a grand and imposing spectacle, which must have been truly gratifying to the feelings of the High Sheriff. . . . "The procession, which stopped at Moss Pit (short of Stafford), the customary place for the Sheriff to receive the Judges, was joined soon after six o'clock by Mr. Justice Best; and immediately on its arrival at Stafford the Commission was opened. The High Sheriff afterwards gave a sumptuous entertainment at the Swan Inn (Stafford) to his numerous friends . . . ." The Rev. John Clare was his chaplain and preached from 2 Pet. iii. 17 (but not at the dinner).

Thus though approaching his 65th summer, James Hordern was set fairly in the public eye. "She stoops to Conquer" is performed at the Theatre under his immediate patronage; a complimentary dinner at the Swan Hotel with tickets at one guinea, to begin at 5 o'clock exactly, claimed him on 14 April. It could be counted a success, for 120 were present and the Rev. Mr. Tindall in the chair rose to the occasion and the toast. Again, on the King's Birthday (24 April) with Mr. James Olarenshaw in the chair, he attended the dinner of the Society of the True Britons and their Friends at the New Hotel. Later in the year it is reported, on Sunday 10 August, the judges, Sheriff and his chaplain dine with Lord Talbot (the Lord Lieutenant) at Ingestre.

Politics too called upon him in a neutral capacity, when he convenes a meeting (14 July) of the "Gentlemen, Clergy and other Freeholders of the County of Stafford" to nominate a person proper to represent the County in Parliament in the place of Sir John Fenton Boughey, Baronet, deceased. The candidate was Sir John Wrottesley, Bt. (another banker, but an aristocrat) who was escorted by his friends and supporters from the Lion Inn, in this town, to Stafford where the nomination took place from three waggons in the Market Place.

Fortune favoured him, as did the selection committee, for there was no contest. How different when he tested public opinion at a previous bye-election in 1812, when Sir Edward Littleton was his opponent, and the canvass had gone against him. He did not neglect the warning; he remembered his eleven children and counted the cost. "In this case," he wrote (1 June 1812) to the electors, "the Question is no longer who is the properest man, but who is the richest". And so, on the auspicious occasion good order and unanimity reigned; yet the trusting Rev. Mr. Walker of the Old Church had his pocket picked of his watch, which being "of Platina metal" might (it was thought) have been mistaken for gold.[1] The new members' election followed in due course (23 July) and on his return from Stafford he was met at the entrance of the town (for which as part of S. Staffs. he was now Member) by a large concourse of people, who, taking out the horses, drew his carriage through the principal streets. He remained M.P. (Whig) until 1837, and lived to be first Lord Wrottesley.[2]

A love of punctuality may have prompted Mr. Hordern to give a bell (1790) to the Grammar School, but his sons, Alexander and Henry, were afterwards sent there and were able to benefit by its tone. Both afterwards became Justices and Deputy Lieutenants for the county, and occupied Oxley Manor and Dunstall Hall respectively, two houses demolished in modern times. James Hordern died 3 April 1825, and was buried at Bushbury. Lord Hatherton writing later on the death of his brother, Joseph Hordern of Saredon (February 1838) his oldest tenant, says:—"I have never known two shrewder or more able men. Their liberality in many matters to those to whom they gave their confidence was unbounded."[3]

1 Wolverhampton Chronicle, 13 July.
2 Wedgwood Parliamentary History: S.H.C. 1933.
3 MS Journal, per the late Mr. M. Wright.

WOLVERHAMPTON RACES — 1825

It is perhaps rather curious that the reign of George III lasting as it did until 1820, witnessed no established races for horses at Wolverhampton. The wish was there, for Races of a kind took place, upon occasion, at Walsall, Penn, Compton (1812), Albrighton, Shifnal and Brierley Hill, and the Morfe Coursing Club operated at no great distance.

Baser amusements flourished: Pugilism (a "Severe Contest took place near the town on Thursday 22 September 1814, indecisive after 50 rounds): Bull baiting (since the Town Act of 1777 illegal, and so moved over the town boundary—the town ending where the houses ended, at Chapel Ash—particularly at the Tettenhall Michaelmas wakes). The constables of Wolverhampton again and again in the baiting season remind the public that the penalties will be strictly enforced; but there are often convictions (Canal Street case 16—17 October 1815; ib. 29 November).[1] There was Cock Fighting too.

It was a private Act of Parliament introduced by Mr. Martin M.P. for Galway, for the protection of animals in 1822, and the Society for Prevention of Cruelty to Animals (1824) which awakened the interest in providing an alternative occupation. A well organised fixture had its attractions even to those who protested that artisans "already celebrate so many Saint Mondays,[2] in addition to one useless, noisy, long-lasting Holiday Fair (of one week) and an almost weekly occurrence of wakes, Horse and Donkey Races", and so on. But the decision was made and March 1825 at a meeting at the Lion Inn the collection of subscriptions began. T. W. Giffard, Esq. and Henry Hordern, Esq. were appointed Stewards and Mr. Francis Marshall clerk of the Course. The dates 15—16 August 1825, coincided, curiously enough, with another movement; for at a Meeting of the Inhabitants held on 30 June, Francis Holyoake in the chair,[3] it was resolved that it would be highly beneficial to the Town and Neighbourhood were a Bank for Savings established; and that it should be established; with Treasurers Hordern & Co. and about 125 Directors. It was to open at No. 1 Queen Street on Monday 15th August. (The boom in the iron trade due to railway building had started the flow of money).[4]

The races took place on the flat meadow land below the hill to the west of the Town: "Broad Meadows" belonging to the Earl of Darlington as lessee of the Deanery, partly where the Park is now; but then open and bleak. Four races on each day were proposed. Among the counter attractions was the "Main of Cocks" to be fought in the New Pit at the back of Darlington Street (presumably near the new Methodist Meeting House, just opened, but a little lower than the angels): the gentlemen of Staffordshire versus the Gentlemen of Shropshire.[5]

A vast concourse of spectators attended, though the first day was wet. Stands and booths were strung out for one quarter mile and completely filled, while the meadows were thronged with carriages from the large equippage with positilions to the humble trap, also horsemen and pedestrians. A great number of pickpockets were present. Thus with a certain amount of give and take, and the good humour of a British mob, the occasion passed harmoniously, and orators at the luncheon "Ordinaries" at the Lion on Monday (under Mr. Giffard) and at the Swan on Tuesday (with Mr. H. Hordern in the chair) were able to congratulate the Town upon the inauguration of these Races "an object of material importance both in a moral and political point of view, and one likely to encourage the

1 Wolverhampton Chronicle, 13 Oct., 1819.
2 Letter, 8 Sep., 1824.
3 Wolverhampton Chronicle, 18 May.
4 This Bank, after a successful career, closed on 20 Nov., 1866. Depositors were paid to their last penny in December.
5 Wolverhampton Chronicle, 10 Aug.

Early Seals

17th and 18th century Wolverhampton Tokens

Carving on Saxon Pillar in Churchyard

Saxon Column in St. Peter's Churchyard

rational enjoyments of the people and tending to keep up harmony and friendly feeling between all classes". In time for next year there had been prepared a view of the Race Course "beautifully coloured", 25×15", price one guinea, after a drawing by Robert Noyes.[1] This is of extreme rarity but shows the lively scene. A larger view of the course as it appeared in 1839 can be seen in the Art Gallery. An oil painting by George Wallis is also known.[2] A permanent Grand Stand was built in 1827, and the Wolverhampton Races continued on this site until 1878, when the ground then open and private was taken over and enclosed for a Public Park. This was regarded as a step in the right direction by the Rector (Rev. J. T. Jeffcock) who in his preface to the second edition of Steen's Guide (1884) rejoiced in the change which daily afforded "fresh air and recreation to hundreds, in the place of the race week which did but little good to few, and a decided amount of harm to many".

At one time there was a fear that prize fights were becoming too prevalent in the town and in 1833 the constables, one of whom was G. B. Thorneycroft who became first mayor, prosecuted, and in a letter to the Clerk of the Course forbade it in future, as it introduced rough elements into the town. Lawyer Thomas Wood, upholder of lost causes answered evasively; but clearly prize fights were on the wane.

ST. GEORGE'S CHURCH 1830

IF Public Races satisfied to some small extent the popular appetite for amusement, there remained also the more serious side of public reclamation.

This was not entirely neglected; a long standing Act of Parliament more or less compelled attendance at Public worship. The Rev. John Clare, vicar of Bushbury, a magistrate, fined a butcher's servant 20s. for driving cattle through the town on a Sunday. (W. Chron. 2 June 1830). Householders, indeed, had a sort of freehold in their pews or seats, which were allotted in accordance with their property qualification. Devoted worshippers from a newly acquired residence were sometimes taken aback on finding that the pew, which they thought was theirs, had lapsed by the non-user of their predecessor.

But all said and done it was evident that church accommodation, as well as parsons, was insufficient for all the population, being in 1824, 36,838, of which the churches could seat 3,000.[3] The Government had, however, recently provided power and limited funds for extension through the "Commissioners for Building Additional Churches" and the church-wardens called a meeting to consider the matter on 5th June 1825.

In his application for funds, dated 22nd November 1825, the Rev. Thomas Walker, chairman of the Committee which had been formed, set out, in a printed circular,[4] "a correct Statement of the melancholy situation in which the great Body of its Inhabitants" were placed. He computed that the number of persons in this Township were 25,000 and that the old and new churches (if every seat were filled) did not afford accommodation for 2,500. He asked "The Sons of Affluence and Wealth" to consider for a moment that they had around them more than 20,000 of living souls "who never hear the name of God but in the faulty and abasing language of profanation".

His aim was a "New Free Chapel" and the finding of "a respectable Clergyman" (had he foresight here?) with a salary to suit. The Dean had surrendered his right of patronage "most kindly and liberally"; the galleries were reserved for subscribers and the whole of

1 W.S.L. Collection.
2 Possessed by the late Sir Charles Mander.
3 Wolverhampton Chronicle, 4 August.
4 Art Gallery Collection.

the body of the church for the poor; thus all parties were satisfied according to their station, and the scheme was set in motion.

It must not be forgotten that the Nonconformists were also aware of their duties in spiritual welfare, and some special activity on their part is visible at this time. The New Wesleyan Chapel in Darlington Street (also new) was opened for public worship 26 August 1825; while Noah's Ark Chapel[1] was re-opened on Sunday, 20 November by the Calvanistic Independents, of which Mr. Charles Mander was treasurer. Presumably this was a somewhat narrower gathering than that in the Old Chapel, St. John's Street, under Rev. John Steward of a presbyterian persuasion, but not so narrow as that at Temple Street (no longer Grey Pea Walk) under Mr. John Godwin, who had a most despondent view upon the condition of his flock. He was a most censorious man and very eccentric.[2] It is said, on good authority, that the sacrament was never administered during all his 30 years ministry as he did not consider his Congregation christians.[3] His church was re-formed 24 October 1832 and Mr. Godwin died 14 June 1835 aged 80.[4]

But Nonconformity, though many sided, was too restricted to cover much ground, and the town was preponderantly heathen, ignorant and unhealthy.

The site chosen for the new church, which was bought by levying a rate upon the inhabitants, was off Bilston Street, at the back of Turton's Hall. This it fronted, and the new line of the Holyhead Road bounded it on the south.

The Architects chosen was James Morgan from London. It was said to be his first effort; a proud man was he therefore when he walked in the procession to the stone-laying. At that date, 20 August, the newspaper postponed, until it was less pressed for room, an account of him; but later when its grim aspect "plain and almost devoid of ornament", with (as it seemed to Rev. J. B. Owen, Vicar of St. Mary's Bilston) "a collapsed roof and spire" were visible to all, words were not forthcoming and Mr. Morgan would have been forgotten, like the architect of St. John's, but for the fact that he had taken steps to prevent it. His name is recorded on a "Commemoration Medal" which was prepared and struck in three metals, silver, bronze, and pewter, on its front a picture of the church, on the back a many worded account of the circumstances of its erection.

Built of brick cased with Tixall stone, it is described as being in the "Grecian style of architecture of the Doric Order" it remains an interesting product of that period of strange pseudo-classical and Aegyptian edifices (that gave London St. Pancras Church, and New York "The Tombs" prison) just too early for the Gothic revival.

In August 1828 it was decided that the new church should be called "St. George's" and the foundation stone should be laid by the Hon. and Very Rev. H. L. Hobart, D.D., Dean of Windsor and Wolverhampton, on Monday 18th.[5]

The appointed day was a fine one and began with bell-ringing at 6 a.m. After a crowded service in the Collegiate Church a procession was formed. This was headed by the two constables and the Town Crier, and included a band, the children of the Blue Coat School (each wearing a medal), 3 beadles, the churchwardens, 12 clergy of the neighbourhood in cassocks and gowns two and two, the M.P.'s for the county, E. J. Littleton and Sir John

1 It was advertised as To Let, 4 Nov., 1789 (Wolverhampton Chronicle) "very convenient for carrying on the Public Line". In March, 1791 it was in the hands of William Horton, Rum and Spirit dealer. (Ibid. no. 80).
2 W. H. Jones.
3 Note by SSM. in their Church Book (now in possession of Sir G. Le M. Mander).
4 Staffs Advertiser, 27 June.
5 Wolverhampton Chronicle, 6 and 13 Aug., 1828. The ceremony is fully described in its issue of 20th.

Wrottesley Bt., the architect, committee, subscribers and visitors, the (town) constables and their deputies, men bearing banners and so forth. But centre of all, and object of rare and special interest, and wearing his insignia as "Register" of the Most Noble the Order of the Garter, was the Dean of Wolverhampton (the last dean) in his robes, walking with the perpetual curate, Rev. T. Walker, and escorted by sidesmen. No wonder the streets and windows were packed by a "vast concourse" at this edifying spectacle.

On the ground itself within a temporary enclosure, banks of seats had been set up and there "elegantly dressed ladies" added "charm and animation to the scene".

We learn that amid the respectful attention and great decorum of the crowd, the dean performed his task in the usual manner with "much feeling and devotion". Prayers ended with the singing of the old Hundredth Psalm and the benediction, when the procession was re-formed and proceeded to the Assembly Rooms in Queen Street "where female beauty and loveliness again shone conspicuous". In the course of speeches the silver trowel was presented to the Dean and cake and wine were handed round. A dinner at the Swan Hotel followed.

It was two years before the church was ready for consecration, but before this there was an opportunity of testing its capacity. There were 2,300 sittings and these were completely filled for a curious debate promoted by the Rev. William Dalton under the cloak of the British Reformation Society on the 6th July 1830. Mr. Dalton, who was soon to build his own church (St. Paul's) had already fixed the attention of his hearers by sermons at St. Peter's and St. John's and now the subject of discussion was "the supremacy of the Pope", a matter upon which others than he could be eloquent. It proved of such interest that, beginning at 11 o'clock, it was necessary to adjourn the debate until 4 p.m.[1]

Here was an energetic man who could fill a church, but it was fated that one should be chosen who could keep the church empty. The church-wardens, Thos. H. Ward and Jas. Underhill, meanwhile announced the date of Consecration by the Bishop of Lichfield and Coventry on Thursday at 10 a.m. (Books of the service).[2] Dinner at The Swan at 3 p.m.

The presentation of a suitable vicar hung fire. This right the dean seems to have retained. It is significant that he preached in the Collegiate Church on Sunday, 23 September. A month later it was known that he had nominated the Rev. George Boodle Clare, B.A. of Worcester College, Oxford, to the vacant living, the son of the redoubtable Rev. John Clare J.P. Vicar of Bushbury, with whom he lived at the Deanery House. It was intended to open the church for divine service on Sunday, 5 December; in the meantime pew letting could proceed[3] but both were postponed.[4] The congregation had fled! General William Dyott, in deploring the slackness of the Established Church in bringing religion to the lower orders, cited the case of St. George's as a "strong proof" of that neglect. "As soon as it was known" he writes,[5] "That a clergyman of irregular, idle habits was appointed, every person who had subscribed for seats withdrew their names, and one and all relinquished their subscription".

So the best-laid schemes of men went awry, but Mr. G. B. Clare continued on. He has no memorial at St. George's; but at Shareshill, which he served in plurality, there is a tablet:—"In memory of George Boodle Clare B.A. Thirty four years incumbent of this parish. He died November 16 1859 Aged 60 years."

1 The speakers were Mr. Dalton, Rev. Mr. McDonnell (R.C.) and "Mr. Falvey".
2 Wolverhampton Chronicle, 18 Aug. An account of the ceremony is given in the issue of 1st September.
3 Wolverhampton Chronicle, 17 Nov.
4 Ibid., 24 Nov.
5 Diary, vol. ii, 90—29 Oct., 1830.

THE FIRST WOLVERHAMPTON ELECTION

UNTIL 4th June 1832, Wolverhampton had not by itself the power to return a member to Parliament. Nor had Birmingham, Manchester, or Walsall, so it was not alone in its neglect. It was qualified to return a Member for the County: two members; but these matters could be arranged, and there had not been a county election in Staffordshire since 1747, 85 years ago. So Wolverhampton, due to obtain two members, was directly interested in, was part of, the Great Reform Bill. When therefore the Lords in Parliament assembled cast out the Second Reform Bill 8 October 1831, and rioting broke out, the Editor of the Wolverhampton Chronicle probably voiced the general opinion in noticing the gravity of the event:—"We write in awful times. The Rejection of the Reform Bill by the House of Peers has created an exitement which no wise and no good man can view without emotion."[1] The Third Reform Bill, introduced in March 1832 was urged on by shouts of open sedition and the flames of Bristol and Nottingham. A County Member, Mr. E. J. Littleton, had helped to draw round Wolverhampton Parliamentary boundaries suited for a two member borough. It comprised the old parish, including Wednesfield, Willenhall and Bilston, but part of Sedgley was included as a make-weight.

Electiontide was a period of gloom for the Tory Party, Reform gained all the air-waves; only Reformers were heard, and these vied with each other in the extremity of their views. Richard Fryer, Radical, now came in to his own and was the pivot of the Reformers, Wolverhampton was marked however by other radical politicians, for the new constituencies, unused to the elaborate payments which made the older boroughs so ruinous an investment, were each counted an inexpensive prize. Earliest of these wooers, a total stranger, was Fortunatus William Lilley Dwarris (1786—1860) barrister-at-law and authority on the West Indies where he had been born. His lengthy election address appeared in the Times (September 8) and was thought to be "one of the most sound and manly expositions of the political principles of a candidate we have ever seen". With this certificate it was inserted in the Wolverhampton Chronicle on 19th September. Reform and revision was his only theme: to prevent revolution, to uphold the Throne, to save the Church, to restore our languishing trade and manufacturers. Currency Corn Laws, tithes: all must undergo revision. He knew; for "his years had not been few nor idle". Unluckily he had written a five act play "with a Shakespearean latitude" which provided powder for an attack while he kept his distance.[2]

The Tories put in the field Mr. Francis Holyoake a name honoured in the town and neighbourhood. He was joined by Mr. William Woolrych Whitmore of Dudmaston, near Bridgnorth, which he had hitherto represented "as one of the landed interest" with his cousin Thomas Whitmore of Apley, esquire. He had recently incurred some odium among the farmers for his views on the Corn Laws, and to his sorrow he had found them "exerting themselves strongly in favour of a stranger" against him "a neighbour in point of residence, and a friend in inclination".[3] His pamphlet of 84 pages in which he argued reasons for a *revised* taxation (1826) was intended to conciliate them; but now he saw a chance of going where his views were welcome, and events proved him right.

Mr. Holyoake started his attack with "an elegant breakfast" to his friends at the Swan Inn (28 September)[1] and so primed and with influential support he commenced a "very active canvass". Mr. Whitmore who had intended to address the electors at the Public

1 Wolverhampton Chronicle, 12 Oct., 1831.
2 Wolverhampton Chronicle, 14 Nov
3 Pamphlet, p. 6.

Office, in Princess Street, on October 1st, found there a crowd so dense that he adjourned to the Market Place and addressed them from the balcony of the Swan Hotel. He was introduced by Mr. Joseph Pearson "in a neat speech" who being able to speak of him by past experience, knew no man better qualified to represent them. Mr. John Barker, a wealthy ironmaster, seconded the nomination. Mr. Whitmore followed the usual reform programme with one exception; he advocated only the complete alteration in the present system of their Corn Laws. He did not think it wise or safe, all at once, without preparation, to remove the whole duty. It would injure the farmers and not benefit the manufacturers. This was not a popular announcement, and there was some inclination towards heckling, but he stood his ground. An altercation however arose in which some personalities were exchanged between Mr. Barker and Mr. Joseph Walker a supporter of Mr. Fryer. The former had remembered an *obiter dictum* of Mr. Fryer's that a reduction of taxes meant lower wages. It went home, Mr. Barker was reminded of his Tommy Shop. This thrust also told. An extreme radical, Mr. Simkiss considered Mr. Whitmore was not sufficiently explicit. He would have him pledge himself to vote for the appropriation of Church property to liquidate the National debt (laughter and cheers). The Rev. John Roaf from Queen Street Chapel said he did not come forward as an elector: he would take no part in local politics—but as a man, a christian and a minister of religion. He wishes every exertion to be made "to wipe away that foul stain from the land—negro slavery".[2] A luncheon was then given to the friends of Mr. Whitmore, after which he proceeded to canvass, which was highly successful. His welcome was particularly noteworthy at Sedgley where he was met by a party of 40 gentlemen on horseback and escorted into the place, where he was warmly received. He subsequently polled heavily there. Sir Horace St. Paul, Bt. a candidate for Dudley was met (Tuesday 23 October) by more than 300 gentlemen on horseback and a procession of 1,200 on foot. (But Sir John Campbell, the popular candidate, was elected by a narrow majority). Mr. Holyoake is said to have had an equally favourable reception at Bilston (ibid 13 October). But whatever successes they met with did not lessen the confidence of Mr. Fryer's friends in the certainty of his return. (W'ton Chron. 17 October). He also had been well received at Bilston. (Monday 22 October Staff. Adv. 27 October).

On Monday 12th November, Mr. Fryer addressed a large body of the electors so as to acquaint them with his political sentiments, though these were not in doubt; but the plaudits of the mob may have fallen sweet upon his ears. The things that troubled him has made him restive for twenty years: the repeal of the Corn Laws which, he said were "brought by the devil from hell"; the ballot, triennial Parliaments, church reform, abolition of slavery and monopolies. He cannot have favoured Mr. Whitmore who was one of that "oligarchy of Land-owners who had a monopoly of Food". (Election letter W. Chron. 3 October). Indeed there were those who considered the Liberal vote should be cast in favour of "two real reformers". By the end of the month the tide of opinion had flowed so strongly for Fryer and Whitmore, that Holyoake, who had had an uneasy canvass, withdrew from the contest (Staff. Advt. 8 December). Meanwhile an invitation had been sent by the Wolverhampton Radicals to Mr. John Nicholson, a London tea-man of approved principles, and his acceptance came on Tuesday, December 4th; but not alone, for Fortunatus Dwarris, Esq. came too ("As we go to press"—W'ton Chron. 5 December). He addressed the electors from the Swan Hotel Window on the same evening, and being a barrister, knew how to present his case. His views were sweeping. There should be no

1 Staffs. Advertizer, 29 Sep.
2 Do. Sat., 6 Oct., 1832.

corn laws, no taxes on agriculture, no unreformed church no church rates, he "would restore church property to its primitive uses". He would vote for the repeal of repressive taxes, such as window and inhabited house duty; he would remove bishops from the house of Lords and clerical magistrates from the benches. Sinecures he would abolish, "but not rewards earned for services performed" (his own case). He stood up to the catechism of Mr. Simkiss and answered questions "in a very candid and manly way", and left his fate in their hands. (Staff Advert. 8 December). But he had no local backing; he came and went, a meteor which generated little heat at Wolverhampton but collected a Knighthood from Queen Victoria in 1838. (D.N.B. In his own circle he was not undistinguished).

Mr. John Nicholson made his public entry into the town on Saturday 8 December, attended by a band and a large procession bearing colours. There was an immense concourse before the Swan when he appeared on the balcony. He was proposed by a Mr. Bywater, who declared it was the last time he should step forward in public life: his blood boiled within him to live in such a town (laughter). Let them send him free of expense to the poll; let them subscribe, his mite was ready. Mr. Brooks seconded. He wished to test the power of the Liberal Party in Wolverhampton. Nicholson and Fryer were their men. Mr. Nicholson's sentiments were "quite of an ultra character" (Staff. Advert. 15 December). He was at one with the other candidates in that he had "no personal interest to gratify or ambition to serve", a stock phrase. He had had 30 years of public life, and though connected with the tea trade, was against the East India monopoly. He did not come there to threaten Mr. Fryer, he should retire if he did so (loud cheers). "Mr. Fryer was the man of the people (he is, he is)". They were right in selecting a man from among themselves, and one they knew. Like Caesar and the crown, he put away the thought of proceeding to the poll, lest he should endanger the election of Mr. Fryer (tremendous cheers). Thus the "immense assemblage" showed a strong feeling in favour of Mr. Nicholson, and cheers for Fryer and Nicholson rent the air. This loving union, the split radical vote, had the immediate effect of bringing Mr. Francis Holyoake back into the field. He may have judged that the voteless mob who cheered was ineffective at the poll. He republished his address:— He had always supported Reform, and had opposed the Borough System (now dead); he hated slavery, was against injurious monopolies, disliked taxation, welcomed Law Reform, supported no class of the community at the expense of the rest. The good of all ranks must now be the governing principle; the present Corn Laws required revision, but farmers needed protection, that in substance was his political faith. He did not say he was a Tory; the reforming fever had claimed him as a victim; yet he would recover.[1]

There were now four candidates in the field for two seats, and the position was interesting: who could predict what a poll would declare? The pace quickened, excitement was aroused, and argument gave way to force.

On Monday night, 10th December Mr. Fryer's friends marched in a torchlight procession through the town, and afterwards through the windows of the committee room, Mr. R. Fryer, Mr. J. Walker and Mr. W. Walker addressed the crowd. The trouble which they had been nursing for years was now coming to a head. To preach peace and quiet could have little effect to the disorderly. It appeared that both Fryer and Whitmore's friends had adopted the *laurel* as their badge, and ill-feeling had been excited; but Mr. Whitmore's party decided to fight without laurels; they would crown his success. The hustings was

1 Wolverhampton Chronicle, 12 Dec.; St. Adv., 15 Dec.

erected in St. James's Square which, drear and neglected as it is today, made history then. The senior constable, Mr. William Lott Ryton presided, and the nominations were due to take place on Tuesday 12th, midday. About eleven o'clock Mr. Fryer's friends in Wolverhampton, attended by a band and flags bearing various devices, went out to meet him (coming from the Wergs) at Chapel Ash, and conducted him to the hustings. Mr. Whitmore's friends in like manner set out to meet their candidate (coming from Bridgnorth) at the Swan Inn, Compton. A sorry array wounded and contused survived the journey; for the mob set upon them tore their flags, broke their instruments, threw stones and mud. It was deemed a disgraceful affair. Meanwhile Mr. Holyoake with Mr. Giffard and others in his carriage arrived at the hustings, but met with an attack which made them seek refuge, Mr. Giffard bleeding from a cut near the eye. It was organised violence, and the large force of special constables could do nothing. They were overwhelmed, their staffs-of-office thrown about the Square amid the jeers of the mob.

Mr. Nicholson and his friends walked quietly into the square and took their place about 12 o'clock on the hustings with Mr. Ryton and Mr. Fryer. News was brought from Mr. Whitmore that he did not consider it safe to venture there; his friends feared for him and he feared for his friends. "I should have made the attempt to address you at the hustings" he wrote, "but I did not feel myself justified in exposing my friends to the outrages and danger of which, I grieve to say I have witnessed more than one lamentable instance."[1]

Amid banners inscribed "No Corn Laws", "Triennial Parliaments", "Peace, order and union", and cries of "No Whitmore", Mr. Ryton sat embarrassed and undecided. He was not without advisers, Mr. Simkiss among them, who told the Returning Officer to do his duty and proceed with the nomination; he had not power to adjourn the business; a walk-over for the Radicals was envisaged. On the other hand Mr. Ryton would not sign a certificate that a riot had taken place, nor had he sent for the military but only a constabulary force. Eventually it was found there were those on the hustings who would propose and second the absent candidate, and Mr. Price (probably the same Mr. Price who heckled at the County election, a manufacturer; "poverty made men politicians" was a mot of his) rose and proposed Mr. Fryer as a fit and proper person to represent the borough. Mr. Walker "in an able speech" seconded. Mr. Sidney then amid discordant yells nominated Mr. Holyoake and Mr. George Robinson (afterwards second Mayor of Wolverhampton) seconded. Mr. Thorneycroft (afterwards first Mayor of Wolverhampton) nominated Mr. Whitmore and the Rev. Mr. Hill seconded. Mr. Brooks proposed and Mr. Crockett seconded John Nicholson Esq. of London. Then a curious thing happened. A show of hands was called by Mr. Ryton, and there appeared for Fryer and Nicholson a moving forest of palms and the clapping of them together had a very singular effect. At the names of Holyoake and Whitmore not a hand was raised in the Square, but they were greeted with the loudest yells and hisses. Several ladies however in the adjoining windows applauded and waved their handkerchiefs. The reformers had forgotten them, perhaps rightly, for had they the vote, it is undoubted from this demonstration that Wolverhampton would have returned a Tory as its first M.P. As it turned out he was a whig.

Mr. Ryton however being closer to the event justly observed that the election appeared to him to have fallen upon Richard Fryer and John Nicholson. He could not have said anything more popular; but a poll was demanded by Mr. Sidney for Mr. Holyoake and Mr. Thorneycroft for Mr. Whitmore. No time was lost. Thursday and Friday were the days appointed, from 9 till 4. Booths were erected for the Wolverhampton and Wednes-

[1] Letters to electors, 11 Dec., Wolverhampton Chronicle, 12 Dec.

field voters at "Mr. Tudor's Coach Repository" (Snowhill); for Sedgley, at the schoolhouse, for Bilston at the Dispensary, and at the schoolhouse for Willenhall. Nor did the Magistrates neglect the public peace. The Tuesday outrages induced them to take the unusual course of swearing in nearly the whole of the householders in the town, whether electors or not; but this did not touch the mob where trouble lay. This began early on Thursday morning, when as the crowd grew to watch the voting, their insolence increased the proportion, and whenever Mr. Whitmore's or Mr. Holyoake's friends approached the gate of the enclosure, they were met with a rising opposition, first of groans and hisses, but afterwards of showers of stones. About 9-30 the road was filled with a vast crowd who pressed upon the gate and palings of the enclosure so much that they had to be strenghtened and barricaded by additional timbers. Special constables who attempted to clear a way, were roughly handled by the mob, and several were hurt. The friends of Mr. Holyoake demanded a suspension of polling alleging that they could not bring up any of their men; but Mr. Fryer's party opposed this. They tried indeed to obtain order, but were unsuccessful. Eventually Sir John Wrottesley read the Riot Act, and sent for a detachment of the Scot's Greys, which were at Tettenhall; and these soon dispersed the crowd. Their presence however continued to be necessary, for violence was never far away, and the windows of the Swan Hotel were broken as a gesture of disapproval. (Staffs. Advert. December 15 p. 4).

The exingencies of the press prevented an account of the Friday's polling but a provisional result (the polling then was public) was known at the close of the poll. A surprise was in store. The examination of the polling books began at 8-0 on Saturday and the result was announced by Mr. Ryton soon after noon (ibid 22 December). It was a victory for the moderate man, who had no sympathy with the extremist (but the extremist had few votes). The figures were:—[1]

Mr. Whitmore	..	(Whig)	..	850
Mr. Fryer	..	(Radical)	..	810
Mr. Holyoake	..	(Tory)	..	657
Mr. Nicholson	..	(Radical)	..	358

Mr. Whitmore could only regard his return with considerable satisfaction. He valued it, as he told the electors, "more than anything that Kings had it in their power to bestow". They had placed him in the proud situation of representing a free, enlightened, and intelligent constituency. No corrupt influence had been used on his behalf. He was not, as he had been represented, an enemy of the poor man, and he hoped when he next appeared before them he should not stand quite so low in the opinion of the non-electors. In the past he had been a farmer, but he would now be attentive to the manufacturing interest. They cheered him. Mr. Fryer then came forward to give thanks, not too pleased, it would appear, to find himself but second string. The methods of address used by the old parliamentary hand were not his. He had heard Mr. Whitmore he said, and had learnt nothing; perhaps it was from want of understanding; he had not Mr. Whitmore's ability in speaking, but he hoped he said something when he did speak (loud cheers). They would excuse him; he was a plain speaking man—his speech was quite unvarnished, so he hoped they would bear with him. What a change he had seen in public opinion in his life-time through forty years when the Tory faction ruled the country with a rod of iron. But he, the old jacobin, was now member for Wolverhampton (laughter and cheers). What had they sent Mr. Whitmore to Parliament for? He had never told them. But he (Fryer) would

1 Wolverhampton Chronicle ;19 Dec., 1832; Staffs. Adv. 22 Dec. where details are given of each polling place.

tell them what he intended to do. No *ifs* and *buts* and *time to consider for him*. They had sent him to Parliament to reform the church . . . . and so on, Mr. Fryer was well away. He would not bolster up the old lady in Threadneedle Street, and make her mistress instead of servant. He spoke of "the selfish oligarchy of the landlords who ruled the country with a rod of iron, and made the agricultural districts one vast truck-shop" (tremendous cheering). Mr. Whitmore could answer that: He was sorry that tumults had occurred; it was too often the case at elections; but he maintained there had been less violence there, than at any contested election in the Kingdom. There was no greater injustice to electors than to bring in the military; it was a high degradation to the town that they had been obliged to give their votes at the point of the sword; that indeed was a terrible thing. (Confusion). Mr. Simkiss here mounted the table and put a string of questions to Mr. Whitmore; but Mr. Parker and Mr. Pearson protested at this irregular proceeding, and Rev. Mr. Leigh, the cholera hero of Bilston, stepped forward; but cries for Mr. Nicholson were so loud that he could not at first get a hearing. He said that he, though a clergyman and a clerical magistrate, was not blind to abuses and would wish to see them reformed. He had been appointed a magistrate 20 years ago, after being 3 years vicar, at the desire of the inhabitants who had appointed him. He did not approve of clerical magistrates. He had voted for Mr. Whitmore his friend. He was popular and received an ovation. Even Mr. Simkiss was quelled. He regretted that they could not ungown Mr. Leigh and send him to parliament instead of Mr. Whitmore. Mr. Nicholson then spoke. He had come among them as a perfect stranger, and did not blame them for placing him bottom. He unlike Whitmore, had stated his sentiments clearly. "The necessity of the ballot (secret voting) had been most satisfactorily proved within that week in that very county. Stafford and Dudley, and he might add Walsall, had presented the disgraceful and iniquitous scenes of men being publicly bought, like cattle . . . . at a price of from £1 to £20, and the man that waited longest got most." He continued with a long address. There is no account of a speech by Mr. Holyoake, but he published a letter stating that he considered his position on the poll under the circumstances in which it took place, "a glorious triumph to the principles which he came forward to support". The swing of the pendulum and the cries of the mob were against him; but nevertheless he was soon to sit at Westminster (for a Stafford by-election) not as a colleague of Richard Fryer, his fellow banker, for whom one Parliament was enough, but with a fresh young Tory, one W. E. Gladstone, the son of a Liverpool slave owner, who had with the Reformed Parliament commenced his career as M.P. for Newark. And was not the day at hand when Richard Fryer, no longer at Westminster, mellowed rather towards landlords and devoted attention to his own landed estate at the Wergs. (By right of his wife, Mary Fleeming). His sons in law, Stubbs Wightwick and Robert Thacker were with him on the platform. The latter made a Gretna Green marriage, 2 November 1827 (W. Warner's Diary). A third daughter married (1829) Rev. Thomas Walker, Preb. of St. Peter's—one wonders how he voted: for the two winning candidates probably. His son, William Fleeming Fryer, built the present house at the Wergs. This estate was offered for sale in August 1872, and valued at £11,300. It included Palmer's Cross, Cronkhall, the Birches and Woodhall. Fryer's Bank had recently become Lloyd's. He sported a coat-of-arms, granted 1835. The jacobin was reformed.

CHAPTER XI

DR. OLIVER AND HIS TIMES

IN THE Dictionary of National Biography Dr. Oliver is dismissed with a few dates and a list of some 33 of his "works"; but of his doings at Wolverhampton nothing is said, and this phase of his life which covers the decline and fall of the Collegiate Structure (in more senses than one)[1] forms a running commentary on a deplorable period of church history in the town. No account of Wolverhampton can neglect him: he was anathema to his churchwardens and the centre (as surely his was) of the conversaziones.

At the time of his appointment as Perpetual Curate and Sacrist to succeed the Rev. Thomas Walker in 1834, he was past 50 years of age and of settled habits and convictions. Besides, having long been a schoolmaster at Grimsby, he was accustomed to command rather than be rebuked. He was and continued vicar of Clee and Scopwick in the county of Lincoln; had been Domestic Chaplain to the Right Hon. Lord Kensington, and styled himself M.A., S.E., but had seen no more of University life than having his name on the boards of Trinity College, Cambridge, as a "Ten year man", which was followed in 1835 with a Lambeth degree of D.D. The appointment proved unfortunate, but this could not be foreseen and he may not have realized that he was filling a post which a reforming government had only to observe to condemn and, by Act of Parliament, to sweep away.

In 1834 the last church rate was granted without opposition. In August 1838 a poll was taken and the rate lost by a large majority, a phenomenon not peculiar to Wolverhampton and a sign of the times. Vainly did the incumbent (who might justly have regarded it as a vote of "no confidence") attempt to show that the proportion was small compared with the population and that church rates could be traced to the Laws of Ina (six Letters, p. 10). The vote was final and a church rate was never again levied in the town.

What Dr. Oliver's intentions were is not in doubt. They were plausible and proper and are set out in two Addresses to the Inhabitants (1834—5) and six Letters to his curate, published in 1838, the writer being then at Scopwick and "precluded by inadequate health from . . . . active co-operation". But he was still able to write; he liked writing, and produced a steady output with fluency and ease of which only his useful and readable "Account of the Collegiate Church" need be mentioned here. This he compiled in a very short time (for the Preface is dated February 1836) and its illustrations by Robert Noyes must always be valued and redeem his faulty text. Jealous of his rights as sacrist he upheld them with pertinacity, and soon put himself in the wrong with his churchwardens and the inhabitants generally by becoming involved in a dispute respecting the fees of St. Georges Church.

His 28 pages of "Candid Statement" on this occasion which was intended to excuse him was demolished by the incumbent, the Rev. G. B. Clare's 28 pages of "Reply". In short the inhabitants could recognise a Mother Church, but not double "surplice fees". The question was an old one and Dr. Oliver should have read the past and have taken warning.

1 Dr. Oliver in his exuberant style mentions "the west wall (of the church) is falling periodically by masses of a ton and upwards." Second Pastoral Address (1835) p. 10.

Rebuffed in this question the sacrist turned to the old church-yard and "piled Pelion upon Ossa" by reopening it for burials. The unsightly rows of brick vaults are owed to his action and the distaste the inhabitants had for the "new" burial ground after the recent cholera scourge. He approved even of intra-mural burial: "The old fable, that this practice is unwholesome", he wrote, "has vanished before the light of science". (Second Pastoral Address, p. 10). With the new-pewing he was more happy in his advocacy (and with a view of the old pews before us, there can be no two opinions about the marked improvement) and the pews remain; but other alterations and restorations made about the church during 1837—9 have all been removed.[1]

One interesting change took place in 1839 when black gowns were substituted for the blue coats and red collars of the vergers which Dr. Oliver thought "unbecoming".[2] Besides writing "Hints for improving the Societies and Institutions connected with Education and Science in the town" (1836), he was President of the Literary and Philosophical Society of Wolverhampton, and the Society of Antiquaries of Scotland had made him an honorary member. But he still remained not fully appreciated, and taking his pen with him, he surrendered his pulpit in August 1836, to a solitary curate, John Boyle, B.C.L., who soon lost himself in this vast parish. A storm of troubles and correspondence gathered strength during the following years, which is set out in detail with disarming candour in a pamphlet entitled "An Address to the Inhabitants . . . . in Reply to the misrepresentations in a Circular issued by Messrs. Thorneycroft and Parke" (1840).

From comparative calm things had become greatly confused. The curate was overworked. Weddings had found no parson; women were sent away unchurched, children unbaptised, the sick unvisited. The churchwardens protested only to be reminded that "the affairs of the church are under my management" and "threats would be without effect". Dr. Oliver regarded the suggestion that he should come into residence as offensive, and the churchwardens' activity a "persecution" which nevertheless he would "patiently" endure.[3] The movement to supersede him became definite in April 1839. The churchwardens were two strong and prominent men who having renovated the church hoped to renew its ministers. It was no simple task. The Official wanted particular and not general accusations of insufficiency before he took action and Dr. Oliver was generally and not particularly obnoxious.[4] In April 1840 the churchwardens prayed the Official, Mr. Birkett's attendance at the ensuing Visitation, "for his doing so is the only hope we have (of) seeing like peace restored to our distressed church. Dr. Oliver is again here in lodgings with a new Curate and nothing but confusion reigns to the utter disgust of all the friends of the church".[5] But the appointment of new churchwardens made an opening for peace, and order was restored; the pamphleteers rested and the learned incumbent took comfort in Histories of Masonry. Signs and portents were not wanting. Early on Sunday morning 3 January 1841, during a heavy fall of snow the cross on the tower of the church (a massive oak structure 40 feet in length and 15 inches in diameter) was struck by lightning and quickly became a glowing mass of flame, an awe-inspiring object for those who were up and about at 2 a.m. in unsettled weather.[6]

1 The total bill, 1839, amounted to £2,500.
2 Letter of 8 April 1839, quoted in his Address in Reply to the Churchwardens, 1840, p. 12. There may have been too much of the parish officer in this uniform for church tastes.
3 Ibid. p. 1. 4. 26.
4 It would seem that Dr. Oliver had obtained a licence for absence from Doctors Commons but the Registrar of the Collegiate Church pointed out "it is good for nothing, as the Archbishop has no jurisdiction within a Royal Peculiar". Letter from John Mott from Lichfield 20 Feb. 1840.
5 Letter from William Parke 11 April 1840.
6 Note by William Parke.

In 1846 the last Dean of Windsor and Wolverhampton died, and though it is difficult to say what, after laying the foundation stone of St. George's Church in 1828, he had done for Wolverhampton, his death was an event of great importance. The legislature got busy with 11 & 12 Vict. cap. 95, and new prospects opened out for Dr. Oliver's future. The Wolverhampton Chronicle remarks upon it with almost unkind terseness (24 March 1847): "We understand that the long talked retirement of the Rev. Dr. Oliver . . . . is about to be effected by exchange with the Rev. J. O. Dakeyne, M.A., Rector of South Hykeham, Lincs." This was actually accomplished on the 10 April; but the exchange being a fair one, very little was gained. The Lord Chancellor had returned a Roland for their Oliver. Still, the "suppression" of the Deanery meant no Sacrist and no Perpetual Curate, for Mr. Dakeyne found that he had only momentarily held this office, being mentioned as such in the Preamble of the Act only to be abolished by a latter clause.[1] So the new Rector could claim no fees (which he very much needed) from the new vicarages, nor could the polychromatic dazzle of the Wellington Memorial window inserted over the west doorway in 1855, blind people to the fact that the Rectory was in a state of sequestration from 1856. The unhappy incumbent died 20th January 1860. Dr. Oliver lived till 3rd March 1867.[2] On the whole the exchange was justified.

1 Counsel's opinion, 14 May 1852.
2 D.N.B. which gratuitously tells us that his voice began to fail in 1854.

CHAPTER XII

ST. PETER'S COLLEGIATE CHURCH

THE Collegiate Church of St. Peter stands in a commanding position on high ground in the centre of Wolverhampton dwarfing the buildings around it. The churchyard, which had been a Christian burial ground for almost a thousand years, is now laid out as a garden having been conveyed to the Corporation for this purpose in 1938. The church, which is cruciform, is dominated by the beautiful late Perpendicular central tower of three storeys which rises to a height of 125 feet and is one of the land-marks of the district.

This tower, which is built of local sandstone, is elaborately panelled on the west, south and east sides. The windows of the clock chamber consist of a single opening in each wall surmounted by an ogee head while the windows of the bell chamber are set in pairs in each wall covered by a single ogee hood mould. Beneath the window in the west wall is a niche containing the figure of St. Peter. The tower is surmounted by battlements and four tall crocketted pinacles.

The entrance to the church is through the 14th century vaulted south porch. It is of two storeys, the upper one, which formed a parvise or solar, having been added in the 15th century. In the porch are two tablets. That on the east wall commemorates the benefactions of Wulfrun and replaces an earlier one which was much decayed. The one on the opposite wall is to the memory of Charles Claudius Phillips, an itinerant musician whose performance on the violin delighted the ears of our 18th century ancestors.

Near this place lies
Charles Claudius Phillips
Whose absolute contempt of riches,
And inimitable performances upon the violin,
Made him the admiration of all that knew him.
He was born in Wales,
Made the tour of Europe,
And, after the experience of both kinds of fortune
Died in 1732.

Exalted soul, thy various sounds could please
The love-sick virgin or the gouty ease;
Could jarring crowds, like old Amphion, move
To beautious order and harmonious love.
Here rest in peace, till angels bid thee rise,
And join thy Saviour's concert in the skies.

Shortly after the memorial was placed here the epitaph, the work of Dr. Richard Wilkes the Willenhall antiquary, was recited by David Garrick to his friend Dr. Samuel Johnson[1] who on hearing it remarked "I think, Davy, I can make a better". "Then stirring about his tea for a little while in a state of meditation, he almost extempore produced the following verses:—[2]

1 Boswell's "Life of Johnson" edited by Roger Ingpen, 1925. Vol. I p. 80.
2 Mr. J. Enoch Powell, M.P. detects a number of differences in these lines from those reputed to have been written by Johnson.

Phillips, whose touch harmonious could remove
The pangs of guilty power or hapless love;
Rest here, distress'd by poverty no more,
Here find that calm thou gav'st so oft before;
Sleep, undisturbed, within this peaceful shrine,
Till angels wake thee with a note like thine."

Sometime during the last century this second epitaph, also carved on slate, was placed beneath the original memorial.

The oak vestibule at the south door was erected as a memorial to Alderman Sir Charles Tertius Mander, 1st Baronet, a Freeman and former Mayor of the Borough who died in 1929. It is a fine piece of modern woodwork in two storeys, heavily carved with crockets and canopy work, and blazoned with shields of arms. On either side of the central door are statues of St. Thomas of Canterbury and King Charles I both of whom had associations with Wolverhampton.

In the centre of the church stand the four arches which support the central tower and are the only part of the 13th century building which has survived. To the east is the chancel wholly rebuilt by Ewan Christian in 1867 as part of the restoration which he supervised. The open chancel roof is carried on principals supported on corbels carved with angels and the part over the apse is carved, gilded, and coloured. The Altar is of the Early English type with riddel posts and curtains and the pews, which are of oak, have carved bench ends ornamented with poppy heads and kneeling angels. The stained glass in the windows of the apse dates from the rebuilding of the chancel.

In the large windows on the north and south sides of the chancel has recently been fixed some ancient glass which originally adorned the east window of St. Mary's Church, Wolverhampton before its closure in 1948. It was given by Miss Theodosia Hincks of Tettenhall who built and endowed St. Mary's about 1840 and was a great collector of antiques. Nothing is known of the early history of this glass but from examination it would appear to have come from at least two sources, Flemish and German, and was probably acquired by Miss Hincks during one of her many journeys on the Continent.

The Flemish glass probably came from one, or possibly two, windows and depicts various events in the life of Our Lord. From the design of costumes it would appear to date from the first two decades of the 16th century. The scenes depicted are the Miracle at Cana, the Anointing of Our Lord by Mary Magdalene, the Entombment, the Resurrection, the Appearance to Mary Magdalene in the garden and the Ascension. Across the bottom of the window was an inscription too fragmentary now to be deciphered but probably in Flemish.

The German glass is a little later than the Flemish and consists of pictorial panels, roundels and shields. The shields display various German coats of arms many showing the double headed German eagle and there are one or two small panels composed of glass fragments. One bears the quaint inscription "Negotiuminde liberatum facillime poenitentia sequitur septemvir XIX Apr. MDXXXVI". Translated this reads 'Business which has been too easily transacted brings sorrow in its train 19 April 1536".

The pictorial panels show a knight, a bishop in chasuble and mitre and the raising of the daughter of Jairus by Our Lord. There are also two roundels; one portrays St. Jerome wearing a cardinal's hat around the edge the following inscription "HERONIMUS . RECH . LIEBEN . SCH STER PIT . GOT . H . FUR . MICH . 1533." The other roundel displays a shield of arms and is also surrounded by an inscription in German.

Some of this ancient glass has not yet (1958) been fixed in the church.

The south transept of the church is now fitted up as a Lady Chapel and in it can be seen both Decorated and Perpendicular styles of architecture. The beautiful Decorated east window was at one time much larger than it is now the lower part having at some time been filled in. It is now filled with stained glass by Eden depicting the descent of Our Lord from Jesse and was placed here in memory of the men who fell in the First World War. It takes the place of a similar window which stood here in pre-Reformation days.[1] The Altar table in this chapel dates from the Stuart period and was probably the one then used as the High Altar which was consecrated by Archbishop Laud in 1635.[2] The window in the south wall was inserted at the time of the reconstruction of the transept in the middle of the 15th century and consists of three lights under a four centre arch. The mouldings of the jambs are identical with those of the most eastern window in the south aisle and the hood mould finials are carved with quaint heads. Beneath this window is a 14th century piscina much mutilated. It is the only one in the church which has survived.

In the south east corner of the chapel stands the table tomb of John Leveson, who died in 1575, and his wife Joyce.[3] In the opposite corner stands the bronze statue of Vice Admiral Sir Richard Leveson and is all that now remains of a large monument the work of Hubert le Sueur Court sculptor to King Charles I. The admiral died in London in August 1606[4] and was brought to Wolverhampton for burial. The monument was not constructed until 1634 and the contract for its erection is recited by Stebbing Shaw.[5] What remains is but a small part of the original which stood in the old chancel. In the agreement we are told that the Statue stood on a black marble base 6½ feet long 2½ feet wide and 5½ feet high with bronze tablets attached to this pedestal. The sword held by Sir Richard has disappeared as also the compass and anchor held by the two cherubs. The inscriptions record the parentage of the admiral and in turgid Latin tell of his many naval exploits including his participation in the action against the Spanish Armada in 1588. During the Commonwealth the statue was removed from the church with the intention of sending it to Stafford to be melted down for gunmetal but Lady Leveson of Trentham succeeded in obtaining it and kept it at Lilleshall until 1714[6] when it was returned to its original home in St. Peter's chancel.

Over the tower arch is a large painting on canvas recording the benefactions to the Charity School of Wolverhampton and on it are depicted a boy and a girl dressed in the quaint costume of the period. The priest's desk is of oak and is said to have come from Halesowen Abbey at the time of the Dissolution and the seat is part of the misericord seats brought here from Lilleshall Abbey.[7]

The chapel is enclosed by two 15th century parclose screens brought here from other parts of the church and altered to fit the openings. They are much restored but still display a great deal of their original carvings.

The north transept, now fitted out as a War Memorial Chapel, was the last part of the pre-Reformation church to be completed and dates from about 1510. It is built in the late Perpendicular style and still retains the original oak roof. It is panelled, with moulded ribs and quatrefoil rosettes at the intersections. Around the sides are angels bearing shields. This chapel was originally dedicated to St. Catherine and St. Nicholas and probably the large niches on either side of the east window were designed to contain the statues of

1 See Shaw's History of Staffordshire Vol. II p. 161.
2 See p. 76.
3 For description of this monument see p. 156.
4 The date on the inscription is incorrect.
5 History of Staffordshire Vol. II p. 158.
6 Wolverhampton Antiquary Vol. I p. 178.
7 For a comprehensive account of all the Stalls from Lilleshall including the Clergy Stalls the nave see Wolverhampton Antiquary Vol. II p. 64.

these patron saints. After the Reformation the chapel fell into disuse and later about 1660 the font was placed here. As the north side of the church was used by the people of Willenhall this chapel became the burial place of the important families from that district—the Lanes of Bentley, Wilkes's of Willenhall and the Hopes of Nechells. This part of the church presents some very interesting architectural problems. The style of the window openings in this chapel, with the central mullion, is unusual and seems to point to a departure from the original design. This view is supported by a find that was made when the Lane monument was removed from the centre of the east wall in 1947. Part of the original cill of the east window was revealed and the remains of a stump of a mullion close to the large central mullion came to light. It could also be seen that the interior side of the cill which is now a hollow mould originally had a dentil motif but this was cut away probably owing to its decayed condition. The remains of the mullion indicates that at some time the east window was of five lights but whether it was altered to its present style after the Reformation or is all that remains of the pre-1500 building it is difficult to say with any certainty. The central mullion shaft of the north window descends to the ground and forms an integral part of the stone panelling with which the walls of the chapel are adorned. We know that there were extensive repairs and alterations to the church in the 17th century and alterations in this chapel may have taken place at that time.

The present altar occupies the site of its mediaeval predecessor and the stone panelling of the east wall was interrupted to allow of this original arrangement. After the destruction of the old altar the tomb of Thomas Lane of Bentley occupied the site and on the east wall an inscription in black Gothic lettering was painted but when uncovered it was so decayed as to be illegible. The tomb was removed to its present position in the corner of the chapel about 1678 and was replaced by the monument to Colonel John Lane. Thomas Lane's tomb is the work of Robert Royley the famous 16th century maker of alabaster tombs at Burton-on-Trent many of whose monuments are to be found in the Midlands.

This tomb stands on a raised stone base the top paved with black and white slate and marble squares. The chest measures 7 ft. 9 ins. long, 4 ft. 5 ins. wide, and 3 ft. 1 ins. high and around the chamfered top string is the following inscription "Here lieth the bodies of thomas lane of bentley in the countie of Stafford esquier and katheren his wyffe, wch katheren deceased ye VIIIth daye of October in ye yeare of our lord god 1582". Thomas[1] is shown dressed as a knight, bearded, and with short curly hair, with his head resting on a mantled helm and his feet on a small dog. On his right side near his feet lie his mail gloves. On his left lies his lady, her head resting upon a cushion, and wearing a late pointed coif; the gown is tightwaisted, and the skirt is split showing the petticoat. Small dogs nestle on either side of her skirt and hanging on a chain from her girdle is a pomander box. The fine underlinen rises from the V-shaped neck of the gown to be gathered up in a large ruff. The sleeves are padded at the shoulders with a double twisted band of material, and the under sleeves have frills at the wrists. The head panel of the chest bears three shields. The one below the man bears the Lane arms: party per fesse or and azure, a cheveron gules between three mullets counter-changed. The shield below the lady bears Trentham: argent, three griffins' heads erased sable and the centre shield shows the Lane arms impaling those of Trentham. The side panel shows their children, five sons and seven daughters, and over each little figure was at one time carved and painted their names but these are now almost illegible. The eldest son John supports a shield showing the Lane arms with six quarterings: 1, party per fesse or and azure, a cheveron gules between three mullets

1 For a more detailed description of this tomb see Wolverhampton Antiquary Vol. I p. 239 et seq.

counter-changed (Lane); 2, a lion rampant ermine (Hyde); 3, gules, two bars or (Harcourt); 4, ermine a fesse fretty or (Edgerton); 5, gules a scythe argent (Partrich); 6, argent three griffins heads erazed sable (Trentham); Impaling Littleton *i.e.* Argent, on a lion rampant sable, a fesse counter-componee or and azure (Burley); 2 and 3, argent a cheveron between three escallops sable (Littleton); 4, or, three piles sable, a canton ermine (Wrottesley). The eldest son John is dressed in armour and the other children in the costume of the period. Two are shown as chrisom children. The panel which formed the foot of the tomb is now fixed on the east wall and displays the Lane arms in six quarterings supported by two cherubs.

The other Lane monument is to the west of the last one and is to the memory of Colonel John Lane who died in 1667 and who was one of the protectors of King Charles II when he was a fugitive after the ill-fated Battle of Worcester. It was erected somewhat later than 1677 when the King granted to Thomas Lane of Bentley the honour and privilege of bearing a canton of the Royal Arms on the family coat. A shield with this blazon surmounted by Col. John Lane's crest and with two cannon as supporters appears on the top of the monument which is contructed of slate and marble. The upper part of the monument consists of an inscribed tablet flanked by two columns, the inscription a long one in Latin. The following is a translation:—

The mortal remains
Of the distinguished soldier, John Lane, Esq.
In hope of a joyful resurrection
Are here deposited:
A man superior to titles, and to whose merits
There are none more entitled.
In the troubles of the late civil war, under Charles the First,
And afterwards in the Dutch war, under Charles the Second,
He discharged most honourably the duties of a Colonel in the Army.
He was the deliverer of both King and Country;
For when Charles II after the battle of Worcester,
Had escaped with extreme difficulty, and was strictly searched after,
With exemplary loyalty, fidelity, courage,
And imminent hazard of capital punishment
From the snares of a tyrannous usurper, and the treachery of partisans
He bravely rescued him.
Among the eminent deeds of the age,
This was the most eminent.
To these services the King himself gave a clear testimony,
By the grant of the Royal Arms as an augmentation
To the Arms of the ancient and noble family of the Lanes,
To his son, Thomas Lane, Esq. (the heir of his father's virtues)
As a badge of distinction well merited by the deceased.
His remains, moreover, from a sense of pious and grateful affection
The King would have interred with great funeral pomp,
In the Royal Tombs at Westminster,
Had not the hero's modesty, in his dying moments,
Resisted so great an honour.
Born March 24th, 1609,
And on August 31st, 1667
Died greatly lamented.

The lower part of the memorial is in the form of a chest the front panel of which is heavily carved with the accoutrements of war and on the left hand side a tree surmounted by a crown an allusion no doubt to the King's secretion in a tree at Boscobel when Parliamentary soldiers came there to search for him after the Battle of Worcester. This panel is very much like that on the tomb chest of Sir Thomas and Lady Wentworth at Silkestone, Yorks., whilst the cannon at the top are reminiscent of those on the memorial to the elder Dr. Plot at Borden in Kent. Both these monuments are of the same date as the one to Col. Lane and are thought to be the work of Jasper Latham who may well have been responsible for the one at Wolverhampton.

The Lane vault occupies almost a quarter of the area of the chapel and lies in the north east corner. The arch of the vault stood about 18 inches above the floor of the chapel but this has been cut away, (except for the part which forms a platform on which stands the tomb of Thomas Lane), and reduced to floor level. When the vault was opened in 1947 it was found, contrary to the evidence recorded by R. P. Walker, that it still contained the coffins of the Lanes, the last one to be interred being Sarah wife of Thomas Lane who died in 1784 and whose elaborate coffin plate of copper silverplated and beautifully engraved in a copperplate hand was then examined.

On the east wall is a mural monument to Thomas Lane who died in 1782 and his wife Sarah, daughter of Richard Fowler of Pendeford, who died in 1784. Also in this chapel is a mural tablet with medallion portrait to Richard Fryer of the Wergs a wealthy banker and a Radical who became one of the first two Members of Parliament for the Borough after the passing of the Reform Act in 1832.

The chapel was rededicated in 1948 as a memorial to the men and women of Wolverhampton who gave their lives in the second World War. All the furniture and fittings are modern with the exception of the priest's desks which have been reconstructed from part of the misericord seats from Lilleshall Abbey. The bench ends display fish and animal motifs. The reredos is of carved panelled oak with a central canopy. The following figures are carved on it:—St. Peter, Wulfrun, St. Michael the Archangel, St. Alban, St. Paul, St. Joan of Arc, St. George, and the Blessed Virgin. The chapel is enclosed by two carved oak screens; the one in the western arch is a memorial to Alderman Levi Johnson, J.P. past Mayor and Freeman of the Borough and the one in the tower arch is to Canon Alfred Penny, M.A., Rector of Wolverhampton 1895—1919 and afterwards a Canon of Lichfield.

The nave of St. Peter's consists of five bays with a north and south aisle. The pillars are lofty and octagonal with octagonal moulded caps and the arches are composed of three hollow moulds with hood moulds on both sides except on the north side of the north arcade which is plain. Over the centre of each arch on this side is a carved corbel which supports a lesser roof truss. Four of these corbels represent the symbols of the evangelists the other one being carved as a grotesque. They are the work of the same carver or school of carvers who carved the figures on the font, at the foot of the pulpit steps, and the corbels which support the main roof of the nave. The corbels on the south side of the clerestory display heads of bishops, kings and angels, and one shows a pope wearing his triple crown. The ones on the north are grotesques. The clerestory windows were at one time ablaze with heraldic glass and some of it actually survived until the time of Huntbach who records for us details of several of the shields. They perpetuated the names of the families of the town and district who were benefactors at the time of the great rebuilding of the church. The finials of the arcade hood moulds consist of crowned bearded heads. On the piers of the south arcade can be seen a masons' mark in the form of a triskel, a kind of three legged swastika. This mark is only to be found on the south arcade and on the staircase leading to the rood loft. Beneath the tower or just in front of the west arch stood the Jesus Altar in pre-Reformation times. The altar which now stands beneath the tower is used for the celebrations of the Sung Eucharist each Sunday. The Jesus Altar was a necessary feature of all collegiate churches in the middle ages and had a light perpetually burning before it. The niche in which this light stood can still be seen cut in the eastern half pier of the south arcade though now partly obscured by the organ console. It may well be that the wardens of the Light of St. Peter mentioned in 1385[1] in one of the Wodehouse deeds and in the now lost churchwardens' account book in 1551[2] no doubt refer to the men responsible for the maintenance of this light.

The finest ornament of this beautiful church is undoubtedly the sandstone pulpit which was built around the eastern pillar of the south arcade in the middle of the 15th century. It may have been the gift of Humphrey Swynnerton of Hilton a generous benefactor of the rebuilding of that time whose coat of arms, an angel bearing a shield on which is blazoned a cross flory, can be seen on the balustrade of the staircase. The pulpit, which is octagonal, and the sides of the staircase are panelled. The moulded heads of the panels are cusped, the ends of these cusps being formed into small rosettes. Around the top of the pulpit is a band of flowers and leaves and around the bottom the motif consists of vine leaves and clusters of grapes. Both of the bands are heavily undercut and still bear traces of the colouring and gilding with which the whole of the pulpit was originally adorned.

At the foot of the staircase balustrade sits a grotesque lion put there no doubt by our mediaeval ancestors to protect their preachers from the forces of evil. Over the western arch of the tower now stands the organ in the place once occupied by the rood loft. The staircase to the loft is now in use as an access to the organ.

At the western end of the south aisle stands the font[3] placed in the church towards the end of the 15th century. Its date is about 1480. Around the base are eight small figures each in a niche which can be recognized as follows:—St. Peter, St. Paul, St. John Baptist, an Apostle (probably St. John), a King, a Bishop, A Priest in chasuble, and St. Anthony (patron saint of Windsor). The upper part of the font is very much restored in cement and on it is "ROBERT COX RICHARD GREEN 1660" and "RESTORED 1839". After the Restoration the font stood in the north transept and the present baptistry was panelled with wainscotting and used as the Consistory Court of the Wolverhampton Peculiar. As a rule the Court met here and then adjourned to the more congenial atmosphere of the Swan Inn. The present panelling is modern.

The three windows of the south aisle are glazed with stained glass by Kemp the famous early 20th century window painter. The subjects are as follows. Easternmost window:—Saints of the church St. Augustine, St. Jerome, St. Gregory and St. Ambrose, Middle Window:—The four Evangelists—St. Matthew, St. Mark, St. Luke and St. John, and the Westernmost Window:—St. Anne, St. Simeon, Malachias and Enoch.

At the west end of the nave stands the gallery erected in 1610 by the Merchant Taylors' Company for the use of the boys of the Free School (now Wolverhampton Grammar School) of which they were the trustees. The front is beautifully carved as are also the pillars which support it; these latter still show in places the decoration which once adorned them. The front panel displays coats of arms of Sir Stephen Jennings and the Merchant Taylors' Company and between them the following inscription:—

1 S.H.C. Vol. 1928 p. 131.
2 Wolverhampton Antiquary Vol I p. 272 where John Cowper is described as Jesus Warden.
3 See Wolverhampton Antiquary Vol. I p. 328 for a complete description of the font.

This Gallary : was : built : at : the : prop
costes : and : charges : of : the : worll.
company : of : Merchant : Tailors : in
London. Anno : Domi : 1610 : in : the tym
of : Mr. Thomas : Rowe : Master : and : John
Wooller : Randulf : Woolley : Raph : Hamor
and : Thomas : Johnson : Wardens : of :
the : same : Society : : W: Baily : Official.

The gallery was extensively restored in 1939 when it was entirely repewed.[1]

In the nave also are a number of mural monuments of interest. In the north aisle is a small wooden tablet with the following quaint inscription:—

> Here lyeth the body of William Walker, gent. of the Castle of Windsor, whoe served childe of the Chappell of St. George 7 yeares to Queene Elizabeth, and six yeares to King James, and deceased organist of this place, Anno Domini 1634, the 18th of January, at the age of 52.

Near it are two tablets to the family of Bracegirdle, one of them to Rev. Henry Bracegirdle who was Sacrist during the closing years of the 17th century. At the west end of this aisle is a large tablet of wood and canvas recording the qualities and virtues of Dr. William Gibbon who died in 1728 and was for some years Court Physician to Queen Anne.

Although the church has a wealth of silver much of it is modern and no pre-Reformation plate has survived. The earliest piece is a silver Chalice dated 1706 which was given to the church by Rev. Henry Bracegirdle. For many years it was missing and was recovered by one of the churchwardens about 80 years ago having been found in an inn in old Berry Street. Another interesting piece is also a small chalice dated 1703 to which a modern paten has been added and which was given by Rev. Canon John Brierley the present Rector. It has the following inscription:—

"R. T. Church w. Cottam 1703"

and probably came originally from Cottam in Nottinghamshire.

The present registers of Wolverhampton covering marriages, baptisms and burials start in 1603[2] although we have evidence that they originally commenced in 1538 and were examined by Huntbach the antiquary who made extensive extracts from them.[3] Although the church, as a Peculiar, had jurisdiction over the whole of the ancient parish of Wolverhampton very few archives have survived. The following documents are to be found in the Registries of Lichfield and Windsor:—

Lichfield Diocesan Registry.

Wolverhampton Act Book upon the Installation of Prebendaries:—one volume 1752—1818.
Subscription Books:—1719—1800 and 1800—1841.
Royal Free Chapel of Wolverhampton—Lease Book 1800—1839.
Wolverhampton Court Books, three volumes:—1728—1731, 1819—1839, 1822—1845.

Windsor—St. Georges Chapel.

XV 58 C.42
Appointments, Admissions, etc., to prebends and other offices within the Deanery 1673—1703.
IV B.26
Dean Keppel's Book. It includes fees and expenses of the Deanery of Wolverhampton 1765—1777.
IV B.27
Dean Legge's Book. Includes commissions granted at Wolverhampton 1806—1814.
IV B.28
Wolverhampton Book of Appointments to Prebends 1677, 1714, 1729.

1 For further details see "History of Wolverhampton Grammar School" by G. P. Mander p. 87.
2 The early part of these registers has been printed by the Staffs. Parish Register Society.
3 See Wolverhampton Antiquary Vol. I.

THE CHURCHYARD PILLAR

ANY history of Wolverhampton and its ancient church would be incomplete without some reference to the churchyard pillar, the oldest object, fashioned by man, in the town. It stands a few yards south east of the south porch of the church and is the largest and most imposing of these monuments now in the country.

There are two schools of thought regarding its age. For many years it was the opinion of experts that it was not older than the 12th century but in the light of modern archaeological research this idea has now given place to the view that it is pre-Conquest in origin. As early as 1877 Charles Lyman expressed the opinion[1] that "its profile was certainly not Norman but of classic type with a classic entasis". Sir A. W. Clapham confirmed this view[2] and writes "It has been usual to assign this fine accomplished work to the 12th century but in form it certainly belongs to the pre-Conquest age, and its decoration combine the Carolingian acanthus with the Anglican beast".

Professor G. Baldwin Brown[3] is more cautious about the date of this column suggesting the late tenth century but Sir T. D. Kendrick thinks it much earlier[4] and asserts "the Wolverhampton shaft is unquestionably the noblest monument that has come down to us from the pre-Alfredian sculptures of the West Saxon supremacy and it illustrates, better than anything else, the gaily ornate style of the period of Ethelwulf and his sons, a style that sought so often to express itself in the terms of the then fashionable continental art. There is nothing quite like it in England, though it is possible that the heavily decorated round shaft crosses in the north, such as that at Marham, may to some extent reflect an analogous contemporary taste in another province". He considers that part of the decorative arrangement is characteristic of the 9th century.

Mr. M. M. Rix[5] who has done much research on this subject suggests an even earlier date for the Wolverhampton shaft and considers it a late 8th century example of this type of monument. The stumbling block to this view is the acanthus decoration which is not usually found in Saxon carving before the late 9th century. It has however been found on 8th century manuscripts, one outstanding example being the copy of the Gospels now in the British Museum (British Museum Royal 1. E. VI) where the acanthus is used as a border decoration on folio 30 much as in the centre zone of the Wolverhampton pillar. This manuscript was written in Mercia or Kent at the end of the 8th century. Other objects of this period reinforce this evidence.

The column which we see today is but part of a large cross, the upper portion above the knop being entirely gone. The shaft is similar in style to the one at Leek, though larger, but what the cross proper was like can only be conjectured. It may have been of the wheel head type similar to the Leek cross. An interesting feature of the Wolverhampton cross shaft is that it has stood undisturbed through the centuries on its original foundation. This base is now about 3 ft. 6 ins. below the present level of the churchyard and when excavations took place in 1949 it was found that it consisted of a circle of roughish large stones in the form of steps and that these in turn rested on a glacial deposit of sand and gravel. There is no evidence whatever that any burials have ever taken place below the base of the shaft although many were so near as to cause some subsidence and a conglomerate mass of stone rubble was, at some period, cemented round the base to check this.

1 From the Transactions of North Staffs. Field Club Vol. LXXXII p. 82; quoting a paper in Journal of the British Archæological Association.
2 English Romanesque Architecture before the Conquest. 1930 p. 131.
3 Art in Early England 6.II 1937 p. 272.
4 Anglo Saxon Art to A.D. 900. 1938 p. 192.
5 I am indebted to Mr. M. M. Rix and also to the author of the article in North Staffs. Field Club Transactions for much of the information in this chapter.

The cap on top of the pillar, which is 9 ins. thick, has evidence of ornamentation and of therefore being part of the original monument. It is probable that it formed a knop dividing the cross proper from the shaft. The shaft is 14 feet high from the base to the underside of the cap and is 22 ins. in diameter at the top and 30 ins. at the bottom. The circular base is from 6½ to 7 feet in diameter and 1ft. 8 ins. deep. These sizes are identical with those of the pillars of the forum at Viriconium, near Wroxeter, and it may well be that the Wolverhampton shaft was a column pillaged from that city and carved in Saxon times. The stone is a fine textured sandstone, much finer and harder than that to be found in the Wolverhampton area and more like the stone found around Grinsill which was used by the Roman builders for some of their cities in that district.

Atmospheric pollution has caused the pillar to become greatly decayed in recent years but fortunately, in 1877, casts were taken which are now in the Victoria and Albert Museum. They show much of the ornamentation which has now perished. In 1913 a drawing of the whole circumference was made from these casts which is here reproduced (*Fig.* 0).[1] The design is zoomorphic and typically Saxon, showing animal and bird forms, most of these creatures having their heads turned rearwards. The decoration is divided into zones or bands of varying widths which are separated by a cable mould or a fillet.

The top band, 13 ins. deep, consists of a series of handsome spiral scrolls surmounted by a fillet and divided from the next zone by an enriched fillet. The next zone is 16 ins. deep and consists of five nearly circular panels occupied alternately by birds and beasts each looking inwards. Beneath is a band of cable moulding. The next zone is 19 ins. deep and is filled with boldly cut scrolls of conventional foliage. The following zone, divided from the one above by a narrow fillet, is only 7 ins. wide and filled with formal acanthus sprays. Another narrow fillet divides it from the next zone which is 19 ins. deep and consists of five lozenge shaped panels each occupied by a beast with its head turned inwards. Small creatures occupy the spaces between the panels. Beneath this wide panel is a band of cable ornament beneath which are five pendant triangles each filled with birds beasts or foliage.

These pendant triangles are reminiscent of the ornamentation to be seen on the lower part of the metal socket of some early processional crosses. The lower part of the pillar, some 7 feet, is plain and although decayed bears no evidence of ever having any carving on it.

The pillar bears silent witness to the fact that in Wolverhampton we still have a Christian monument erected in remote Saxon times probably not long after the death of that famous missionary to Mercia, St. Chad, first Bishop of Lichfield. It was old when Wulfrun built and endowed her minster on the hill of Hantune and no doubt she saw it when she came to view the progress of the work on her new church. From its presence here we know that for almost twelve centuries the Christian message has been proclaimed from this hallowed spot.

1 By kind permission of the Society of Antiquaries.

Index

INDEX

C

G

H

I

J

K

L

M

N

R

S

W